First Founding Father

First Founding Father

RICHARD HENRY LEE
AND THE CALL TO
INDEPENDENCE

HARLOW GILES UNGER

DA CAPO PRESS

Da Capo Press
Hachette Book Group
1290 Avenue of the Americas, New York, NY 10104
dacapopress.com

Printed in the United States of America

First Da Capo Press edition 2017
Published by Da Capo Press, an imprint of Perseus Books, LLC, a subsidiary of Hachette Book Group, Inc.

The Hachette Speakers Bureau provides a wide range of authors for speaking events. To find out more, go to www.hachettespeakersbureau.com or call (866) 376-6591.

The publisher is not responsible for websites (or their content) that are not owned by the publisher.

Print book interior design by Trish Wilkinson

Library of Congress Cataloging-in-Publication Data

Names: Unger, Harlow G., 1931– author.
Title: First founding father: Richard Henry Lee and the call to independence / Harlow Giles Unger.
Description: First Da Capo Press edition. | New York, NY: Da Capo Press, 2017. | Includes bibliographical references and index.
Identifiers: LCCN 2017040744 (print) | LCCN 2017041656 (ebook) | ISBN 9780306825620 (e-book) | ISBN 9780306825613 (hardcover: alk. paper)
Subjects: LCSH: Lee, Richard Henry, 1732–1794. | Revolutionaries—United States—Biography. | Politicians—United States—Biography. | United States—History—Revolution, 1775–1783—Biography. | United States. Declaration of Independence—Signers—Biography. | Virginia—Biography.
Classification: LCC E302.6.L4 (ebook) | LCC E302.6.L4 U54 2017 (print) | DDC 973.3092 [B]—dc23
LC record available at https://lccn.loc.gov/2017040744

ISBN: 978-0-306-82561-3 (hardcover)
ISBN: 978-0-306-82562-0 (e-book)

LSC-C

10 9 8 7 6 5 4 3 2 1

Frontispiece: Portrait of Richard Henry Lee
by Charles Willson Peale, in the National Portrait Gallery.

To Sarah Hopkins
With deep appreciation and affection
from the author and his family

Contents

List of Illustrations

Acknowledgments

My deepest thanks to Robert Pigeon, executive editor at Da Capo Press of the Hachette Book Group, for the care, the skills, and the time he invested in this and all my other books. My thanks also to the publishing and editorial team at Da Capo Press: John Radziewicz, publisher; Lissa Warren, vice president, director of publicity; Kevin Hanover, vice president, director of marketing; Cisca Schreefel, manager, editorial production; Justin Lovell, editorial assistant; Trish Wilkinson, designer; Josephine Mariea, copy editor; and to the Hachette Book Group sales team. Thanks as well to website developer Tom Bowler for his skills, artistry, hard work, and patience with a low-tech author.

Introduction

BEFORE WASHINGTON, BEFORE JEFFERSON, BEFORE FRANKLIN OR John Adams, there was Lee—Richard Henry Lee.

First of the Founding Fathers to call for independence, first to call for union, and first to call for a bill of rights, Richard Henry Lee was as much a Father of Our Country as George Washington. For it was Lee who masterminded the political and diplomatic victories that ensured Washington's military victory in the Revolutionary War. And after the nation took shape it was Lee—not James Madison— who conceived of the Bill of Rights our nation enjoys today.

Richard Henry Lee was a scion of one of Virginia's—indeed, one of North America's—wealthiest and most powerful families, a fabled dynasty akin to Europe's Medici, Habsburgs, or Rothschilds. He and his blood—and relatives by marriage—ruled over hundreds of thousands of acres across Virginia, western Maryland, Pennsylvania, and present-day Ohio and Indiana; their fleet sailed the world carrying American tobacco to the farthest corners of the earth. At the peak of their wealth and power the Lees controlled Virginia's government and economy and helped develop Virginia into North America's largest, richest, and most populated British colony.

Needing nothing to fill his needs as a young adult, Richard Henry Lee absorbed a library of learning before entering public service—an avocation that became a lifelong commitment and turned him against his own class as he encountered government corruption and widespread deprivation of individual rights. His conflicts with corrupt officials and petty tyrants metamorphosed into demands for individual liberties, human rights, and, eventually, American independence from Britain. As a fledgling member of Virginia's legislature, he shocked the South by declaring blacks "entitled to liberty and freedom by the great law of nature" and planting the first seeds of emancipation in Virginia.

Twelve years before Britain's colonies declared independence, Lee was the first to threaten King George III with rebellion if he did not annul a new stamp tax. Later Lee worked with Boston's firebrand activist Samuel Adams to organize committees of correspondence in each colony, uniting the independence movement and bringing colony leaders to Philadelphia for North America's First Continental Congress.

In 1775 Richard Henry Lee stood with Patrick Henry demanding war with Britain, if necessary, to obtain redress of American grievances against Parliament's governing ministry. A year later he invited his own execution on the gallows with a treasonous resolve before Congress "that these United Colonies are, and of right ought to be, free and independent States."

Three weeks later, on July 2, Congress approved Lee's resolution declaring independence from Britain. Newspapers sent the news streaming across the nation and the world, with banner headlines proclaiming America and her people free of British rule and hailing Richard Henry Lee as Father of American Independence.

A year later, when British troops seized the capital at Philadelphia, Lee rallied a band of twenty congressmen, led them westward to Lancaster, then York, Pennsylvania, and while Washington held the remnants of his army together at Valley Forge, Lee kept the remnants of Congress together and reestablished the fledgling American government. Assuming leadership as de facto chief executive, Richard Henry Lee ensured the new government's survival, supervising military affairs, foreign affairs, and financial affairs and ensuring the needs of Washington's army. John Adams called Lee the Cicero of the Revolution, in contrast to George Washington, the unquestioned Cincinnatus.

Three of Lee's brothers, bound by mutual love of country—and of their older brother—reinforced Richard Henry's every effort. Francis Lightfoot Lee stood by Richard Henry as a firm ally in Congress, while Arthur Lee and William Lee served as surrogates in Europe, to provide intelligence, find financial aid, and work out secret deals to smuggle French arms, ammunition, and materiel to Washington's army. The surreptitious shipments would supply Washington with 80 percent of his army's needs for more than a year until French king Louis XVI recognized American independence and sent his army and navy to America to seal American victory and independence from Britain.

John Adams hailed the Lees as a "band of brothers, intrepid and unchangeable, who, like the Greeks at Thermopylae, stood in the gap, in the defense of their country, from the first glimmering of the Revolution in the horizon, through all its rising light, to its perfect day."[1]

In 1779 Richard Henry Lee—forty-seven years old, with four fingers blown away by a flintlock explosion—displayed his heroism in battle, leading his home-county militia in a charge against British troops landing along the Potomac River near Lee's home.

After the Revolution Lee joined Patrick Henry in opposing ratification of the Constitution, fearing that, without a bill of rights, it would concentrate the nation's power and wealth in the hands of oligarchs. Although they lost their struggle, Lee continued the fight, winning election to the US Senate in the First Congress, where he led efforts to add a Bill of Rights to the Constitution.

But after two years in the Senate, including service as president pro tempore, the struggle wore him down. Spent and ailing, he retired to his Virginia home and died two years later, surrounded by his wife and nine children. The words on his gravestone expressed their loss and that of the nation: "We cannot do without you."

CHAPTER 1

Evolution of a Dynasty

FOR ALMOST ALL OF HIS LIFE THOMAS LEE HAD BELIEVED—AND perpetuated—the family myth that the Lees had landed among the Norman knights at Hastings in 1066. Although his boys were fourth-generation Virginians, the Lee family's evident importance in English history made it imperative that he send them "home" to England for a proper education—much as his own father had sent him there, and as his father's father had sent his sons to English schools.

"Not one of the pupils has died here," headmaster Joseph Randall assured Thomas Lee at England's Wakefield School in 1744, when Lee was touring England in search of appropriate boarding schools for his younger sons. "This village," Randall added, "is happily retired from those Temptations which Youth are exposed to in *Towns* . . . out of the reach . . . of vice . . . and corruptions of the age."[1]

As important as the safety of its boys, Randall pointed out, the curriculum at Wakefield was identical to but less costly than its exalted competitor, Eton College, which Thomas Lee himself had attended as a boy. Although Henry VI had founded Eton in 1440 to educate poor boys without charge, it expected wealthy eighteenth-century parents to pay enormous sums—indeed, exorbitant sums—to educate, house, and feed its students.

That was to be expected for English noblemen grooming their oldest sons to rule the British Empire, but it seemed inappropriate for their younger boys, bound for only the military or the church—with little or no inheritance to take with them. Like members of England's ruling class, Virginia's Thomas Lee had routinely enrolled his oldest son and primary heir, Philip Ludwell Lee, in Eton several years earlier, but his next in line, Richard Henry Lee and his younger brother Thomas, would have to make do with a somewhat less costly education.

Under the universal rule of primo geniture, Thomas Lee would bequeath the vast Lee empire in America to his oldest son, leaving only scattered tracts in the wilderness to Richard Henry Lee and his four other younger sons. With the primary estate that Philip Ludwell Lee would inherit came a seat on Virginia's ruling council of state, with powers second only to the royal governor. Richard Henry Lee and the younger boys would not share such powers and would need no academic or social credentials from Eton College to work their small plantations in the Virginia wilderness.

But the Lees, in fact, owned no armor and, although Thomas Lee would never admit it even to himself, neither he nor his forebears were high born. Their family name had metamorphosed over generations from *de Lega*—old French for "of the law" (perhaps a sheriff or notary by trade)—then *de Le'*, *Leigh*, and finally *Lee*. Subsequent generations were largely tradesmen: some peddled clothes, but one was a wine merchant who accumulated small royal land grants in America—all but worthless at the time—as token payments by the crown for his grapes.

Those grants, however, thrust the Lees into the landed gentry, and when Virginia settlers learned to grow tobacco and feed the sudden British craze for the weed, the value of Lee holdings soared—warranting a coat of arms. Described in heraldic terms as "fesse

Lee

1. *The Lee family coat of arms shows a "fesse chequy," or wide checkered bar across the center of the shield, with ten "billets," or vertical rectangles, above and below the central bar.*

chequy and ten billets,"* it carried the title "Gentleman"—a rank above "Goodman," or landowner who obtained his holdings from a king's vassal rather than the king himself.

In 1640 Richard Henry Lee's great-grandfather Richard took advantage of his rank by sailing across what Britons called "The

---

*A wide, checkered bar (fesse chequy) across the center of the shield, with eight "billets," or vertical rectangles above and below the central bar.

2. The first Richard Lee in America sailed from Britain in 1640 with "headrights" to 1,000 acres in Virginia—a property he expanded to more than 15,000 acres before he died.

Virginia Sea"* to claim his land grants and become the first Richard Lee in the New World.

Before sailing, he bought enough slaves and indentured servants to acquire "headrights" to a thousand acres in York County, Virginia.

---

*To flatter their Virgin Queen, Elizabeth I, mapmakers depicted Virginia sprawling across North America from Florida to Canada and westward to the "South Sea," or Pacific Ocean. As the oldest and largest of Elizabeth's colonies, Virginia has claimed status as "The Old Dominion" ever since.

Conceived earlier in the seventeenth century to ease labor shortages on Virginia's tobacco fields, a landowner could obtain rights to an additional fifty acres from the Virginia Company of London for each person—each "head"—he brought to America to work the land. British taste for tobacco seemed limitless at the time, and headrights let Virginia plantation owners expand their properties and tobacco production by buying slaves or paying the passage of indentured white workers to come to America in exchange for a fixed number of years (usually five) of involuntary servitude on the buyer's plantation. The impending outbreak of an English civil war made it a good time to leave.

With Virginia's population barely 10,000 in the mid-seventeenth century, the 1,000 acres owned by Richard Henry Lee's great-grandfather thrust him among Virginia's largest property owners—and onto the governor's Council of State, an oligarchy of property owners who ruled the colony. By 1653 Richard Lee had acquired enough headrights to claim 15,000 acres of tobacco land along the Virginia coast—including the site of present-day Mount Vernon.

Far from the Garden of Eden they had envisioned when they left England, the first Richard Lee and his family in America lived in an ugly collection of primitive log cabins north of the York River.

3. *Jamestown's population in 1640 had spilled beyond its original triangle of protective walls, but Indian raids remained common.*

Poisonous serpents outnumbered apple trees, and swarms of mosquitoes and other injurious insects harassed settlers day and night. Although the Lees lived within riding distance of the colonial capital at Jamestown, Powhatan Indians called the land theirs and burned Lee's settlement to the ground three times in the years after his arrival, slaughtering dozens of slaves and servants. Lee himself survived each assault and kept rebuilding and expanding his empire.

Before the first Richard Lee died in 1664 (of natural causes), he sired ten children, including a second Richard Lee, who sailed to England to attend Eton as his father had done, then returned to America to rule over and expand the Lee family holdings. By then they included about seven dozen slaves, herds of cattle and sheep, parts of two shipping companies, and an interest in a tobacco trading company in London. In modern terms the Lee plantation was an "integrated" enterprise that combined growing, harvesting, shipping, and trading tobacco, then the most lucrative crop in the British Empire. Like his father, the second Richard Lee in America assumed political offices, privileges, and powers that came with his lands.

Although the second Richard Lee was born in Virginia, he—like other colonial "aristocrats"—called England "home" and remained English, heart and soul, a bulwark of the royal governor's ruling oligarchy. When, therefore, a group of shabby, small-property owners from the frontier demanded government protection against Indian raids, the governor—with the support of Lee and other powerful plantation owners—refused. None was willing to disrupt the profitable trade they had established with friendly Indians who gladly exchanged skins and furs for rum.

Led by planter Nathaniel Bacon, the frontiersmen took matters into their own hands and formed a militia that marched to the Roanoke River and slaughtered Susquehannock Indians, whom they deemed responsible for the attacks. Declared a traitor by Governor Sir William Berkeley, Bacon responded by leading his men into Jamestown, setting the town ablaze, burning the governor's home to the ground, and taking Richard Lee prisoner.

4. *The ruins of Jamestown after planter Nathaniel Bacon retaliated against the royal governor for failing to protect nearby plantations against Indian raids. Bacon died shortly thereafter, and the governor hanged twenty-three of his followers.*

Bacon died a month later, but Berkeley ordered men from a British naval squadron to crush the rebellion, freeing Richard Lee, hanging twenty-three insurgents, and seizing their properties. After British king Charles II learned of the rebellion, he recalled Berkeley to England, allegedly saying, "As I live, the old fool has put to death more people in that naked country than I did here for the murder of my father."[2] With that, the king calmed Virginia tempers with tax reductions and stepped up defenses against Indian incursions.

When the second Richard Lee died, his oldest son—the third Richard Lee—was still living in England, with no inclination to leave for the Virginia wilds. He never got the chance, dying a year later at thirty-nine without male heirs and leaving the Lee empire in America to his brother Thomas Lee, Richard Henry Lee's father.

5. *Thomas Lee negotiated the first peace treaty with hostile Indian nations at the historic Lancaster Conference, earning a royal land grant of 500,000 acres in the Ohio Territory.*

Thomas married the wealthy American heiress Hannah Ludwell, whose dowry helped expand Lee-family holdings in Virginia to more than 50,000 acres. On January 29, 1729, however, raiders broke into their home as the Lees slept, stole their silver and other valuables, then set fire to the house, barns, and outbuildings. One servant died in the blaze, but Thomas and Hannah swept up their young son, Philip Ludwell, and daughter, Hannah, and leaped out a second-floor window to the ground. Pregnant with her third child, Hannah survived the fall but miscarried. The raiders escaped and were never found or identified.

The Lees moved north to higher ground on Virginia's Northern Neck Peninsula and built a fortress-like home on the cliffs overlooking the Potomac River. Named Stratford Hall—the name of the first Richard Lee's home in Britain—the new Lee manor and its austere exterior housed a palatial interior, where Hannah gave birth to six more Lees: Thomas, Richard Henry, Francis Lightfoot, Alice, William, and Arthur.

All but adjacent to Stratford Hall, Thomas Lee built a separate two-story brick schoolhouse—in effect, a small boarding school—and hired a well-educated Scottish clergymen to teach his boys reading, writing, literature, science, Latin, proper behavior, morality, religion, Bible, and catechism. Like other plantation owners, Thomas Lee had little time for "fathering" his boys. Supervision of his agricultural enterprise kept him busy most of the year, and obligations in the colonial legislature—the House of Burgesses—and the executive Council of State in Williamsburg occupied the rest of his time.

Unlike New England, where most villages boasted a church with a minister who taught local children on weekdays, almost nothing

6. *Stratford Hall, the magnificent home that Thomas Lee built on Virginia's Northern Neck, housed a luxurious interior behind an austere, fortress-like exterior aimed at discouraging attacks by thieves and Indian raiders.*

but plantations blanketed the South; the road out of one plantation led only to the road into the next. Slaves usually raised the master's boys until they were five, when a tutor took charge of their upbringing and education until they were twelve and old enough to sail to England and attend boarding schools such as Eton or Wakefield.*

Richard Henry Lee and his brothers slept in a dormitory on the second floor of the Stratford Hall schoolhouse, adjacent to the tutor's private quarters. More than just an instructor, their tutor served as a surrogate parent, ministering to the boys on Sundays, escorting them to social and sporting events, and teaching them a variety of social and recreational skills ranging from dancing to horsemanship. The tutor roused the boys at seven each morning for an hour of lessons before breakfast and morning chores. Lessons resumed at nine and, except for an hour for dinner, continued until five. In the hour of free play that followed, Richard Henry Lee—far more than his older brother Philip—embraced a leadership role that earned him the lifelong devotion of three of his younger brothers, Francis Lightfoot, William, and Arthur.

After the personal and financial disaster Thomas Lee had suffered with the loss of his first home, he decided to strengthen Virginia against Indian raids. All but seizing command of Virginia's government from a timid royal governor, Lee organized a peace conference with leaders of the Six Nation (Indian) Confederacy in Lancaster, Pennsylvania, in early summer 1744. Plying them with wampum, whiskey, rum, and rhetoric, Lee convinced Indian leaders to cede much of western Maryland, Pennsylvania, and the lands east of the Blue Ridge Mountains to the British. Language differences, however, left Thomas Lee convinced he had restored British control over

---

*While their brothers acquired formal education, the Lee girls stayed at the sides of female slaves and, later, their mothers, growing up unlettered and learning only "women's work" and "lady-like" behavior. A few of the wealthiest learned "decorative arts," such as embroidering or playing a musical instrument to entertain their future husbands.

territory Britain had claimed in 1609 that "extended to the South Sea" (Pacific Ocean)—or so he wrote to the king.

The king expressed his gratitude by granting Thomas Lee 500,000 acres in the Ohio Valley, with which Lee and a group of friends, including George Washington and his brothers, formed the Ohio Land Company, with plans to sell land to would-be settlers in the ensuing decades.

By then Thomas Lee had expanded his property adjacent to Stratford Hall from its original 1,500 acres to about 4,000 acres, with vineyards, orchards, tobacco fields, and fields of grain stretching to the horizon. And at its core stood the magnificent manor, Stratford Hall, atop a bluff overlooking the Potomac River, on Virginia's Northern Neck, the northernmost of three giant peninsulas that reached eastward into Chesapeake Bay (see map, page 19). Below, on river's edge beneath Stratford Hall, stood a mill, a warehouse, a landing for ocean-going transports, a ship's store, and a fully equipped shipyard to build, repair, and service ships. Scattered about the property was housing for as many as one hundred slaves, servants, and workers, including weavers, carpenters, coopers, blacksmiths, shipwrights, millers, herdsmen, weavers, tailors, shoemakers, and other craftsmen. In effect, Thomas Lee—Richard Henry Lee's father—had transformed a corner of Virginia into a thriving, self-sufficient, English waterfront community, which he intended bequeathing to his oldest son, Philip Ludwell Lee. With Philip already studying law in London, Thomas Lee went to England to see about educating his other sons and sought to enroll Richard Henry Lee in Wakefield School.

"A young nobleman or gentleman may have a room to himself and eat at a private table with the [Randall] family," Wakefield headmaster Randall assured Thomas Lee. An additional £35 a year (just under $5,000 in current dollars) would assure him "the best masters" to teach him the basic curriculum, along with "natural philosophy [physics], fortification and gunnery, logic, dancing, fencing, music, and drawing.

"It must be observed," Randall added, "that washing is not included in the board. The usual price is fourteen shillings (about $135 today) a year . . . for which they have three shirts a week. Each pupil finds his own sheets alternately with his bedfellow."[3]

Randall's presentation evidently convinced Thomas Lee, who enrolled thirteen-year-old Richard Henry. The boy was still there four years later in 1750 when both his parents died—his mother, Hannah, in January, his father, Thomas, in November. As expected, Thomas Lee left the bulk of his wealth to his oldest son, Philip Ludwell Lee, twenty-three by then and still at the Inner Temple in London studying law. As primary heir and executor of his father's estate, he immediately returned to Virginia.

Richard Henry Lee was approaching nineteen and in his last year at Wakefield. With no responsibilities in the settlement of his father's estate and far too late to attend the burial, he chose to finish his studies at Wakefield, then set off to see the Western world. He left for the continent after graduating and spent the next several years touring Europe—including France and especially Paris, which had evolved into a center of arts and letters. "Noblemen, judges, and men of finance perfected the art of conversation with philosophers, artists, and men of letters" in the many salons. The rarity of a visit by so polished and cultured an American as Richard Henry Lee made him a popular figure and left him with little inclination to return to the isolated Virginia hilltop of his childhood.[4]

Besides the family fortune, however, his older brother Philip Ludwell Lee had inherited the task of caring for his six minor siblings and managing their inheritances until they each reached the age of majority. Richard Henry had no choice but return to claim his share of the family wealth.

Thomas Lee had left his minor children with handsome, if not extravagant, assets in either land or money. He bequeathed his sons Thomas, Richard Henry, and Francis Lightfoot several hundred acres each—in Stafford County, Prince William County, and Loudon County, respectively. Each property came with thirty to fifty slaves along with more than adequate sums of money to build substantial homes. He left his two youngest boys, William, eleven, and Arthur, ten, £1,300 pounds ($175,000) each—enough to live on and even build modest homes when they reached their majority. In the meantime their oldest brother, Philip, was to raise the two "religiously and virtuously and, if necessary, bind them to any profession or trade, so that they may earn their living honestly."[5]

As sole executor of the estate, Philip Ludwell Lee controlled the bequests of the four minor boys along with bequests of £1,000 each ($136,500 in current dollars) that Thomas left his two daughters as dowries to ensure marriages to husbands of standing. The older daughter, Hannah Lee, was already twenty-one when her father died and married a prosperous planter. His other daughter, Alice, fourteen, would later marry Philadelphia's renowned physician Dr. William Shippen, the future surgeon general of George Washington's Continental Army.

Twenty-year-old Richard Henry Lee sailed home to Virginia in 1752. More interested in scholarship than commercial trade or agriculture, he returned to his boyhood home at Stratford Hall, where his brother Philip—still unmarried—welcomed his brother's companionship, giving him his own apartment along with access to the more than 300 books in the Stratford Hall library. While Philip focused on running the family enterprise, Richard Henry immersed himself in history, political philosophy, political science, and law, absorbing the works of John Locke, Sir William Blackstone, and the Baron de Montesquieu.

"From the works of the immortal Locke," his grandson Richard Henry Lee II recalled, "he acquired an ardent fondness for the principles of free government; and from those of Cudworth, Hooker, Grotius, and other writers . . . he drew maxims of civil and political morality.

He read . . . the histories of the patriotic and republican ages of Greece and Rome, which animated his love of his country and of liberty. . . . His taste was refined by . . . Homer, Virgil, Milton, and Shakespeare. . . . The best histories of every age were within his reach, and a vast fund of political wisdom derived from them . . . when, in future life, he called for its use in the service of his country.[6]

Lee did not, however, devote himself exclusively to study. A consummate southern dilettante by then, "he mingled cheerfully in society," according to one of his grandsons. He attended all the festivities at great homes of other planters nearby, including Belvoir,* the stately mansion of Lord Fairfax and his family up the Potomac on the Northern Neck not far from Mount Vernon. Recipient of one of the largest royal grants in American history, Lord Fairfax could claim ownership of more than 1 million acres stretching over the entire Northern Neck in eastern Virginia, westward to the base of the Shenandoah Mountains. Lee was "affable and polite," his grandson noted, and "became very popular upon entering into the active scenes of life."[7]

It was at Belvoir that Richard Henry Lee met the young George Washington, at twenty-two, a year older than Richard Henry. Washington had just assumed control of what had been his older brother's plantation at Mount Vernon, upriver from Stratford Hall. In contrast to Richard Henry Lee, young Washington was a professional surveyor, an experienced wilderness explorer who loved gardening and farm work, and an officer in the Virginia militia. Ostensible opposites, Lee and Washington formed an instant friendship, with each—the scholar and the rugged outdoorsman—lacking yet admiring the other's experiences.

In the spring of 1755 the first clouds of war darkened American skies when French troops from Canada invaded what Virginia had long claimed as its territory in western Pennsylvania and the Ohio River Valley. Virginia's governor ordered Washington to lead

---

* The ruins of Belvoir are on the grounds of the military installation at Fort Belvoir, near Mount Vernon, Virginia.

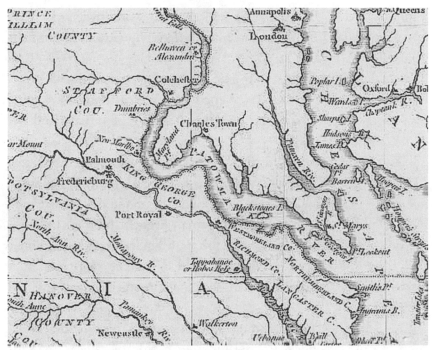

Map 1. Virginia's Northern Neck. The peninsula between the Potomac (spelled Patowmack on this antique map) and Rappahannock Rivers was one of several jutting out from mainland Virginia into Chesapeake Bay. Richard Henry Lee's boyhood home, Stratford Hall, and Chantilly, the home he built for his family, stood in Westmoreland County on the north shore opposite Blackstone's Island. George Washington's Mount Vernon stands overlooking the Potomac upriver at the first bend beneath Alexandria, in Fairfax County.

150 militiamen to demand surrender of Fort Duquesne, which the French had built on the site of present-day Pittsburgh. After a short skirmish in which the French humiliated Washington and his men, the Virginians staggered home to await the arrival of British general Edward Braddock with 1,400 regular British troops.

When Braddock's ships sailed up the Potomac River past Stratford Hall, Richard Henry Lee decided to emulate his friend Washington and take up arms. He galloped off with other volunteers to join Braddock in Alexandria—only to have Braddock reject the young

Virginians as ill trained and ill equipped. In words Richard Henry
Lee described as "coarse and rude," he ordered them to return to their
homes.[8]

Braddock was also ready to reject Washington and his 450-man
troop until junior officers intervened, citing Washington's experience in the backcountry and his understanding of Indians and Indian warfare.

Days later, however, as Braddock and his force reached Great
Meadows near their destination, the general ignored—indeed,
rejected—Washington's warning about "the mode of attack which
he would likely face against the Canadian French and their Indians.

"So prepossessed were they in favor of regularity and discipline,"
Washington explained in disbelief, "and in such absolute contempt
were these people [Indians] held, that the admonition was suggested
in vain."[9]

Confident the Indians would not dare attack his sparklingly at-
tired troops, Braddock ordered his men to advance linear style toward Fort Duquesne. Suddenly crackling shots and blood-curdling
war whoops engulfed the woods. A mob of half-naked French and
Indians materialized among the trees, emitting a ceaseless staccato
of shouts and shots. Dozens of British troops fell dead. Before survivors could turn and flee, a second wave of attackers succeeded the
first, letting loose another blast of blood-curdling brays and bullets.
In and out they sprang, left, right, front, rear, one after another
emerging from the trees, firing, then disappearing. Confusion and
terror gripped the British ranks. The slaughter lasted three hours:
977 of the 1,459 British troops and 66 of the 86 officers dropped
to the ground dead or wounded, including General Braddock, who
died from his wounds four days later. The French suffered 17 casualties, the Indians maybe 100.

As news of Braddock's humiliation filtered back to Alexandria
and, from there, to Stratford Hall, both elder Lee brothers, Richard
Henry and Philip Ludwell, determined to reshape Virginia's policies.

As a landowner, Philip was eligible to run for election to the House of Burgesses and won a seat, joining George Washington's brother Augustine and an imposing number of Lee cousins and their in-laws already sitting in the legislature. Owning no land in Westmoreland County, Richard Henry was ineligible to run, but brother Philip—now addressed as "Colonel Phil"—saw to his younger brother's appointment as a county justice of the peace. Although Richard Henry would not influence colonial policy for the moment, it was a first step into Virginia's political machinery until he settled on his own property and became eligible for election to the colonial legislature.

By the time George Washington and his crippled force emerged from the wilderness, rumors had listed him—and most of his troops—as casualties. Experienced as he was in wilderness warfare, however, he escaped unhurt and even added a touch of humor to his macabre adventure.

> "As I have heard a circumstantial account of my death and dying speech," he wrote to his brother Jack, "I take this early opportunity of contradicting the first and assuring you that I have not yet composed the latter. But by the all-powerful dispensation of Providence, I have been protected beyond all human probability and expectation, for I had four bullets through my coat and two horses shot under me yet escaped unhurt, although death was leveling my companions on every side of me."[10]

Washington's prowess as a horseman had allowed him to remount horses of dead officers during the battle and effect his own escape. On his return to Virginia, however, he raged as he reported details of "our shameful defeat" to the House of Burgesses in Williamsburg. Washington excoriated the British high command for having failed to train troops to adapt to unconventional, Indian-style warfare. He made it clear that a handful of individuals firing behind the cover of trees, shrubs, and rocks had a clear advantage in the wilderness over

7. *Colonel George Washington owned the Mount Vernon plantation upriver from Stratford Hall and commanded a unit of the Virginia militia who suffered a humiliating defeat at the hands of the Indians and French in western Pennsylvania.*

large columns of troops firing from upright positions in traditional linear-style warfare designed for the wide, open fields of Europe.

With that, the burgesses, led by a disproportionate number of supporters among the Lees, unanimously named Washington commander of the Virginia militia and voted to raise a 1,200-man force for him to command. "It is probable they will determine for 4,000," Richard Henry Lee's cousin Philip Ludwell told Washington. "Every one of my acquaintance profess a fondness for your having the militia

[and] whilst I am serving so deserving a man [as you], I think with pleasure that I am serving my country as well."[11]

With the French and Indians threatening to overrun the American West, Britain declared war on France on May 17, 1756, and ordered an expeditionary force far larger than Braddock's to sail to North America to halt French incursions into territory Britain claimed as her own. Until it arrived, Washington, his militia, and the rest of the Virginia population could do nothing but wait and hope the French and Indians would not march eastward.

In the meantime plantation life proceeded as normally as possible, with three Lee brothers—Philip, Richard Henry, and Thomas, who had returned from England by then—engaged in the usual family quarrels but nonetheless wooing eligible young ladies at the neighboring plantation. Brother Philip had been first to make contact with the owner, Colonel James Steptoe. While courting Steptoe's daughter Elizabeth Steptoe, he introduced his two younger brothers to his future wife's half-sisters, Mary and Anne Aylette. Tom married Mary and immediately whisked his bride upriver to the property he had inherited in Stafford County, midway between Stratford Hall and Alexandria. Richard Henry married Anne Aylette but had no inclination to farm the acreage he had inherited in Prince William County, upcountry on the Northern Neck near Mount Vernon. Intent on staying put among the books and luxuries of his boyhood surroundings, he gladly accepted Colonel Phil's invitation to remain in Stratford Hall with his bride, who became de facto mistress of the household and bore two of her children with Richard Henry there.[*] In addition to caring for infants Thomas and Ludwell, she and Richard Henry also took a hand in guiding the two youngest Lee boys, William and Arthur, both in their teens by then and still devoted to their older brother Richard Henry.

---

[*]Thomas and Ludwell were her second and third children, respectively, the first being Elizabeth, who died in infancy.

Colonel Phil had already discerned William's talents in mathematics and planned to bring him into the family business to learn international trade and banking. The youngest boy, Arthur, seemed an impractical intellect, however, and Richard Henry convinced Colonel Phil to send him to Eton and, from there, to medical school.

As Colonel Phil himself drew closer to marrying, he and Richard Henry recognized the potential for conflict between two matrons living in and governing the same household. Phil agreed to lease Richard Henry 500 acres high on a nearby bluff overlooking the Potomac, where Richard Henry designed a home he called Chantilly, after the Château de Chantilly north of Paris that had entranced him when he visited in 1751.

Richard Henry Lee's Chantilly was far less elaborate—but more practical—than the original, which had been built in 1560 for the French king's constable. Although Lee's home commanded a breathtaking view of the Potomac River, it was standard Virginia—a three-and-a-half-story, rectangular frame house, with front and rear doors placed in the center of the ground floor to let breezes flow through and cool the interior in summer. One Lee relative called the house commodious but not elegant. Its ground floor, clad in a veneer of brick, housed an entrance hall, parlor, library, and a twenty-by-twenty-four-foot dining room. The second floor, with its wooden clapboard exterior, held four bedrooms and a lookout room where Lee kept two telescopes to follow ships as they sailed on the river below, bound, as often as not, to the landing beneath Stratford Hall. The third floor, squeezed beneath a sloping roof, housed a large classroom, where a tutor would educate Richard Henry Lee's children, just as one had educated him at Stratford Hall.

Formal gardens reminiscent of those he had seen at Chantilly in France enhanced the lawns around the house, and a "great walk" led to the spectacular panorama at the edge of the bluff. A cellar held three dozen bottles of port wine, five dozen bottles of Virginia wine, a dozen bottles of gin, and ample supplies of madeira, muscat, claret, and champagne. Outbuildings included a kitchen, dairy,

8. *The magnificent Château de Chantilly, built in the sixteenth century north of Paris for the constable of France, entranced Richard Henry Lee when he visited it after graduating from Eton College. He would give the name to his own home in Virginia. (LPLT/Wikipedia Commons)*

blacksmith's forge, stables, barn, laundry, slave quarters, and, of course, a "necessary"—or outhouse. A landscaped path wound its way down to the river's edge, where a barge waited to take the Lees and their guests on river cruises.

With no interest in farming or commerce, Richard Henry opted for a career in public service, in which Colonel Phil agreed he could best serve the Lee enterprise and its interests in international commerce and land development in the west. Envisioning a life of reading, travel, contact with interesting public figures, and the joys of raising a family, Richard Henry wrote to friends far and wide seeking an interesting, if not taxing, government sinecure, of which there were many.

"I know not any person to whom I can, with more propriety, apply for an application on my behalf, that I may be appointed to fill the next vacancy in his majesty's council," he wrote to General James Abercrombie, commander of British forces in America. "The desire I have to do my country service is my only motive for this solicitation."[12] On the same day he wrote to a former schoolmate from Wakefield School to "entreat the favor of you . . . to apply to your noble friend Lord Halifax. . . . If an ardent desire to serve my country . . . [is] considered in this application, you may safely declare yourself my friend."[13]

He ended his efforts to obtain government appointments in 1757, however, when George Washington's older brother Augustine retired from politics and urged Richard Henry to run for his seat in the House of Burgesses.

As Richard Henry sought election in Westmoreland County, his younger brother Francis Lightfoot Lee, who had settled on a farm in Loudon County, fifty miles northwest of Alexandria, also sought election to the House of Burgesses. Both brothers won, and, when the three Lee brothers—Colonel Phil, Richard Henry, and Francis Lightfoot Lee—strode into Virginia's House of Burgesses, they joined eight in-laws and cousins to form the largest, most powerful voting bloc in the legislature, with more than 10 percent of the votes at most sessions. Their commercial dynasty had evolved into a political dynasty, and Richard Henry Lee, the dilettante scholar, suddenly found himself a powerful figure in Britain's most important colony.

Nor would Richard Henry Lee's younger brother Francis Lightfoot Lee—or Frank, as his brothers called him—long remain in the seclusion of his farm. Once in the sociopolitical swirl of Williamsburg, he met the magnificent Rebecca Plater Tayloe—at seventeen, she was half his age but nonetheless as attracted to him as he was to her. Her doting father was John Tayloe, a burgess and master of the 20,000-acre Mt. Airy plantation that stretched along the Rappahannock River on the south side of the Northern Neck, across the peninsula from Stratford Hall and Chantilly. The owner of 320 slaves, he also owned an enormous iron works that would supply Virginia's militia and navy with cannonballs and pig iron during the

9. *Richard Henry Lee won election to the House of Burgesses in Williamsburg, Virginia, bringing to eleven the number of Lees in the colony legislature—enough to dominate proceedings and direct the colony's destiny.*

Revolutionary War. Tayloe—the origin of the spelling is unclear—fully approved of his daughter's choice in marriage but refused to consider allowing her to leave for the Loudon County wilderness. He offered her fiancé, Francis Lightfoot Lee, 1,000 acres of Mt. Airy land as his daughter's dowry if he agreed to build a home and remain there with his wife. He did and they did—happily so. They were

10. Francis Lightfoot Lee, Richard Henry Lee's younger brother by a year, supported his brother's political quests in Virginia's House of Burgesses, its Assembly, and the Continental Congress. Always working on his brother's behalf behind the scenes, he almost never displayed the oral histrionics that lifted his brother Richard Henry to national fame.

near not only her family but also his brothers at Stratford Hall and Chantilly.

As these three Lee brothers and their eight cousins and in-laws took their seats in the House of Burgesses for the 1757 session, they joined a group whose names would become some of the most illustrious in American history: George Washington, George Mason, Benjamin Harrison, Peyton Randolph, and George Wythe, among others.

Once seated, the more than 100 burgesses ruled over the largest, wealthiest, and most heavily populated English colony in the New

World, with 800,000 people, or nearly 27 percent of the 3 million people in the thirteen colonies. Nearly three-fourths of the burgesses owned properties of more than 10,000 acres, with the median holding 1,800 acres with forty slaves. Washington owned more than 20,000 acres—with more than 300 slaves—and Speaker John Robinson, 30,000 acres and 400 slaves. Some 85 percent of burgesses had inherited their properties and what they deemed their right to rule the colony.[14] Of the 116 members, 40 had attended the College of William and Mary and nearly 100 had served as justices in their home counties before entering the House. Almost all had won election to the House without opposition. During the fifty previous years, four families—the Randolphs, Carters, Beverlys, and Lees—had dominated House voting.

Together the burgesses not only ruled Virginia—they *were* Virginia.

The only political division between burgesses reflected the split between Tidewater aristocrats like the Lees, who owned the large tobacco plantations in eastern Virginia, and the isolated upland farmers and backwoodsmen from the Piedmont hills to the west. Thirty-five of Virginia's fifty-six counties were in the Tidewater region, and only twenty-one were upland, giving the closely connected Tidewater aristocrats all-but-absolute control of the House.

All, however, paid obeisance to the politically conservative John Robinson, who had filled dual roles as both Speaker and colony treasurer since 1738 and held almost all the older burgesses in his thrall.

Robinson welcomed Richard Henry Lee and his brothers, expecting them to fall in line with the other burgesses who had marched in political lockstep behind him for a generation. Nothing in Richard Henry's boyish smile and warm demeanor signaled his intention to shatter the older man's career and bring Virginia's century-old political house crashing to the ground.

CHAPTER 2

Egyptian Bondage

As Richard Henry Lee entered the House of Burgesses the French and Indian War was raging in Canada, western Virginia, and other American provinces. Involving only Britain, France, and American Indians at first, it spread across the Atlantic to Europe, where it evolved into the Seven Years' War, with six more nations joining the conflict, expanding it into the planet's first "world" war.

In September 1758 the French and Indians staged raids that reached into eastern Virginia, threatening the Lee holdings at Stratford Hall and the Northern Neck. Newspapers blamed Washington and his misadventure in the West as having caused the conflagration: "When raw novices . . . who have never been used to command . . . are honored with commissions in the Army," the *Virginia Gazette* asked rhetorically, "how wretchedly helpless must a nation be?"[1]

As British reinforcements landed in America, they met with nothing but disaster. French forces swept southward from Quebec into New York, capturing three key English forts north of Albany while a hurricane destroyed a British fleet attempting to seize the French fortification at Louisbourg at the entrance to the St. Lawrence River.

British forces went on the offensive in some areas, however. In the waters off Nova Scotia they eventually forced the French to surrender Louisbourg. In western Pennsylvania a large force of British troops expelled the French from Fort Duquesne near the site where the French had humiliated General Braddock. In Europe British troops raided the French coast, and Britain's Prussian ally defeated and occupied Saxony, a French ally.

Although the war would continue in Europe until 1763, the capture of Fort Duquesne ended the immediate threat to Virginia. British forces all but ended the war in North America in September 1759 with a surprise assault on Quebec City that forced the French to surrender all of Canada to Britain the following year.

Although Virginians celebrated the British victory, they paid a heavy price in added taxes to pay for their participation, all but pushing some of Virginia's wealthiest plantation owners to the brink of financial ruin. Colonial treasurer John Robinson, the wily Speaker of the House of Burgesses, found a way to pay for the war, however, without bleeding his friends, the colony's property owners. He simply issued and sold government notes, which spread the burden for repaying costs of the war across America and Britain. Virginians hailed Robinson as a financial and political genius.

"His reputation was great for sound political knowledge and . . . a benevolence which created friends and a sincerity which never lost one," the future Virginia governor Edmund Randolph testified. "In the limited sphere of colonial politics, he was a column. The thousand little flattering attentions which can be scattered from the chair operated as delicious incense."[2] Robinson was everyone's hero.

Everyone's hero but Richard Henry Lee and his family.

Richard Henry Lee and his brothers did not dislike Robinson— no one could dislike him—but Robinson was a partner in the Loyal Land Company with, among others, Benjamin Harrison V, a wealthy Virginia planter-merchant. Their company had staked out lands south of the Ohio River and waged a long, bitter war for control of Ohio River rights with the Ohio Land Company on the opposite bank of the river. Washington, Lee, and their families were among the founder-partners of the Ohio Land Company, whose 200,000 acres were part of a 1612 royal grant. Both companies intended reaping huge profits from the sale of furs and other easily harvested wealth and the reselling of sections of land to would-be settlers. To open the region, however, they needed control of lands along the Ohio River waterway to carry men and materials to their holdings. Years of bitter family feuding had left both companies unwilling to compromise.

When Richard Henry Lee entered the House of Burgesses, he feigned obeisance to Speaker Robinson—politics and good manners demanded nothing less. Lee nonetheless grew suspicious of Speaker Robinson's grandiosity in providing colleagues with financial assistance in the form of Treasury notes. Backed by his family, Richard Henry moved that the House sever ties between the offices of the Speaker and the treasurer. To his surprise—indeed, to the surprise of most other burgesses a curious looking, ill-clad burgess stood to second Richard Henry Lee's resolution.

In stark contrast to burgesses in formal morning clothes and powdered wigs, he had entered the hall in drab work clothes—a working farmer from the Piedmont hills upcountry. Sentries had stopped him at the outer gate, but when he displayed his official papers and election certificate, the sergeant at arms had to let him pass, albeit reluctantly. His name was Patrick Henry, the owner of a simple 1,700-acre farm with no slaves. Although a few other upcountry farmers in homespun clothes sat scattered along the back benches of the House, Patrick Henry stood out in what seemed like a black shroud. He did not fit in, but Speaker Robinson had no choice but to recognize him.

By seconding Richard Lee's resolution, Patrick Henry drew the support from the other farmers and ensured passage of Lee's resolution to reform the House of Burgesses. He also established a "lasting friendship" with Richard Henry Lee, according to William Wirt Henry, Patrick Henry's grandson and biographer. "Mutual admiration and coincidence of views on public questions soon made them bosom friends."[3]

Energized by his first major political victory, Richard Henry again took aim at Robinson, this time noting the large number of slaves who worked the Speaker's 30,000-acre plantation. Suggesting that Robinson was profiting from the slave trade, Richard Henry set some burgesses aghast by moving "to lay so heavy a duty on the importation of slaves as effectually to put an end to that iniquitous and disgraceful traffic within the colony of Virginia."[4]

In what may have been the first—and certainly one of the earliest—public speeches on the subject in American history, he warned of slave rebellions to come, saying, "slaves must be natural enemies to society and their increase consequentially dangerous . . . because they see us enjoying every privilege and luxury . . . and because they observe their masters possessed of liberty which is denied to them, whilst they and their posterity are subjected forever to the most abject and mortifying slavery."

As Burgesses roared in collective outrage, calling on Lee to sit down, he grimaced, indicating he was far from finished.

"Not the cruelties practiced in the conquest of Spanish America," he thundered above the din, "not the savage barbarity of the Saracens can be more big with atrocity than our cruel trade with Africa.

> There we encourage those poor, ignorant people to wage eternal war against each other: not nation against nation but father against son, son against parents, and brothers against brothers, whereby parental, filial, and fraternal duty is violated, that . . . we *Christians* [he emphasized the word] may be furnished with our fellow creatures, who are no longer considered as created in the image of God as well as ourselves and equally entitled to liberty and freedom by the great law of nature, but they are to be deprived, forever deprived, of all the comforts of life and to be made the most wretched of the human kind.

Lee claimed that Christianity had introduced humane principles, universal benevolence, and brotherly love in Europe and "happily abolished slavery. Let us who profess the same religion," he pleaded, "practice its precepts, and . . . pay a proper regard to the dictates of justice and humanity."[5]

Lee himself owned forty slaves, his brother Philip more than one hundred at Stratford Hall, and neither had any inclination to emancipate them. Nor did Virginia law allow them to do so. Slaves were property, to be bought and sold with the land, not to be freed to run loose any more than livestock. Although Quakers hailed Lee's proposal as a step toward emancipation, Robinson supporters, whose plantations depended on slave labor, shouted Lee down, accusing him of planning to profit by breeding and selling his own slaves to fill slave shortages that his proposed duties would create.

Northern Neck plantation owners like the Lees, however, had seen the number of slaves balloon to 50 percent of the population and create an economic burden for their owners. Unlike cotton, which any child able to crawl could harvest to earn his keep, tobacco required skilled hands to plant, harvest, and cure. Newly arrived slaves, however, were not only unskilled, they were illiterate and, because they could not speak English, often proved difficult to train.[*]

In addition to difficulties training adult workers, almost one-third of the slave population on many plantations were infants too young to be productive, while an equal number were often too old

---

[*]Tobacco plant seeds required specially prepared beds, a careful daily watch over each plant, and careful "topping," or removing flowers by hand to force the flow of nourishment into the leaves. Harvesting leaves required a sixth sense—difficult to teach to anyone without language skills. A day or two too soon or too late reduced leaf quality and the market price. After harvesting came curing—a difficult process that required termination at the exact moment the leaf was pliable without being dry and brittle nor moist and soggy. Misjudgments could cost a planter his profits for the year and mean ruin.

or crippled to be productive but nonetheless cost their owners for food, clothes, and shelter. What Northern Neck planters feared most, however, was an increase in the slave population to numbers strong enough to stage a rebellion. Lee's proposed tariff increase was a way of stemming the growth of that population by making it too costly to import more slaves. By adding principles of Christianity to his address Lee hoped Quakers would join the Northern Neckers in support of his proposal.

In the end his political strategy and eloquence won the day, planting some of the first seeds of emancipation in Virginia and giving Lee the potential to become a powerful political force in Virginia.

As the Speaker's hold on leadership weakened, Richard Henry sought to wrest control of the House from Robinson and his supporters. It was not long before he learned that, instead of destroying Virginia government notes after repaying them from the Treasury, Robinson had kept them on the books as outstanding before parceling them out to cronies to cash in at the colonial treasury a second time.

Without disclosing his evidence of the Speaker's malfeasance, Lee moved "that a committee be appointed to inquire into the state of the Treasury," according to his grandson. "The Speaker fixed his eyes with a dark and terrible frown upon Mr. Lee. . . . The most able and influential members of the House opposed his motion, yet he refuted with great force all objections to the inquiry and seemed to gain strength and ardor from the very means taken to defeat it. The resolution was finally adopted."[6]

As Robinson and his cronies held their breath, Lee then "brought the matter to a close," saying he would not demand that a date be set for the inquiry and, in effect, "saved the colony from great fiscal embarrassment and the people from additional burdens." Although he had not sought leadership, Lee nonetheless acquired enormous political standing—in effect, a leader in spite of himself. Adding to the admiration for his political discretion was the quality of his speaking skills.

"Richard Henry Lee was by far the most elegant scholar in the House of Burgesses," recalled William Wirt, later to be attorney general. "His face itself was on the Roman model; his nose Caesarean; the port and carriage of his head, leaning persuasively and gracefully forward; and the whole contour noble and fine."[7] (See frontispiece, page v.)

Lee was also among the most well-educated members of the House, having studied every area of literature and science. "He possessed a rich store of historical and political knowledge," Wirt recalled. "He reasoned well, and declaimed freely and splendidly. The note of his voice was deep and melodious."[8]

Robinson retained his hold on the speaker's seat until his death in 1766, but his passing set off an immediate inquiry, which found at least £100,000 (about $13.5 million today) in outstanding loans to Robinson cronies—including some of Virginia's most prominent figures. As Lee suspected, Robinson himself had removed £10,000 (about $1.3 million today) from the Treasury to invest in his father-in-law's lead mines.

In 1765 Lee again displayed his eloquence, joining fellow burgess Patrick Henry in denouncing the British Parliament's stamp tax, the first direct tax ever imposed on American colonists. In effect for decades in England, the stamp tax required the purchase and affixment of one or more revenue stamps—often worth less than a penny—on all legal documents (wills, deeds, marriage certificates, bills of lading, purchase orders, etc.) as well as on newspapers and periodicals, liquor containers, decks of playing cards, and many other industrial and consumer goods.

All but negligible when added to the cost of any individual item, the stamp tax nevertheless amounted to a considerable—and reliable—revenue source for the government after collections from tens of thousands of documents and products poured into the Treasury. British chancellor of the Exchequer Lord Grenville estimated that stamp tax collections in America would reap about £60,000 a year, or about 20 percent of troop costs there.

At the time years of war had left England's treasury nearly bankrupt, with a national debt of £130 million (nearly $8 billion today) and £300,000 in annual costs of military garrisons to protect American colonists against Indian attacks. To pay for the garrisons, Parliament first raised taxes at home but sent 40,000 Englishmen plunging into debtor's prisons and provoked widespread antitax riots. Threatened with a national uprising, Parliament rescinded some tax increases at home and compensated for revenue declines by raising duties on America's imports and exports. Still facing huge deficits, it extended the reach of the British stamp tax to the colonies. Parliament—and, indeed, most Englishmen—believed Americans deserved to pay for their own military protection, and the stamp tax seemed the most innocuous way to do so.

Lee argued that Virginians had already paid a heavy tax of sorts in the sufferings and lives lost repelling Indian attacks, in the hardships endured settling and developing the wilderness and extracting its natural resources to benefit British shippers and industry.

The eloquent British parliamentarian Edmund Burke agreed. "Your scheme yields no revenue; it yields nothing but discontent, disorder, disobedience," he warned Grenville. "And such is the state of America, that after wading up to your eyes in blood, you could only end just where you began; that is, to tax where no revenue is to be found."[9]

Burke pointed out that for generations Parliament had only collected indirect "hidden" taxes such as import duties from the colonies. It had always allowed each colony's elected legislature to impose direct taxes such as sales taxes and property taxes to pay costs of colonial administration. The Stamp Act was the first direct tax Parliament had ever imposed on American colonists, and Richard Henry Lee joined other colonial critics in calling it "unconstitutional."*

---

*Then, as now, Britain's "constitution" referred to so-called case law—that is, the collective decisions handed down by the courts over generations.

Joining them in criticizing the Stamp Act was first-time burgess Patrick Henry. "The General Assembly of this colony have the only and sole exclusive right and power to lay taxes . . . upon the inhabitants of this colony," Henry all but shouted as Robinson blanched and reached for his gavel. "Every attempt to vest such power in any person or persons . . . other than the General Assembly . . . has a manifest tendency to destroy British and American freedom."[10] Reflecting views shared by Richard Henry Lee, Henry argued that Americans did not need the British military to protect them, that American militiamen could defend themselves by themselves.

Coming as it did after Parliament had doubled duties on non-British imports, the stamp tax sparked protests along the entire Atlantic coast, beginning in Boston and spreading to New York, Philadelphia, and southward. As it was, increased duties were already strangling the American economy in the spring of 1765. Importers were collapsing under the weight of debts to English suppliers; shopkeepers and craftsmen closed their doors; even the largest merchants struggled to stay in business, leaving farmers without their usual outlets for crops and at the mercy of speculators. Although personally unaffected by the Stamp Act, Richard Henry Lee stood in the House of Burgesses to support Patrick Henry. Ever the scholar, Lee cited John Locke's assertion that nature had created all men "equal and . . . no one ought to harm another in his life, health, liberty, or possessions . . . [or] take away, or impair the life, or what tends to the preservation of the life, the liberty, health, limb, or goods of another."[11]

As the debate in the House of Burgesses intensified, Henry raged at both the tyranny of the Stamp Act and the elders who had long ruled the House of Burgesses under Speaker Robinson. "Caesar had his Brutus, Charles the First his Cromwell, and George the Third may profit by their example!"[12]

Robinson interrupted, shouting, "Treason, sir!"

"Treason!" echoed the older burgesses, some standing to shake their fists at the insolent renegade farmer. "Treason! Treason!"

11. Patrick Henry, a newcomer to Virginia's House of Burgesses, raged against the British Parliament's attempt to tax Americans as a threat to freedom.

Henry arched his back and stood tall as he let the shouting subside.

"If *this* be treason," he sneered in defiance, "make the most of it!"

The House erupted in a cacophony of angry shouts and jubilant cheers. "Violent debates ensued," Henry recalled. Until then "many threats were uttered, and much abuse cast on me. After a long and warm contest, the resolutions passed by a very small majority, perhaps of one or two only."[13]

Richard Henry Lee and George Washington had stood as the intrepid "one or two" who formed that "very small majority" and tightened the bonds of friendship with Patrick Henry.

By the time the House of Burgesses recessed, Henry's eloquent arguments against the Stamp Act had ignited Richard Henry Lee's hitherto dormant interest in protecting Virginia and Virginians against parliamentary excesses. For him taxes simply meant an all-but-unnoticeable reduction in the income he and the Lees derived from growing and shipping tobacco. Until he encountered Patrick Henry, taxes had no grander meaning. Now they did.

"As bad as Egyptian bondage is now become the fate of every inhabitant in America," he wrote to his brother Arthur. "Every man in America hath much reason to lament . . . the loss of American liberty . . . the mother country being converted into an arbitrary, cruel, and oppressive step-dame."[14]

Richard Henry Lee returned home to Chantilly intent on building support for Patrick Henry and the tax protests by writing and publishing the provocative—indeed, subversive, if not treasonous—Westmoreland Resolves of 1766 (see Appendix A). The resolves reiterated his "allegiance and obedience to our lawful Sovereign, George the Third, King of Great Britain" but asserted that a British subject "cannot be taxed, but by consent of a Parliament, in which he is represented by persons chosen by the people, and who themselves pay a part of the tax they impose on others.

> If, therefore, any person or persons shall attempt, by any action, or proceeding, to deprive this Colony of these fundamental rights, we will immediately regard him or them, as the most dangerous enemy of the community; and we will go to any extremity, not only to prevent the success of such attempts, but to stigmatize and punish the offender.

Richard Henry intended presenting the resolves to Northern Neck planters at Leedstown on February 27 and threaten "danger and disgrace" to anyone collecting or paying the stamp tax. The resolution warned Parliament that Virginians would fight the Stamp Act "at every hazard and pay no attention to danger or to death."

But just as Richard Henry Lee was to present the resolutions and reach the pinnacle of political influence in Virginia, his political star suddenly crashed to earth when an ally of Speaker Robinson won the competition to become collector of stamps. Calling himself "An Enemy of Hypocrisy," he sent two articles to the *Virginia Gazette* exposing Richard Henry Lee as one of the losing applicants for the post as stamp collector.[15]

It was a devastating revelation. Lee had told no one that he had applied. Indeed, he regretted doing so immediately after filing it, but had no way of withdrawing it once it left on the boat to London. Red faced, embarrassed, ashamed of an action motivated solely by his greed for extra money, Lee hemmed and hawed and claimed unconvincingly that he had not realized the significance of the Stamp Act when it passed.

Finally he took the only action he could in the circumstances. He publicly apologized: "It was but a few days after my letters [applying for the collector's job] were sent away," he wrote to the *Virginia Gazette*, "that reflecting on the nature of the application I had made, the impropriety of an American being concerned in such an affair struck me in the strongest manner and produced a fixed determination . . . to prevent the success of a measure I now discovered to be in the highest degree pernicious to my country. I considered that to err is certainly the portion of humanity, but that it was the business of an honest man to recede from error as soon as he discovered it."[16]

By then the meaning of "my country" for some Americans had changed from Britain to the colony in which they lived. In Lee's case "my country" now meant Virginia.

With that, Richard Henry Lee pledged all his energies to fighting the stamp tax and presented the Westmoreland Resolves to a gathering in Leedstown. He then led three of his brothers, two cousins, four members of the Washington family, and more than one hundred others in signing the Resolves and exposing themselves to arrest by British authorities for subversion and imprisonment if not death. Colonel Phil's name was noticeably absent. Intent on maintaining warm relationships with British merchants, he resisted allying himself with American malcontents—even his own brothers. Although he resented the Stamp Act as much as any of them, he preferred to work for its repeal by sending gentle warnings to English merchants with whom he traded, illustrating in pounds and pence how the Stamp Act would raise costs of American commodities and leave American merchants with fewer profits with which to buy British goods.

With Richard Henry's name at the top of the Westmoreland signatories, he leaped back to leadership among those his brother called malcontents—only to have tragedy mar his political success. In a ghastly hunting accident Richard Henry fired his gun, and it exploded, blowing the fingers off his left hand. After a long, slow healing process, he covered all but the thumb of his deformed hand with black silk, an accessory he would wear the rest of his life. To add to his misery, his wife, Anne, fell ill and died just before Christmas, leaving him to care for four young children—two girls, two and four, and two boys, eight and ten. Within a year, however, he found another wife, "a pretty little widow" who, Richard Henry enthused, proved "a most tender, attentive, and fond mother to my dear little girls."

Also named Ann, his second wife lacked only the second "e" of her Christian name to match his first spouse in the love she lavished on the family. She not only embraced him and his children but would also increase his brood to nine, five girls and four boys, none named Richard Henry Lee.

Arthur, twenty-eight by then, had earned his MD from Edinburgh Medical School—then, the English-speaking world's finest—and toured France and Holland, where he stayed to earn a second MD at the prestigious University of Leyden before returning to London. There, with Benjamin Franklin's endorsement, he won membership in the renowned Royal Society of London, added the exclusive FRS to the two MDs after his name, and joined Britain's most distinguished intellectuals and physicians. The prestige of his appointment reached across the Atlantic, where he won election to the American Philosophical Society in Philadelphia and the Board of Visitors (trustees) at the College of William and Mary in Williamsburg, Virginia.

12. Arthur Lee, seven years younger than his brother Richard Henry Lee, studied at Eton College, then earned an MD and a law degree in England before evolving into a champion of American independence and the most important spy for the American independence movement.

During Arthur's years in medical school Colonel Phil had continually dipped into the cash inheritances of his younger brothers to finance trade opportunities, thus forcing him to ignore requests from Arthur (and William) for money that was legitimately theirs—and angering both brothers. Often in desperate need to pay for his education, Arthur, of necessity, turned to Richard Henry, who proved himself a generous brother, dispensing money as well as wise counsel, cementing his role as a trusted mentor.

"Every man in America hath much reason to lament . . . the loss of American liberty," Richard Henry Lee wrote to Arthur in July 1766 after Arthur had returned to London and Parliament had passed the Stamp Act. Richard Henry said the Act had transformed "the mother country" into "an arbitrary, cruel, and oppressive step-dame." He urged his brother to return to America to join the family's struggle for repeal. America, he wrote, "has a parent's claim to her descendants and a right to insist that they shall not fix in any place where, in so doing, they may add strength to cruel and tyrannical oppression." He signed it, "I am, my dear brother, ever your affectionate friend."[17]

Although he had not intended doing so, Arthur responded immediately to his brother's call and returned to Virginia, ready to plunge into battle. He did not have to wait long, although it was not the battle he had anticipated. He arrived just as Richard Henry drew harsh criticism for his public apology over the stamp collector's post from George Mercer, who had won the job as stamp collector. A former officer cited for bravery serving with George Washington in the French and Indian War, Mercer was a crack shot. His articles exposing Richard Henry's hypocrisy so infuriated Arthur Lee that he challenged Mercer to a duel. With no experience firing pistols, he nonetheless appeared at the appointed dueling ground at 5 a.m. on the appointed day ready to die—indeed, certain to die—for his brother's honor.

Arthur waited in vain.

Later Mercer claimed he had been delayed and that by the time he arrived, Lee had left. In truth, a discreet word from George Washington, a warm friend of both the Lee and Mercer families, coaxed Mercer to spare Arthur Lee's life.

In the spring of 1765 Boston lawyer James Otis sent a letter to each of the colonial assemblies asking them to send representatives to convene in New York City to formulate a colony-wide protest against the Stamp Act. Four provinces failed to respond or send representatives, but state representatives who did appear adopted Richard Henry Lee's Westmoreland Resolves and sent copies to the king and to both houses of Parliament. Both the king and Parliament ignored the documents.

When the Stamp Act went into effect on November 1, 1766, Americans refused to purchase a single stamp. And after 200 New York merchants pledged to stop buying imported goods, merchants elsewhere followed suit—400 in Philadelphia, 250 in Boston. Anglo-American trade came to a halt, making Colonel Phil's warning seem prescient. British exports to America plunged 20 percent. Ordinary Britons, addicted to American tobacco, raged at the shortages the Stamp Act produced. Facing bankruptcy with no American raw materials to sell, British merchants hammered at the doors of Parliament demanding a return to normal trade with the American colonies. Almost a year to the day after it had passed the Stamp Act, Parliament retreated and repealed it, without a single stamp having been sold in America.

As Richard Henry Lee and other opponents of the Stamp Act rejoiced, Parliament avenged its humiliation, however, by passing a Declaratory Act, asserting that Parliament "had, hath, and of right ought to have full power and authority to make laws and statutes of sufficient force and validity to bind the colonies and people of America . . . in all cases whatsoever."[18]

A year later it used that power to pass the Townshend Acts, imposing import duties in the colonies on glass, lead, paints, paper, and tea. The first four items were essential to constructing homes and businesses in America, and the last item—tea—was a staple of the American diet in Boston and other major towns. Unnoticed at first, a series of twelve *Letters from a Farmer in Pennsylvania* appeared in newspapers across the colonies alerting Americans to the Townshend duties and arousing their collective furor.

Written by the wealthy Pennsylvania lawyer and legislator John Dickinson, the *Letters* conceded Parliament's authority to impose duties to regulate trade but not to raise funds for the government's treasury. "Every statute relating to these colonies, from their first settlement to this time," he argued, "is calculated to regulate trade.

> Never did the British Parliament think of imposing duties for the purpose of raising a revenue. Here then, my dear countrymen, ROUSE [his emphasis] yourselves and behold the ruin over your heads. If Great Britain can order us to pay what taxes she pleases, we are . . . abject slaves.[19]

Dickinson's *Letters* so gripped Richard Henry Lee that he arranged for a special printing in Williamsburg, writing a preface that condemned Britain's Navigation Act and the "exclusive trade with these colonies." He charged Parliament with trying to seize control of America's most valuable assets by bankrupting those who had uncovered and developed those assets. He then wrote to Dickinson, "As a friend to the just and proper rights of human nature, but particularly as an American, you, Sir . . . have the honor of giving just alarm and of demonstrating the late measures to be, at once, destructive of public liberty and in violation of those rights which God and nature have given us.

> To prevent the success of this unjust system, a union of counsel and action among all the colonies is undoubtedly necessary. How to effect this union in the wisest and firmest manner, perhaps time and much reflection only can show. But well to understand each other and timely be informed of what passes both here and in Great Britain, it would seem that not only select committees should be appointed by all the colonies, but that a private correspondence should be conducted between the lovers of liberty in every province.[20]

In writing to Dickinson, Richard Henry Lee became the first American Patriot to call for establishment of committees of correspondence in all the states and for the British-American colonies to effect a union.

In Boston Dickinson's *Letters from a Farmer* provoked merchants to resume boycotting British imports. Rhode Island and New York followed suit. New York City business leaders developed a scheme to promote domestic production of goods they had previously imported, thus increasing local employment as well as local commerce.

Taking full advantage of the turmoil in Boston, Samuel Adams, a Harvard scholar who had failed in business before becoming a political activist, followed Richard Henry Lee's suggestion and wrote a "circular letter" approved by the Massachusetts House of Representatives that he sent to the legislatures of the twelve other colonies. As Dickinson had done, Adams assailed the Townshend Acts as violations of the constitutional principle prohibiting taxation without representation.

Adams, however, conveniently overlooked the fact that few taxpayers in England had any representation in Parliament. Indeed, only 1 million of the 9 million adult males in Britain were entitled to vote, and there were many valid reasons for Americans not to have a vote. First, they would have too small a number of members of Parliament (MPs) to have any impact on legislation. Secondly, agents such as Benjamin Franklin were already representing American interests and had failed to convince a parliamentary majority that the American colonies should not share the costs of defense. One or two votes in Parliament would have added nothing. And thirdly, MPs went unpaid. Colonists would, therefore, incur new costs of transporting their representatives to and from London and lodging and supporting them and their families there.

"Copyholders, leaseholders, and all men possessed of only personal property choose no representatives," argued Soame Jenyns, a member of Parliament from Dublin who supported limited representation in Parliament and Parliament's right to tax Americans. He cited what he called the principle of "imaginary representation," with Parliament, in effect, representing all Englishmen, voters and nonvoters alike.

Manchester, Birmingham, and many more of our richest and most flourishing trading towns send no members to Parliament and consequently cannot consent by their representatives because they choose none to represent them. Yet are they not Englishmen? . . . Why does not their imaginary representation extend to America as over the whole island of Great Britain. If it can travel three hundred miles, why not three thousand? If it can jump rivers and mountains, why cannot it sail over the ocean? If the towns of Manchester and Birmingham sending no representatives to Parliament are notwithstanding there represented, why are not the cities of Albany and Boston equally represented in the assembly?[21]

But the arguments of Jenyns and other parliamentarians had little effect in Boston, where street demonstrations grew increasingly violent and provoked the British to send two regiments of troops into Boston Harbor, where they landed and imposed martial law.

In Virginia both Richard Henry Lee and his brother Arthur scoffed at the Jenyns argument, pointing out that some 15 percent and more of the MPs in the House of Commons represented pocket boroughs and rotten boroughs, in each of which a small group of landowners—in fact, often only one landowner—controlled the vote of an entire geographic area. The Lees charged Parliament with corruption and intending to bleed American landowners of their wealth. The Townshend duties, they charged, aimed at making it too costly for would-be settlers to buy materials to build homes in America, thus undermining land values and allowing British politicians and their cronies to buy American land at a fraction of its value.

After two years of attempting to establish a medical practice in Williamsburg, Arthur Lee abandoned his efforts. Eight other native Philadelphians with MDs had already established thriving practices in Philadelphia by the time he arrived, and as a Virginian in a state not his own—in effect, a "foreigner"—he faced insuperable competition from them and local "empirics." The empirics were, in fact, quacks, but they concocted tasty alcohol-based syrups they patented and sold as medicines to the sick and desperate as well as the healthy poor who could not afford conventional liquor.

The growing American resistance to Parliament and British rule, however, had piqued Arthur's interest in constitutional law, and he decided to return to London to study law and, where possible, represent the interests of his brother and other opponents of parliamentary rule. To that end he collected letters of introduction while on a junket through the middle colonies and New England to meet leaders of the resistance to British taxation, including Samuel Adams and his Boston associates.

Arthur's younger brother, William, meanwhile, had grown discouraged working for Colonel Phil. Although he had learned all facets of the tobacco trade and kept Colonel Phil's books carefully and faithfully, William's rewards were paltry. Aside from free lodging and meals at Stratford Hall, he received only token pay for his work and found himself continually at odds with Colonel Phil over the latter's reluctance to release funds from William's inheritance. When he learned of Arthur's intent to return to Britain, he asked to sail with him, and Arthur embraced the idea of the two sharing the trip and their lives in London.

In May 1769 George Washington's Northern Neck neighbor, planter George Mason, introduced a set of resolutions in the House of Burgesses asserting that only the governor and the provincial legislature were authorized to tax Virginians. Mason also assailed a parliamentary proposal to bring American malcontents to Britain for trial. The British royal governor disagreed and responded by dissolving the House of Burgesses before it could vote on Mason's resolves. Outraged by the governor's arbitrary dismissal, Richard Henry Lee and the others reconvened the next day at Williamsburg's Raleigh Tavern and adopted Mason's Resolves along with a ban on imports of British goods covered by the Townshend Acts. They also adopted a landmark agreement banning importation of slaves—the ban that had generated outrage when Lee had sought it as a newcomer in the

House of Burgesses twenty years earlier. The Burgesses also agreed to ban importation of European luxury goods from which British merchants had been profiting.

Other provinces followed suit, with Maryland merchants voting for the boycott a month later, followed by merchant groups in all other provinces.

In August 1769, however, a hurricane sent a forty-foot-wall of water crashing over the Atlantic coast, overflowing Virginia's low-lying riverbanks and carrying away houses, outbuildings, and tobacco warehouses that bulged with the previous season's harvest. Ten days of heavy rains followed and washed away the fortunes of Tidewater planters, large and small, leaving many penniless and searching for missing children, family members, and family retainers. Untold hundreds died; thousands of livestock vanished; tens of thousands of acres of fall plantings and topsoil flowed into the maelstrom, leaving direct losses estimated at £2 million—more than $250 million in today's money. James River planters alone lost 2.3 million pounds of warehoused tobacco.

Planters, traders, merchants, and bankers across the flood-ravaged regions could no longer think in terms of boycotts. They would need all the help they could get from Britain in money and supplies. Instead of alienating the British, they now needed—and intended—to embrace every Britisher they knew. For them all thoughts of rebellion had ended.

CHAPTER 3

No Liberty, No King!

WHILE FLOODS DEVASTATED THE LOWLANDS, MOST PLANTERS ON
the Northern Neck escaped devastation. Their homes and much of
their planted acreage stood atop tall bluffs that guided the flood waters harmlessly down streams into the Potomac and Rappahannock
Rivers and into Chesapeake Bay. With George Washington's plantation at Mount Vernon all but untouched, the value of his tobacco
crop soared, increasing his fortune amid surrounding devastation of
biblical proportions.

The storm affected the British as well as Americans, slashing colonial imports from Britain from about £2.2 million the previous
year to only £1.3 million in 1769.

Although Chantilly and Stratford Hall suffered relatively minor
damage, the storm destroyed and washed away the thriving riverside
port facility at Stratford Landing. Richard Henry Lee, his hand and
lower arm still healing, took an indefinite leave of absence from the
House of Burgesses to return to his family, help repair his home at
Chantilly, and lend whatever help he could at Stratford Hall and
Mt. Airy.

By then Richard Henry Lee's "dear brothers" Arthur and William had reached London. He missed them both. "The flame of liberty burns bright and clear," Richard Henry wrote to Arthur, "nor can its luster be impaired by any ministerial art or delusion.

> The Americans from one end of the continent to the other appear too wise, too brave, and much too honest to be either talked, terrified, or bribed from the assertion of just, equitable, and long possessed rights. It is clear beyond question that nothing but just, honest, and friendly measures can secure to Great Britain the obedience and love of America. . . . I have been so covered with affliction this past winter that I have thought little of anything except my own unhappiness. . . . Continue, my dear brother, to love me and to believe that I am and ever shall be your most affectionate brother.[1]

Once in London, Arthur Lee settled into lodgings at Lincoln's Inn, where law students lived and studied because of its proximity to the courts. At the time the study of law was an informal process, with candidates immersing themselves in a prescribed range of law books on their own, attending and learning from court proceedings as much as possible, hiring tutors as needed, and eventually taking the bar examination when they deemed themselves prepared. Lincoln's Inn was—and is—one of four "Inns at Court" where future lawyers (barristers) lived while preparing for the bar, the other three being the Inner Temple, Middle Temple, and Gray's Inn.

Richard Henry sold Arthur Lee's horses to cover his younger brother's initial London expenses, but he would eventually have to carry the entire burden of Arthur's legal education. Theirs was a deep filial affection, strengthened by Colonel Phil's increased coldness toward his siblings. Ever more obsessed with expanding his business and embellishing the palatial interiors at Stratford Hall, he not only distanced himself socially from his younger brothers and sisters, he continually dipped into funds set aside for their inheritances, often making them wait interminably for the money he owed them.

13. William Lee, another of Richard Henry Lee's younger brothers, used his commercial ties while in England as head of his own tobacco trading house in London to funnel secret shipments of arms and ammunition to American revolutionaries.

As Arthur was studying law, William established himself as a to-bacco trader. Already skilled from his years under Colonel Phil, he had signed agreements to serve as London agent for a number of Virginia planters. In addition to tobacco from the 500 fertile acres Richard Henry had leased at Chantilly, he had inherited hundreds of acres of his own upriver that he leased to tenant farmers to produce tobacco. After enlisting other Lee relatives as clients, William sailed into London with an impressive list of growers to supply him with tobacco for his trading business. He could not have picked a better time to set up shop.

Early in 1770 British merchants again forced the British government to cede ground in its conflict with Americans by repealing all

but one of the Townshend duties. Within a year the American provinces ended their boycotts and restored normal trade with Britain,
producing enormous profits for William's new venture. To save face
politically, however, the government retained an all-but-negligible
duty on tea—a symbol of its authority to tax Americans directly.

Before Americans learned of the British turnabout on tariffs,
however, anti-British riots erupted in New York and Boston, with
the Boston disturbance culminating in British troops shooting and
killing five protesters. Civil authorities arrested six British soldiers
and their commanding officer and charged them with murder, but
two renowned Boston lawyers—John Adams and his cousin Josiah
Quincy, both of them Whigs—won acquittals for four of the soldiers
and their commanding officer by a decidedly anti-British jury made
up of local farmers. The jury found two of the soldiers guilty of man-
slaughter, but recognizing that their victims had provoked them, it
exacted only a token punishments (a brand on the thumb) and released them. With the end of the trial peace returned to the streets
of Boston and the rest of the American colonies.

By then William's tobacco trading business was prospering and
adding to the profits of both Philip Ludwell's Stratford Hall and
Richard Henry's Chantilly. With William acting as their London
broker, they eliminated unrelated middlemen, allowing their tobacco
to travel on Lee-owned ships to a Lee-owned warehouse in London,
where William would sell the tobacco to English merchants—often
in exchange for household goods and other items the Lees needed in
America. With William's newfound wealth came access to London
society. He was, after all, still British.

Like Arthur, William adored his brother Richard Henry, and
aware of the financial burdens Richard Henry faced with his growing family, William invited Richard Henry to send his two oldest
boys to England, where he would see to their education.

Attending a British academy remained the hallmark of Virginia
gentlemen, and William enrolled them in St. Bees, an adequate (if
not Etonian) English boarding school in Lancashire. Founded in

1583 by the Archbishop of Canterbury, it experienced good years and bad and would manage to survive until 2015.

"'Tis the care of my dear boys that I recommend to you with true parental warmth," Richard Henry wrote to William. "Their welfare, you may be sure, is deeply in my heart. . . . They are good scholars so far as they have gone. I propose Thomas for the church and Ludwell for the bar. [At] about 15 years old, Ludwell may be entered at one of the Inns of Court and come there to study law . . . so that he may return with the gown at 21. We shall hereafter consider the cheapest and fittest place for the eldest until the time comes that he can be ordained. He is 14 years old next October and Ludwell 12 the same month. . . . Pardon me for not now making you a better remittance."[2]

In fact, Richard Henry's financial reserves were touching bottom. Public service had proved a costly occupation, encompassing nothing but costly outlays and, without a sinecure, no income. He asked William, therefore, to see that "my boys . . . be very frugally clothed. The plainest, to be decent, will please me much the best.

> With five children and another—it may be two—in the stocks, a small estate must part with nothing unnecessary. I take all possible care, but I assure you, if the varying state of politics on your side would enable my brother to fix the profit of some place with me, it would remove many difficulties. Have an eye on the deputy secretary's place.[3]

In the days and weeks that followed, however, Richard Henry applied himself to the family business, consigning 96 hogsheads of tobacco to William in one shipment, 33 in another, 40 in another, 54 in still another, and promising 220 or 230 more. Business was booming for the Lees on both sides of the Atlantic.*

---

*Each hogshead was a barrel four feet high and two and a half feet wide, weighing about 1,000 pounds and containing about ten cubic feet of tobacco.

Like William, Arthur had also been quick to make friends and connections in London, and given his base at Lincoln's Inn, they tended to be in law, politics, and the arts. Both Lees used their ties to publicize Virginia's complaints about British taxation; William established friendships with business men seeking to improve trade relations with America, and Arthur fraternized in the political world with those seeking political compromise.

William displayed the more winning personality, however, and used his status as an Englishman to win election as one of London's two sheriffs in 1773. Not long thereafter he won a post as alderman—a lifetime position as a member of the borough council. Once safely on the council, he announced his intention to run for a seat in Parliament and castigated the British government for its treatment of colonials. To the surprise of both William and Richard Henry, William found enormous support from Londoners in the world of commerce with whom he had business relations as head of the Lee trading operation. The commercial community wanted nothing but peace—and the profitable trade and prosperity it generated.

After Parliament passed an act reasserting its authority over the colonies, William spoke out in defiance, declaring, "The act cannot give a right which does not exist. Parliament had no right to make such an act. Americans had never acknowledged such authority." Lee accused the Ministry of committing "many oppressions of the unoffending Americans such as . . . seizing their property violently, sending an armed force to command obedience by the sword. . . . These proceedings were too much for human nature to bear."[4]

Arthur, meanwhile, defended American interests from a different direction, using a letter of introduction from Samuel Adams to meet Benjamin Franklin—at the time the overworked agent in Britain for both Massachusetts and Pennsylvania. Franklin gladly arranged to reduce his workload by seeing to Arthur's appointment as assistant agent for Massachusetts.

Arthur's ties to Franklin brought him into contact with a wide range of London political characters, including a group of radical, self-professed "friends of America." England's first woman historian, "the Celebrated Catherine Macaulay," was one, and scientist Joseph Priestly another. Other "friends" included cleric Richard Price and essayist Dr. Samuel Johnson along with such politicians as Edmund Burke, Isaac Barre, and the notorious John Wilkes.

Wilkes was a relatively well-to-do and extremely learned son of a British distiller, but he was as ugly as he was rich. Often called England's ugliest politician, he compensated for his facial deficiencies with an insatiable appetite for women, outrageously radical political views, and a charming and disarming personality that won him an army of friends and supporters. After starting a small, opposition newspaper, Wilkes won election to Parliament in 1757 but was expelled for insulting the king. Tried and sentenced to prison, he fled to France but returned in 1768 to serve his sentence. Supporters rioted outside Wilkes's prison, shouting "No liberty, no King," only to have troops fire into the crowd, killing seven and wounding fifteen. Infuriated survivors, however, rallied to reelect Wilkes to Parliament even as he languished in his prison cell.

After his release, Wilkes returned to Parliament to denounce the British government for attempting to tax Americans. "The assumed right of taxation without the consent of the subjects," Wilkes warned, "will lead to the horrors of civil war."[5]

With encouragement from his brother Richard Henry, Arthur Lee joined a Wilkes-backed political group called the Supporters of the Bill of Rights, which also supported the rights of Americans to tax themselves. "My political progress made me acquainted with many of the leaders of all parts of the opposition," Arthur explained his transition from law student to spy.

Then, "by constantly comparing the different ideas of those gentlemen . . . with the plans and proceedings of the ministers," he said, "I was able to form a pretty accurate judgment . . . of the real

*4. John Wilkes, British political leader jailed for in-
sulting the king, won re-election to Parliament while
still in prison and led member protests against taxing
Americans without their consent. The town of Westmoreland, Pennsylvania, honored Wilkes and Irish
member of Parliament Isaac Barre for their support by
renaming itself Wilkes-Barre.*

intentions of the latter and how far America was warranted in relying on the support of the former."[6]

Backed by the Supporters of the Bill of Rights, Arthur wrote
the first of a series of angry editorials under the pseudonym Junius
Americanus—a variation of the anonymous *Junius*, who had written
scathing criticisms of King George III. The original Junius was a
Roman patriot who overthrew a despotic Roman government.

"In the heart of every American," Junius Americanus (Arthur Lee) explained in one article, "the wish for the prosperity of England is second only to that for the liberties of his own country.

> When that cannot be done without submitting their hands to chains and their necks to the yoke, they must be forgiven for the refusal . . . they will never be slaves. . . . It has been my humble, but honest task to warn his majesty's ministers through the channel of the public papers of the fatal consequences of their arbitrary measures. . . . When the acts of this country respecting America are just, they will never be questioned; when they are unjust, they will never be obeyed.[7]

At Arthur Lee's suggestion, Richard Henry established his own links to a few opposition figures, including the controversial, albeit delightful Catherine Macaulay. Unusually well educated for a British commoner, Macaulay had been a prolific reader as a girl and embraced the histories of the Roman and Greek Republics. Calling "liberty" her primary object of study, she wrote the epic eight-volume *History of England from the Accession of James I to the Revolution*—a work that transformed her into "the Celebrated Mrs. Macaulay" by questioning divine right of kings and espousing the rights of citizens to depose their monarch. A harsh critic of British government policies in America, she had grown close to John Wilkes and, eventually, Arthur Lee.

"As a good Christian properly attached to your native country," Richard Henry wrote to Macaulay, "I am sure you must be pleased to hear that North America is not fallen. Nor likely to fall down before the images the king hath set up.

> After more than ten years of abuse and injury . . . the administration is at length determined to try if the sword cannot effect what threatening acts of Parliament had in vain attempted. . . . The inhumanity with which this war . . . (unprovoked as it has been on this side) is prosecuted is really shocking. A few days since, in the midst of

winter's northern climate, did [British] General Howe turn out of
Boston between two and three hundred women and children without even the necessaries of life. Some of them died on the water side
before their hospitable countrymen could relieve them.[8]

Although Arthur Lee continued issuing his tempestuous *Junius*
articles, the British government purposely ignored him. Some calm
was returning to America, restoring British-American trade to pre-
crisis conditions, and Parliamentary leaders seemed content to leave
things that way.

Convinced that the calm presaged another storm, however, Richard Henry Lee insisted that Congress lay the foundation of an intelligence network in Europe, beginning with the appointment of
Richard Henry Lee's brother Arthur as its eyes and ears in London.
"It would be agreeable to Congress *to know the disposition of foreign
powers towards us* [his italics], and we hope this object will engage
your attention," Richard Henry wrote to Arthur on behalf of the
Committee of Secret Correspondence of Congress. "We need not
hint that *great circumspection and impenetrable secrecy* are necessary."[9]

In Boston, meanwhile, the vestigial Townshend duties on tea
imports had provoked a boycott of British tea and rampant smuggling of Dutch tea. At first British authorities paid little attention.
Tea duties were hardly noticeable amidst the flow of revenues from
America. When, however, a group of the boldest smugglers burned
the British customs schooner *Gaspé* near Providence, Rhode Island,
a Commission of Inquiry proposed sending the assailants to England
for trial. Adding to what New Englanders deemed a threat to local
self-rule was a decree subjecting the conduct and pay of the governor
of Massachusetts and all provincial judges to the crown, rendering
the executive and judiciary independent of local control.

By early 1773 the boycott of British tea had left 17 million
pounds of East India Company tea overflowing London warehouses
and onto London docks. Parliament reacted by letting the company
ship tea to America duty-free and sell directly to consumers through

franchised shops. The Act locked the merchants responsible for the American boycott out of the tea business by creating a government-supported monopoly on English tea.

Boston merchants retaliated, sending thugs to terrorize East India Company agents and calling on other provinces to prevent East India Company tea from landing in America.

On Sunday, November 28, 1773, the first Boston-bound ship glided toward the wharf in Boston with its cargo of tea. A few days later a second tea ship tied up beside the first, and a third sailed into port after two more days.

A few days later an angry mob marched down a nearby street shouting, "Boston harbor a tea-pot tonight!" A group of forty to fifty demonstrators, amateurishly disguised as Indians with blankets over their heads and coloring on their faces, boarded the tea ships. Methodically and skillfully they lifted the tea chests from the hold with blocks and tackles, carefully split each open with axes, and dumped the tea and splintered chests into the water—342 chests in all, valued at £9,659, or more than $1 million in today's currency.

As lawyer John Adams rode into Boston the next morning he saw the splintered tea chests and huge clots of tea leaves covering the waters of Boston Bay. "This," he wrote in his diary later, "is the most magnificent movement of all. There is a dignity, a majesty, a sublimity in this last effort of the Patriots I greatly admire. . . . This Destruction of the Tea is so bold, so daring, so firm, intrepid & inflexible, and it must have so important Consequences and so lasting, that I cannot but consider it as an Epocha in History."[10]

In Virginia Richard Henry Lee had mixed feelings about what Americans would later call the Boston Tea Party. Even as he hailed Boston's defiance of the Tea Act, he condemned the destruction of private property. He was, after all, a property owner himself. "Something material may happen in consequence of the well-deserved fate which befell the tea on your quarter," he warned Boston rabble-rouser Samuel Adams. He predicted the British would respond with "harsh measures."[11]

15. *The Boston Tea Party, shown here in Nathaniel Currier's 1846 lithograph, saw the destruction of £9,659 worth of tea, or $1 million in today's currency by American rebels disguised as American Indians.*

Richard Henry Lee's fellow burgess George Washington was more sanguine, disapproving "of their conduct in destroying the tea" but asserting that "the cause of Boston . . . is and ever will be considered as the cause of America." He predicted "a general war is inevitable whilst those from whom we have a right to seek protection are endeavoring by every piece of art and despotism to fix the shackles of slavery upon us."[12]

Samuel Adams ignored Richard Henry's warning and called for colony-wide disruptions of tea shipments and boycotts of English tea in all the colonies. Bostonians responded with a second "tea party," New Yorkers staged their own immediately afterward, and Philadelphians followed suit a few days later.

To halt the spread of insurrection the British government passed the first of the so-called Coercive Acts, or, as others called them, the Intolerable Acts. The first, the Boston Port Bill, passed on March 1, closed Boston's port to all traffic—in and out—threatening to starve Bostonians until they submitted to unconditional British rule and recompensed the India Tea Co. for its losses.

"No shock of electricity could more suddenly and universally move [us]," Richard Henry Lee wrote to brother Arthur in London, using the most colorful metaphor he could devise.

At this time of immense danger to America, when the dirty ministerial stomach is daily ejecting its foul contents upon us, it is quite necessary that the friendly streams of information and advice should be frequently applied to wash away the impurity. Astonishment, indignation, and concern seized on all.

16. *Samuel Adams as a street activist whipped Boston mobs into a frenzy, throwing stones, bottles, and other missiles at British soldiers, provoking them to fire and kill five civilians and wound six others at the Boston Massacre.*

Lee called the British policy "a most wicked system for destroying the liberty of America."[13]

When Bostonians refused to submit to the Boston Port Bill, Parliament passed two more Coercive Acts on May 20. The first stripped the people of Massachusetts of voting rights and empowered the king to appoint and dismiss members of the Massachusetts (governing) Council. It gave the royal governor power to appoint and dismiss all members of the judiciary—the attorney general, all judges, justices of the peace, and so forth.

The second Coercive Act reached beyond the Massachusetts border and established a centralized British government in the former French colony of Canada. Called the Quebec Act, it also extended the Canadian border southward to the Ohio River, incorporating western Pennsylvania, Ohio, Indiana, and Illinois into Canada. In effect, the Quebec Act cost Americans their claims to all the lands in the Ohio Territory, including the hundreds of thousands of acres of Ohio Land Company lands the Lee and Washington families had planned to develop.

Richard Henry might have tolerated some British trade restrictions and taxes that limited his market for tobacco to Britain; he could even tolerate taxes that forced him to share his income with what he considered a corrupt British government. But he could not—would not—tolerate those same officials confiscating lands that his family had owned for generations. This was their land: Lee land. The Quebec Act simply stole it from him. To make matters worse, Parliament passed yet another, fourth Coercive Act on June 2, legalizing the arbitrary quartering of British troops in private homes as well as taverns and unoccupied buildings.

The Quartering Act proved a breaking point.

The Boston Port Bill had warred against Samuel Adams and Boston, the Massachusetts Government Bill had warred against the rest of Massachusetts, and the Quebec Act had warred against the Lees and Washingtons. But the Quartering Act, with its power to station a Redcoat in every home, warred against all Americans, and Richard

Henry Lee strode forward with George Washington to lead Americans to war on the British Empire.

Sensing the need for stronger leadership in the growing anti-British movement, Richard Henry Lee issued a public condemnation of the Boston Port Bill, calling it "a most violent and dangerous attempt to destroy the constitutional liberty of and rights of all North America." He called for a colony-wide congress "to consider and determine ways . . . for securing the constitutional rights of America against the systematic plan for their destruction."[14]

Recognizing Samuel Adams's influence in the besieged Boston community, Richard Henry wrote to Adams to lay the groundwork for the first truly "continental" congress, asking, "Do you not think, Sir, that the first most essential step . . . will be an invitation to a general congress as speedily as the nature of things will admit?

> I hope the good people of Boston will not be dispirited under their present heavy oppression, for they will most certainly be supported by the other colonies, their cause being rightly and universally considered the common cause of British North America. So glorious a one it is . . . that all America will owe their political salvation . . . to the present virtue of Massachusetts Bay.[15]

Although Richard Henry esteemed Samuel Adams as a valuable, popular leader in Boston and a vital ally in the struggle against Britain, he viewed Adams as both parochial and unstatesmanlike—capable of rallying a mob and igniting riots but too outspoken to attract American statesmen to his side. Despite a Harvard education, Adams lacked the subtlety to negotiate with haughty British leaders who had honed their sophistication at Eton and Oxbridge. Moreover, he did not understand the differing needs of thirteen diversified colonies nor did he wield the political skills to unite them as one. Richard Henry realized that independence by itself would not unite them. Adams, moreover, did not possess what Lee had at his command—a network of allies in every corner of the British political establishment.

There were many like Adams in America who could lead a violent revolution, but few could match Lee's ability to lead a nuanced, perhaps even nonviolent revolution to produce political change and restore the constitutional rights of Americans without loss of life.

Thus Lee stepped into the breach, first by calling for a nonviolent day of fasting in support of the people of Boston. This earned him so much national attention that Virginia's colonial governor, Lord Dunmore, punished him and his followers by dissolving the House of Burgesses and charging Lee with defying royal authority.

In doing so, however, Dunmore miscalculated, angering burgesses who had been neutral in the dispute between colonies and crown and even breeding resentment among some otherwise loyal Tories. Lee responded by calling burgesses to reconvene in nearby Raleigh Tavern the next day. With the approval of almost all, he assailed the Intolerable Acts and called for a convention of political leaders from across the colony to meet the following year to respond. To stay informed about the latest schemes afoot in Parliament, he wrote to his brothers in London to establish a flow of information from Parliament's inner sancta—in effect, establishing America's first espionage service, sending letters with pieces torn out and sent separately, thus making each letter incomprehensible unless pieced together with one or more others.

"It is said . . . that the war is to be carried into Virginia as well as in the northern provinces," William Lee wrote from London to brother Richard Henry. "The utmost industry of the Ministry is employed to inflame men's minds here, especially by publishing . . . accusations of savageness and barbarity . . . on the part of the provincials. . . . Thirty thousand men is . . . the estimate of the whole force intended against America. Next year."[16]

"It is essentially necessary," Richard Henry wrote cryptically to brother Arthur, "that you visit Virginia for a few months." Without saying as much, he hoped Arthur would understand his brother's command as a plea to bring Richard Henry Lee's boys back to

Virginia before someone in the British government decided to use them as hostages.[17]

Stepping forward publicly as Virginia's acknowledged political leader, Richard Henry Lee summoned district leaders from across the state to convention, where they approved proposals that included a total ban on trade with Britain and reiterated their opposition to parliamentary levies, including the Tea Tax. They labeled any consumer of East India Tea "an enemy to the rights and liberties of America." The ad hoc convention went on to select delegates to attend Lee's proposed national convention in Philadelphia—or, as historians would call it later, the First Continental Congress. It was an invitation to Americans to unite in a new and independent nation—and an invitation to British authorities to hang Richard Henry Lee for treason.

On September 5, 1774, Richard Henry joined fifty-five other delegates from twelve of the thirteen British-American colonies in Philadelphia's Carpenters' Hall. They were a curious group, differing in modes of dress, depending on their geographic origins. Excepting those whose parents had shipped them to British schools as Lee's parents had done, they often had difficulty understanding each other. Depending on which colonies they inhabited, they spoke a wide variety of English dialects flavored by accents that often made their words indecipherable. Immigrants from many nations had settled in various parts of North America—often sailors who jumped ship and introduced words and accents that infected entire regions. Slaves had affected almost every southerner's accent.

Other factors such as geography worked against cohesion among the delegates to the Continental Congress. Philadelphia lay more than three days' travel from New York, about ten days from Boston, and was all but inaccessible from far-off cities such as Richmond or Charleston. There were few roads, and foul winter weather and spring rains isolated vast regions of the country for many months and made establishing cultural ties difficult at best and often impossible. The

South—and southerners—were as foreign to most New Hampshire-men as China and the Chinese. In fact, only 60 percent of Americans had English origins. The rest were Dutch, French, German, Scottish, Scots-Irish, Irish, and even Swedish. Although English remained a common tongue after independence, German prevailed in much of Pennsylvania, Dutch along New York's Hudson River Valley, and French in Vermont as well as parts of New Hampshire and what would later become Maine.

Author-schoolteacher Noah Webster compared the cacophony of languages to ancient Babel, and Benjamin Franklin complained that Germantown was engulfing Philadelphia. "Pennsylvania will in a few years become a German colony," he growled. "Instead of learning our language, we must learn theirs, or live as in a foreign country."[18]

So except for a handful of delegates who shared a deep resentment against Britain's Parliament—John Adams and Samuel Adams of Massachusetts, for example, or Richard Henry Lee and Patrick Henry from Virginia—there was little camaraderie or unity among the delegates as they gathered in Philadelphia. Indeed, Georgia had refused to send delegates. Dependent on British troop protection against Indian attacks, Georgian leaders had no intention of alienating the British government by attending a congress dedicated to criticizing and perhaps overthrowing British rule.

In addition to Lee and Henry, the other Virginians attending were George Washington, Peyton Randolph, Edmund Pendleton, Benjamin Harrison, and Richard Bland, a wealthy planter, longtime burgess, and, like quite a few Virginia patricians, related by marriage to Richard Henry Lee and Thomas Jefferson.

Having won recognition as America's premier orator, Virginia's Patrick Henry was first to speak at the convention. According to Boston lawyer John Adams, Henry noted that theirs was the first such congress in American history and that they could look to no former congress for a precedent. Every word uttered would itself be a precedent. According to Adams, Henry went on to proclaim,

We are in a state of nature, sir. . . . Government is dissolved. Where are your landmarks, your boundaries of colonies? The distinctions between Virginians, Pennsylvanians, New Yorkers, and New Englanders, are no more. I am not a Virginian, I am an American.[19]

Congress would remain in session seven weeks, during which every delegate had to "show his oratory, his criticism, and his political abilities," John Adams grumbled to his wife, Abigail. Calling some of the proceedings "tedious beyond expression," he told her that if a motion were made that two plus two equaled five, delegates would debate it endlessly "with logic and rhetoric, law, history, politics and mathematics."[20] He had a kinder evaluation of Richard Henry Lee, whom he described simply as "an orator."

"The Virginians," Adams noted in his autobiography, "loudly celebrated . . . the eloquence of Mr. Patrick Henry and Mr. Richard Henry Lee," but according to one delegate, "the most eloquent speech that had ever been made in Virginia on American affairs had been made by Colonel Washington." Adams claimed it "was the first time I had ever heard the name of Washington as a patriot in our current controversy.

I asked who is Colonel Washington and what was his speech? Colonel Washington he said was the officer who had been famous in the late French war and in the battle in which Braddock fell. His speech was that if the Bostonians should be involved with the British Army, he would march to their relief at the head of a Thousand Men at his own expense. . . . We all agreed that it was both sublime, pathetic, and beautiful.[21]

Because of Virginia's importance as the largest and richest American colony, at least two Virginia delegates served on every committee, with Patrick Henry serving on three—including one with John Adams and Richard Henry Lee to prepare a final address to the king.

Adams first met Lee at the home of Dr. William Shippen, who had married Richard Henry Lee's sister Alice. Richard Henry was staying with the Shippens, who had invited the famed Massachusetts lawyer to breakfast along with other dignitaries. Dr. Shippen's taste for fine wines made his elegant home one of the city's culinary centers as well as a salon for intellectuals and sophisticates. John Adams was one of four delegates from Massachusetts visiting the Shippens, along with his cousin Samuel Adams, Thomas Cushing, and Robert Treat Payne. French visitors to the Shippens' home described *conversaziones* reminiscent of the greatest Italian philosophers.

"In the afternoon, we drank tea," a visiting French marquis would recall. "While one of the young ladies sang, a second accompanied her on the harpsichord, a male guest played the harp, and another male guest played violin. This was the first time I had seen music introduced into American society."[22]

"They are all sensible and deep thinkers," Adams said of the Lees and Shippens. Adams called Richard Henry "masterful" and hailed his proposal for repealing all the Intolerable Acts and removing all troops from Boston. He also supported Lee's proposal for a colony-wide "abstinence from all dutied articles. . . . He is absolutely certain that the same ship that carries home [to England] the resolution will bring back the redress."[23]

Among Lee's other resolutions was a ban on imports of all British-made goods, provoking opposition from Pennsylvania delegate Joseph Galloway, a Philadelphia lawyer and staunch Loyalist with close ties to the British government. Striking back at Lee, Galloway warned, "If we will not trade with Great Britain, she will not suffer to trade with us at all. Our ports will be blocked up by British men of war, and troops will be sent to reduce us to reason and obedience."[24]

Galloway called for reconciliation with Britain and adoption of what he called "a plan of union" that would create an American colonial parliament with a president-general appointed by the crown and delegates appointed by colonial assemblies. The colonial parliament would act in concert with Britain's Parliament on most issues, but each parliament could veto the other's decision on matters relating to the colonies.

"I am as much a friend of liberty [as] exists," Galloway averred, "and no man shall go further, in point of fortune, or in point of blood, than the man who now addresses you.

> It is impossible [that] America can exist under total non-exportation. We . . . should have tens of thousands of people thrown upon the cold hand of charity. Our ships would lie by the walls, our seamen thrown out of bread, our shipwrights . . . out of employ and . . . it would weaken us in another struggle which I fear is too near. . . . We want the aid and assistance and protection of our Mother Country.[25]

Although Galloway's Plan of Union offered the colonies greater control of internal affairs, Congress rejected it in favor of Richard Henry's proposal for a Continental Association that would ban all imports from Britain; all exports to Britain, Ireland, and the West Indies; consumption of British products and foreign luxuries; and the slave trade.

Lee then proposed resolutions that went far beyond his mandate from the Virginia Convention. He called on each of the colonies to organize militias and for Congress to arm them in preparation for war.[26] He also demanded that the British remove all troops from Boston. Until then "the free citizens of Boston [should] . . . quit their town and find safe asylum among their hospitable countrymen."[27]

Reconciliationists rose in opposition, calling Richard Henry Lee's proposal "a Declaration of War" against the British Empire—as indeed it was. Like Washington, John Adams, and Patrick Henry, Richard Henry Lee had declared independence.

CHAPTER 4

Poet, Playwright, Watchmaker, Spy

ALTHOUGH CONGRESS HAD APPROVED RICHARD HENRY LEE'S proposal to unite the colonies in a Continental Association, it was unwilling to defend it by warring with the British Empire. In consequence it defeated Lee's resolution on militias along with his proposal that Bostonians quit their city.

"If we demand too much," New York's John Jay argued, "we weaken our efforts, lose the chance of securing what is reasonable, and may get nothing."[1]

In Massachusetts, however, representatives of towns in Suffolk County, which included Boston, met secretly, declared the Coercive Acts unconstitutional, and called for a boycott of all British trade—imports and exports. The group urged citizens to withhold payment of taxes and debts to British merchants until Parliament restored local control of government in Massachusetts. It told people to arm themselves and form local militias to defend their towns against the British army. It was a declaration of open rebellion, and Boston activist Paul Revere, a local silversmith, galloped off to Philadelphia to inform delegates at the Continental Congress.

Electrified by the news, the Congress shouted down the reconciliationists and rallied around Richard Henry Lee, who resolved to
denounce the Coercive Acts and the presence of Britain's standing
army in and about their homes in cities like Boston. With Lee and
the two Adamses—a triumvirate from North and South—urging
them on, a majority in Congress adopted Lee's resolution and ten
others drawn from the Suffolk Resolves, enunciating the rights of
Americans to "life, liberty, and property" and restoring exclusive
powers of provincial assemblies "in all cases of taxation and internal
polity"—subject only to veto by the crown.

After Congress had expressed unanimous consent, Lee led members in declaring thirteen of the parliamentary acts passed since 1763
to have been violations of the rights of British citizens in America.
Congress pledged to impose economic sanctions against Britain until Parliament repealed them all, then agreed to reconvene the following May 10, 1775.

"The proceedings are yet on honor to be kept secret," Richard
Henry wrote to William Lee in London, "but we have great hopes
that their vigor and unanimity will prove the ruin of our Ministerial
Enemies and the salvation of American liberty. About a fortnight
more will produce a publication of our plan after which you shall
have it by the first opportunity."[2]

Knowing that his brother would inform key British officials,
Richard Henry told William that "50,000 men in arms" in Massachusetts and Connecticut were "on the march" to Boston and that
the British would have "no small difficulty . . . [in] forcing submis-
sion from these people and that they are most firmly resolved to die
rather than submit."[3]

John Adams was equally excited. "This was one of the happiest
days of my life," he wrote in his diary. "In Congress we had generous, noble sentiments, and manly eloquence. This day convinced me
that America will support Massachusetts or perish with her."[4]

After Adams and Lee had prepared a suitably obeisant letter to
the king expressing the hopes of Americans to remain his subjects,

Richard Henry drafted a letter on behalf of Congress to colonial agents in London, believing the king would respond favorably: "We desire you will deliver the petition into the hands of his Majesty, and . . . wish it may be made public through the press, together with the list of grievances and . . . to the trading cities and manufacturing towns throughout the United Kingdom."[5]

When Richard Henry returned to Chantilly he learned that his older brother Philip Ludwell—Colonel Phil—was deathly ill at Stratford Hall. During the weeks of agonizing pain that followed, he worked with Richard Henry to set his estate in order, naming Richard Henry executor and trusting his brother to see to the care of his wife, his two daughters, and a third offspring soon to be born. If a boy, he was to become Philip's heir.

Colonel Phil died on February 21, 1775, after which his wife, Elizabeth Steptoe Lee, gave birth to a son and heir, Philip Ludwell Lee Jr., but the boy would live only two years, leaving the great Stratford estate and its associated businesses to Colonel Phil's two daughters. During that time Richard Henry Lee had to oversee a huge commercial enterprise and assume responsibility for raising a second family—in addition to overseeing his own plantation at Chantilly and caring for his pregnant wife and six children.

Before the king could respond to the letter from the Continental Congress the British government acted "to declare all meetings and associations in America illegal and treasonable . . . and to employ military force, chiefly from Canada, if necessary. . . . Added to this," Richard Henry Lee wrote to Samuel Adams in early February 1775, "I understand they propose to forfeit and confiscate all the estates of all those who meet, associate, or combine against the commerce of Great Britain."[6]

By then Lee had seen to implementing Continental Association rules at Stratford Landing, boasting to his brother William that "a ship from London . . . has been forced to return without being suffered to take a single hogshead of [Lee] tobacco [back to England] because she had brought a few chests of tea." He assured

William that "every measure is taken to enforce the Continental Association."[7]

The government ban on meetings, however, infuriated him, coming as it did in the face of the king's apparent refusal to respond to the carefully—indeed, deferentially—worked out appeal for redress by the Continental Congress. What he called the "wicked violence" of the government left no doubt in his mind, he told his brother Arthur, "of the determination to ruin both countries unless a powerful and timely check is interposed by the body of the people."[8]

Like Richard Henry, most Virginians had hoped the king and Parliament would respond favorably to the Continental Congress petition for redress—much as they had responded by repealing most of the Townshend Acts in 1770 in the aftermath of the Boston Massacre. Indeed, all England seemed to support the American petition. When Parliament reconvened in January 1775 petitions from London, Bristol, Birmingham, Liverpool, Manchester, and almost every other English trading city asked for restoration of normal relations with the colonies. Everyone hoped for peace, it seemed, but George III and a small group of ministers in Parliament. On January 12, however, the king dashed the last hopes of the Americans for peace.

After reading the petition of the Continental Congress the king simply sneered, complimented its eloquence, and laid it aside. A fortnight later he rejected it and demanded that Parliament halt trade with the colonies, provide army protection for Loyalists, and arrest protesters as traitors. As the House of Commons debated passage of legislation to transform the king's pronouncements into law, Irish member Edmund Burke pleaded with his colleagues to reconsider.

"The use of force alone is but temporary," he protested. "It may subdue for a moment; but it does not remove the necessity of subduing again, and a nation is not governed which is perpetually being conquered."[9]

Parliament relented only slightly after Burke's speech by offering a blanket pardon to repentant rebels—with the exception of such

17. *George III sneered at American petitions for peace and reconciliation with England, declaring them in rebellion and increasing the number of troops he sent to suppress Americans.*

"principal Gentlemen who . . . are to be brought over to England . . . for an inquiry . . . into their conduct." Among them were George Washington, Patrick Henry, Richard Henry Lee, John Hancock, Samuel Adams, John Adams, and other radicals the government believed were in "a traitorous conspiracy" against a monarch seated by "Divine Providence."[10]

As punishment for such a crime, British law dictated hanging by the neck, and "while you are still living your bodies are to be taken down, your bowels torn out . . . your head then cut off, and your bodies divided each into four quarters"—a fate Richard Henry Lee, for one, did not relish.[11]

When news reached America of the king's rejection of the congressional appeal, Virginia's former burgesses—now calling themselves assemblymen—called for another Virginia Convention. They picked Richmond as their site rather than Williamsburg, where a build-up of British naval strength in nearby waters raised the menace of arrest for Richard Henry Lee, Patrick Henry, and other Virginia political leaders. A town of only 600 residents and 150 homes, Richmond had no assembly hall as such. The largest seating area was in St. John's Anglican Church on Richmond Hill, with space in its pews for about 120 people.

On March 20, 1775, the delegates sidled into the pews—Richard Henry Lee, George Washington, Thomas Jefferson, and other renowned Virginians. Patrick Henry took a seat in the third pew on the gospel, or left, side of the church facing the front. He stood to propose three resolutions, the first two merely parroting resolutions of Maryland's Assembly the previous December: "That a well-regulated militia, composed of gentlemen and yeomen, is the natural strength and only security of a free government; that such a militia in this colony would forever render it unnecessary for the mother country to keep among us, for the purpose of our defense, any standing army of mercenary soldiers . . . and would obviate the pretext of taxing us for their support."[12]

As Washington and Lee listened intently, Patrick Henry broke new ground with a third resolution calling for nothing less than war: "That this colony be immediately put into a state of defense, and . . . prepare a plan for embodying, arming, and disciplining such a number of men, as may be sufficient for that purpose."[13]

Richard Henry Lee shot to his feet to second Henry, as spectators at the rear of the church applauded and a crowd that had gathered outside the door cheered. When the delegates had finished expressing their views, Henry stood "with an unearthly fire burning in his eye," according to a clergyman on the scene.[14]

18. Patrick Henry tells Virginia's former burgesses at a meeting in St. John's Church in Richmond, "If we wish to be free . . . we must fight!"

We have petitioned—we have remonstrated—we have supplicated—we have prostrated ourselves before the throne . . . we have been spurned, with contempt. . . . There is no longer any room for hope. If we wish to be free . . . we must fight!

Henry paused, stood tall, then hurled his arms apart defiantly and looked to the heavens, playing the scene like the veteran actor he was. In loud, triumphant notes he proclaimed, "I repeat it, sir: We must fight!

Gentlemen may cry peace, but there is no peace. . . . The war is actually begun! . . . Our brethren are already in the field! . . . Why stand we here idle? Is life so dear, or peace so sweet, as to be purchased at the price of chains and slavery?

He paused. A frightening silence engulfed the church.

"Forbid it, Almighty God! I know not what course others may take, but as for me. . . . "

He paused again, looked to heaven as if addressing God himself, and called out,

Give me liberty or give me death![15]

The audience sat in stunned silence, unable to think, let alone speak or applaud. Patrick Henry's triumphant words resounded beyond the walls of Richmond's Anglican church, across the colony and continent—and across the sea. "Henry was thought . . . to speak as man was never known to speak before," Williamsburg attorney Edmund Randolph noted. George Washington wrote to his brother, "It is my full intention to devote my life and fortune in the cause we are engaged in."[16]

After delegates had caught their collective breaths Richard Henry Lee again stood to second Henry's resolutions, and the convention passed them, ordering Virginia "to be immediately put in a posture of defense." It appointed a committee to prepare a plan for "embodying, arming, and disciplining" the Virginia militia and elected delegates to attend the Second Continental Congress in Philadelphia in May, among them Richard Henry Lee and George Washington.

On March 27 the convention adjourned, but in every county across Virginia men and boys sewed the words "Liberty or death" on their shirt fronts and rode to their county courthouses to join local militias to fight the British.

Richard Henry Lee received "intelligence from London from our most vigilant, sensible, and well-informed friends" (read, Arthur and William Lee) that the government had compiled a "black list" of thirty-two Americans, including some Virginians, who would be subject to arrest on sight and immediate deportation for trial in London. Apart from himself, other notables on the British black list were Boston activist Samuel Adams and his political ally, the wealthy merchant-banker John Hancock. As Lee learned, Lord Dartmouth, the secretary of state for colonial affairs, had sent blanket orders from London to America's royal governors and commanding generals to use whatever means necessary to enforce the Coercive Acts in Massachusetts and "arrest the principal actors and abettors."[17]

"Some Virginians are in the black list," Richard Henry Lee wrote to his friend and fellow plantation owner Landon Carter. "God put us into the hands of better men and better times, which will surely be the case if we provide ourselves immediately with arms and ammunition, learn the discipline, behave like men, and stick close."[18]

On April 18, 1775, British general Thomas Gage sent troops from Boston to destroy a militia arsenal in Concord, while a detachment went to Lexington to arrest Adams and Hancock, who were hiding there after fleeing Boston. Patriot spies fanned out across the countryside to warn of the approaching British troops, with silversmith Paul Revere reaching Lexington at midnight—in time to warn Adams and Hancock to flee.

As the British approached Lexington, 200 "minutemen"—armed locals determined to repel the British—positioned themselves on the village green to face the dreaded Redcoats.

While the main British force marched to Concord five miles distant, a detachment of 700 troops quick-marched into Lexington. A shot rang out, then another, and still more. When the firing ceased, eight minutemen lay dead and ten wounded on Lexington green, the first casualties in a revolution that would send the world's greatest empire into irreversible decline.

As the main British force in Concord searched in vain for Patriot arms, minutemen attacked a platoon of British soldiers guarding Concord's North Bridge. Realizing the Patriots had removed most of the arsenal, the British commander ordered his men to return to Lexington, only to encounter a growing rain of sniper fire. Minuteman ranks had swelled into thousands. Musket barrels materialized behind every tree, every boulder, every stone wall. One thousand reinforcements arrived to protect the British retreat, but the minutemen had grown to 4,000, then 6,000, 8,000, and 10,000. They came from everywhere; town after town sent 100 men, 200, or as many as they could muster to rally around their fellow countrymen. In the end they slayed 73 British soldiers and wounded 174, suffering 49 dead themselves, with 42 wounded. The decimated British troops wreaked revenge in every town, looting and burning houses, bayoneting anyone who stood in their way, civilian or military.

Incensed by reports of the encounter, Richard Henry Lee wrote to his brother William of the "shameful" British assault, saying, "The wanton and cruel attack on unarmed people after they had brutally killed old men, women, and children . . . roused such an universal military spirit throughout all the colonies and excited such universal resentment against this savage ministry and their detestable agents that no doubt remains of their destruction with the establishment of American rights."[19]

Lee said thousands of colonists from farms and villages and cities across New England, their passions aroused by the incident on Lexington Green, were gathering arms and rallying to the side of the minutemen outside Boston. "The provincials are since increased to 20,000 and lay now encamped before Boston," Lee continued his letter to his brother. "All communication is cut off between town and country."[20]

By then both Samuel Adams and John Hancock had reached Philadelphia safely, joining Samuel's cousin John Adams and Richard Henry Lee at the opening session of the Second Continental Congress. The Patriot propaganda machine that Samuel Adams had organized in Boston sent riders like Paul Revere across the colonies to describe the events at Lexington and heighten American Anglophobia with tales of British atrocities—some true, some tall, all terrible, and many false. Besides accusing the British of setting fires to homes, shops, and barns in Lexington, Samuel Adams told newspapers that the British had "pillaged almost every house they passed.

But the savage barbarity exercised upon the bodies of our brethren who fell is almost incredible. Not content with shooting down the unarmed, aged, and infirm, they disregarded the cries of the wounded, killing them without mercy, and mangling their bodies in the most shocking manner.[21]

In Virginia the Continental Association boycott of British trade was taking hold, with dock hands at Lee's Stratford Landing and other Potomac River and Chesapeake Bay ports refusing to allow any ships to unload cargoes from Britain and forcing them to leave—"scarcely allowing [them] to get fresh provisions," according to Richard Henry.

"All North America," he assured his brother Arthur, "is now most firmly resolved to defend their liberties ad infinitum against every power on earth that may attempt to take them away."[22]

Richard Henry Lee and the rest of the Virginia delegation to Congress were already at war with the British government when they gathered in Philadelphia. Indeed, George Washington appeared in his uniform as a colonel and commander of the Virginia militia, and Patrick Henry had already organized a militia in central Virginia's Piedmont hills where he lived. Although Congress elected Boston merchant-banker John Hancock president, Richard Henry Lee arrived with Patrick Henry and George Washington poised for a military response to the British and boasting that "Virginia's Frontier Men . . . can furnish 1,000 rifle men—men that for their number make the most formidable light infantry in the world."[23]

Knowing that his brother Arthur would pass the information to key political figures in London, Richard Henry Lee sent information he hoped might make British war hawks reconsider.

> The six frontier counties can produce 6,000 of these men who, from their amazing hardihood, their method of living so long in the woods without carrying provisions with them, the exceeding quickness with which they can march to distant parts, and above all the dexterity to which they have arrived in the use of the rifle gun. There is not one of these men who wish a distance of less than 200 yards or an object larger than an orange. Every shot is fatal.[24]

On June 2 Congress received a letter from Dr. Joseph Warren, the new president of the Massachusetts Provincial Congress, urging it to assume control of the disorganized intercolonial army laying siege to Boston. "The army now collecting from different colonies is for the general defense," Warren wrote.

> The sword should, in all free States, be subservient to the civil pow-ers . . . we tremble at having an Army (although consisting of our own countrymen) established here without a civil power to provide for and control them. . . . We would beg leave to suggest to your consideration the propriety of your taking the regulation and general direction of it. . . . The continent must strengthen and support with all its weight the civil authority here; otherwise our soldiery will lose the ideas of right and wrong, and will plunder, instead of protecting the inhabitants.[25]

A week later John Adams proposed that the Continental Congress make the Patriot forces besieging Boston a "Continental Army." Richard Henry Lee and the others agreed and immediately appropriated £6,000 for supplies. Two days later British General Thomas Gage imposed martial law in Boston and declared all Americans in arms and those siding with them to be rebels and traitors. Congress responded by electing a five-man committee to draft rules for administration of the army and to name a commanding general. With each delegation eager to name a worthy Patriot from his state, the committee decided to give the top position to the most qualified man they could find and create subsidiary positions for four major generals and eight brigadier generals, giving each colony at least one general in the combined army.

As for commander-in-chief, John Adams had mingled dis-creetly among the delegates for several days—southerners as well as northerners—listening to and trying to understand every view and sentiment. Teaming with Richard Henry Lee, he concluded that delegates from middle and southern colonies harbored "a jealousy against a New England Army under the Command of a New England General."[26] Connecticut delegate Eliphalet Dyer suggested that selecting a non-New Englander "removes all jealousies, more firmly cements the southern to the northern and takes away the fear of the former lest an enterprising New England general, proving successful, might with his victorious army, give law to the southern or western gentry."

It was evident to all that George Washington had the most "skill and experience as an officer" of any southern candidate.[27] He had commanded the Virginia Regiment for nearly five years during the French and Indian War, gaining an intimate knowledge of wilderness battle tactics.

On June 10 Maryland's Thomas Johnson nominated Washington, with John Adams seconding the nomination. "I had no hesitation to declare," Adams explained, "that I had but one gentleman in mind for that important command, and that was a gentleman from Virginia . . . whose skill and experience as an officer, whose independent fortune, great talents, and excellent universal character, would command the approbation of all the colonies better than any other person in the Union."[28]

John Adams had now joined Richard Henry Lee and a small but growing minority of American leaders in heralding a union of the thirteen provinces. Although the vast majority of Americans and their leaders still claimed that each of the thirteen colonies were independent countries, a handful—Richard Henry Lee, John Adams, and Patrick Henry as the most prominent—envisioned the states eventually uniting as an independent nation.

Congress voted unanimously to name Washington commander-in-chief, then resolved to raise six companies of riflemen in Pennsylvania, Maryland, and Virginia to march to New England to support the troops encircling Boston.

By default Richard Henry Lee took charge of logistics. Seldom did the number of delegates attending Congress exceed fifty. Together they had all the responsibilities of the executive, legislative, and even judicial branches of government. Untrained in waging war, they did the best they could, attempting to divide the workload by forming committees for intelligence, foreign affairs, military affairs, and marine matters, among others. Seldom knowing how to proceed, most committees willingly ceded leadership and responsibility to the few men like Richard Henry Lee whose personas displayed leadership. His education; his travels in Britain and Europe; his ties to Washington, Patrick Henry, and other Virginia leaders; his connections to opposition figures in Britain through brother Arthur Lee; and his links to the powerful Lee family international trading and shipping enterprise all marked him as a leader.

"Ten thousand men are now encamped before the town [of Boston] between which and the country there is no intercourse," Lee told Congress. "[British General] Gage refuses to let the people in or out.

> The besieging army keep the one besieged in constant alarm. . . . Connecticut has 12,000 men in arms, the Jerseys a good many, and the Province [Pennsylvania] at least 8,000. There are 2,000 in this city [Philadelphia] well-armed and disciplined men. In short, every colony this way is well prepared for war.[29]

At Richard Henry Lee's behest, Congress urged Arthur Lee in London to seek the support of the lord mayor of that city, the notorious John Wilkes. There was no need to do so, however. Arthur Lee and Wilkes had already formed a close friendship, and Wilkes was doing his best to help the Americans by demanding Parliament grant Americans representation in that body.

To the English radicals who supported Wilkes, the American struggle reflected their own struggle to vote and offset the votes of a handful of wealthy owners then reaping infinite financial benefits from the pocket boroughs and rotten boroughs they controlled. The fiery rhetoric of Wilkes and his supporters convinced Arthur Lee the radicals were stronger than they were and that the Tories in Parliament were near collapse. He relayed his misassessment to Richard Henry, who passed it on to Washington.

"The ministerial recruiting business in England," Richard Henry assured Washington, "has entirely failed them and now they are driven to their last resort to seek for soldiers in the Highlands of Scotland. But it seems the greatest willingness of the people there cannot supply more than one or two thousand men."[30]

In addition to his English friends, Wilkes's band included a curious Frenchman—a sparkling wit who first gained renown as a brilliant watchmaker. Working as an apprentice in his watchmaker-father's shop in Paris, Pierre-Augustin Caron de Beaumarchais had invented a remarkable new "escapement"—a part of the internal mechanism of clocks and watches that allowed him to produce the first watch small enough to wear on one's wrist instead of carrying it in one's pocket. His invention brought him to the attention of the French court, where King Louis XV converted his passion for unusual timepieces into a deluge of orders for wristwatches and a position in the palace for Beaumarchais as the king's official watchmaker.

Beaumarchais was more than a watchmaker, however. From his mother, an accomplished musician, Beaumarchais had learned musical composition, poetry, and playwriting. By the time he met Arthur Lee in London, Beaumarchais had emerged as France's most renowned playwright and was in London, ostensibly, to oversee the first English production of his highly acclaimed play, *The Barber of Seville*.

After meeting the celebrated Frenchman at a John Wilkes salon and learning of his ties to the French king, Arthur Lee assumed his brother's mantle and asked the playwright to save the American Revolution.

19. Pierre-Augustin Caron de Beaumarchais, the French poet, playwright, and watchmaker, was an effective spy and secret agent for King Louis XV, for whom he masterminded a scheme to defeat Britain by secretly supplying arms and ammunition to American rebels.

CHAPTER 5

An Indispensable Necessity

PIERRE-AUGUSTIN CARON DE BEAUMARCHAIS WAS MORE THAN A watchmaker, more than a poet, more than a playwright. He was also a French spy—French king Louis XV's unofficial "fixer," who used his status as a playwright to cross international borders and fix particularly difficult royal problems that discretion prevented the king from assigning to military aides.

In London to supervise the English production of his sensational play *The Barber of Seville*, Beaumarchais was also on a secret mission for the French king to recapture important state documents from a French turncoat—but not just any turncoat. Beaumarchais's target was Chevalier d'Éon, a fierce swordsman who had served heroically in war as a French army captain and, when the war ended, continued his service to the king as a spy, sometimes appearing as a dashing young officer, other times as a mysterious French beauty. He was a transvestite, and "to serve the king," Beaumarchais admitted later, "I had to make love to a captain of dragoons."[1]

Although Arthur Lee did not know Beaumarchais's official mission in London, the playwright's ties to the French court made him the perfect figure Richard Henry Lee had hoped Arthur would find there. Arthur, therefore, waxed eloquent in expounding the American cause to the Frenchman, pointing out that Americans shared the deep hatred felt by the French court for the British. Knowing how French king Louis XV seethed over the disastrous loss of Canada to the British in the Seven Years' War, Lee said an investment of £100,000 or £200,000 to support the Americans would ensure not only an American victory over the British but the return of Canada to France. Inadvertently or by design, Arthur had uttered the magic words etched on the French royal heart: French recovery of Canada.

Beaumarchais agreed to meet Lee secretly, and in subsequent encounters Lee told Beaumarchais that the Continental Army needed arms, ammunition, and technical assistance as well as funding for its fight for independence. He suggested that the benefits to France of an American victory would stretch far beyond the recovery of Canada. In return for French military aid he promised Beaumarchais that France would reap all the rewards of trade that had enriched England for a century. Then, in what proved a particularly critical meeting between the two, Lee sounded a note that resonated personally in Beaumarchais's heart, pointing out that anyone who engineered a Franco-American alliance would become a wealthy man.

If there was one thing Beaumarchais adored more than theater, music, fame, and intrigue, it was wealth.

Arthur and Richard Henry Lee purposely ended their fraternal correspondence to avoid arousing British suspicions of Arthur's activities in London. William served as intermediary between his two brothers, with Richard Henry sending coded messages often disguised as tobacco transactions that made it difficult to discern whether his instructions dealt with the purchases and sales of tobacco or arms. In fact, the Lees were still observing the trade boycott with Britain, and Richard Henry was probably writing in a code he had invented as a boy playing Robin Hood with his brothers in the woods around Stratford Hall.

Immediately after meeting with Arthur Lee, Beaumarchais wrote to French foreign minister Charles Gravier, comte de Vergennes: "The Americans will triumph, but they must be assisted in their struggle."[2] With that, Beaumarchais then sent a passionate address to the king entitled *La paix ou la guerre* (i.e., *Peace or War*). A little-known landmark in American history, the document steered France onto the path toward a Franco-American alliance that would ensure the birth of a new nation:

> The quarrel between America and England will soon divide the world and change the system of Europe. . . . I am obliged to warn Your Majesty that the preservation of our possessions in America . . . depends solely upon this one proposition: *we must help the Americans.* . . . If the English triumph over the Americans, their victory will embolden them to expand their empire by seizing the French West Indies. If they lose . . . they would seize the French West Indies as compensation. . . . What then is to be done?

Beaumarchais answered his own question, recognizing that France could not afford to war with Britain. But by providing Americans with the right amount of military and financial aid, France could put them "on an equal—but not superior—level of strength with England" and prolong the conflict indefinitely, exhausting them both and rendering them impotent and at the mercy of France "without compromising ourselves. If Your Majesty does not have a more clever man at hand to employ in this matter," he suggested, "I will undertake and answer for the execution of the arrangement without anyone being compromised."[3]

On February 1, 1775, John Wilkes emerged from prison, returned to Parliament, and resumed his attacks on the king, assailing His Royal Highness for declaring Americans to be in rebellion. He called the king's statement "unfounded, rash, and sanguinary"—one that would "most unjustly draw the sword against America.

But before [the] administration are suffered to plunge this nation into the horrors of civil war, before they are permitted to force Englishmen to sheathe their swords into the bowels of their fellow subjects, I hope this House [of Commons] will seriously weigh . . . the cause of this dispute.

Wilkes warned that England was doomed to lose a war against "a hearty and courageous people" fighting for their homes and properties in a limitless wilderness with which they alone were intimate. "Do not deceive yourselves," he shouted at the ministers in Parliament. "The whole continent will be dismembered from Great Britain, and the wide arch of the empire fall."[4]

Republished in newspapers across America, the speech provoked cries of "Wilkes and Liberty"—and a grateful acknowledgment from Richard Henry Lee.

"My Lord," Lee wrote to Wilkes:

Permit the delegates of the people of twelve Antient Colonies [Georgia had not yet attended the Continental Congress] to pay your Lordship . . . a just tribute of gratitude and thanks for the virtuous and unsolicited resentment you have shown to the violated rights of a free people. . . . North America, My Lord, wishes most ardently for a lasting connection with Great Britain on terms of just and equal liberty, less than which generous minds would not offer nor brave and free ones be willing to receive. A cruel war has . . . been opened against us, and while we prepare to defend ourselves like the descendants of Britons, we still hope that the mediation of wise and good citizens will at length prevail over despotism and restore peace and harmony . . . to an oppressed and divided empire.[5]

During the night of June 16, 1775, American troops started building a fortification atop the high ground on Charlestown Peninsula overlooking the harbor across from Boston. When they spotted the structure the next morning, the British ships' high command ordered ships to land 2,400 men in Charlestown to climb to the summit and tear it down.

Slowed by heavy backpacks, the British ran into a rain of murderous fire from Patriot troops at the summit. Falling back to the water's edge, the British dropped their packs, fixed bayonets, and resumed their charge, scratching their way upward until the rain of lead diminished, then stopped: the Americans at the top—about 1,600—had run out of ammunition. As British troops reached the summit unimpeded, shrieks of agony rang out across the sky above the harbor as British bayonets wreaked revenge on the defiant Americans.

Both sides paid a heavy price—1,054 British casualties for the victory and 397 Patriot troops in defeat.

Shocked by the savagery at Bunker Hill, Richard Henry Lee doubled his efforts to supply George Washington and the Continental Army. To that end he instructed Connecticut delegate Silas Deane, an experienced merchant-banker, "to repair to the city of New York and there purchase a ship suitable for carrying 20 nine-pounders [cannons] upon one deck . . . also a sloop suitable to carry ten guns." They were to be the first ships in what he envisioned growing into an American navy. "If you succeed," he told Deane, "you will use all possible expedition to procure them to be armed and equipped for the sea . . . you are to procure powder for both these vessels, and such other military stores as can be had. You will procure cannon . . . officers and men suitable for these vessels . . . and able bodied seamen . . . with all possible dispatch."[6]

Because of their experience buying and selling a wide range of goods and services, merchant-bankers such as Deane were logical candidates among the delegates to purchase arms, ammunition, and other materiel for Congress on behalf of the military. Deane's success in procuring ships for an embryonic navy convinced Richard Henry Lee and the Congress to send him to Europe to purchase arms, ammunition, and other war materiel and, where possible, recruit skilled military officers to train American fighters in the arts of engineering and artillery.

By then Washington had reached Cambridge, Massachusetts, across the Charles River from Boston. Too late to help the troops defending Bunker Hill, he organized as many troops as he could on the Cambridge green. "Between you and me," he wrote to Richard Henry Lee, "I think we are in an exceeding dangerous situation as our numbers are not much larger than we suppose . . . those of the enemy to be . . . and know not where to look for them. . . . Their great command of artillery and adequate sources of powder, & c. give them advantages we have only to lament the want of. . . . If things, therefore, should not turn out as the Congress would wish, I hope they will make proper allowances."[7]

Washington added a "P.S." bemoaning the lack of a hospital with good surgeons for his men. "It rests with the Congress to consider this matter."[8]

While the slaughter on Bunker Hill provoked the fury of Richard Henry Lee and those who favored a war for independence, the brutality of defeat inspired reconciliationists to seek peace. Philadelphia's John Dickinson, the devout Quaker who had stirred colonist resentment against the British with his twelve *Letters from a Farmer in Pennsylvania* ten years earlier, now coaxed Congress to let him address an "olive branch" petition to the king:

> Attached to your Majesty's person, family and government with all the devotion that principle and affection can inspire . . . we solemnly assure your Majesty, that we . . . most ardently desire the former harmony between her and these colonies may be restored. . . . We therefore beseech your Majesty that your royal authority and influence may be graciously interposed . . . to settle peace through every part of your dominions . . . and that such statutes as more immediately distress any of your Majesty's colonies be repealed: For by such arrangements as your Majesty's wisdom can form . . . your Majesty

would receive . . . every testimony of devotion becoming the most dutiful subjects and the most affectionate colonists.⁹

After sending Dickinson's Olive Branch Petition, Congress learned of British plans to send Canadian troops into New York. It responded by authorizing a two-pronged invasion of Canada, one aimed at Montreal, the other at Quebec. Richard Henry Lee, meanwhile, procured twelve to fourteen tons of powder for Washington and proposed "a signal stroke" for installing batteries "at the entrance of the bay of Boston, so as to prevent the egress and regress of any [British] ships whatever . . . to secure the [British] fleet and army in and before Boston so as to compel a surrender."¹⁰

Washington replied in kindly fashion, reminding Lee that the American army lacked enough powder "to give twenty-five musket cartridges to each man and to serve the artillery in any brisk action one single day. Under these circumstances, I dare say you will agree with me that it would not be very eligible to take a post thirty miles distant by land [across the bay] from this place."¹¹

With that exchange Lee abandoned his proposal, telling Washington to "rest assured that Congress will do everything in their power to render your most weighty business easy to you."¹² Rather than devise military strategy, Lee would cede that task to Washington and concern himself solely with filling the needs of Washington's men. To that end he pushed through a proposal to raise the pay of riflemen and their officers before adjourning for a month's respite to escape Philadelphia's summer heat and pestilence by returning to his hilltop home in Virginia.

The break proved a disappointment, however. He had assumed burdens that would crush most men. Besides caring for his own large family in Virginia, he worried about his two sons in England. "I have enclosed a packet for my dear boys," he wrote to his brother William. "On you and my brother [Arthur] I depend solely for the care and protection of my dear boys in this tempestuous season, when I can do little for them. I hope their gratitude and virtue will prevent your having much trouble with them." And he signed it for himself and his wife, Ann, who had just given birth to a son: "Our best love to Mrs. Lee and kiss your little patriot* for me."[13]

While Richard Henry was in Virginia, Patrick Henry had led a force into Williamsburg and made royal governor Lord Dunmore flee the governor's palace and take refuge on a British man-of-war, where he threatened to send marines to crush all opposition in Virginia. Lee rushed to Williamsburg to meet with Patrick Henry and the colony's other former burgesses to assume control of government and end 175 years of British rule. They voted to raise three regiments of 1,000 men each to defend the colony against British troops. They also agreed to print £350,000 in Virginia currency and establish an arms production plant in Fredericksburg near the northern Virginia iron mines.

In Philadelphia the Continental Congress reconvened in mid-September 1775 with delegates from Georgia appearing for the first time and uniting all thirteen colonies in convention. Richard Henry returned from Virginia ready to assume more responsibilities with each passing day. On the road back to Philadelphia he had even stopped at Mount Vernon to see "if your lady had any commands," as he put it to General Washington. "[I] had the pleasure to learn that all were well."[14]

Once in Congress Richard Henry assumed a role as Washington's personal representative and pressed Congress to improve the lot of troops enlisting in the Continental Army. "You will see in the proceedings of our convention," he was able to write to Washington, "that they have agreed to raise the pay of our rifle officers and men to the Virginia standard."[15]

Washington himself, however, was far from happy. "As we have now nearly completed our lines of defense," Washington wrote to

---

*William's newborn son.

Lee, "we have nothing more to fear from the enemy provided we can keep our men to their duty.

> But it is among the most difficult tasks I ever undertook in my life to induce these people to believe there is . . . danger till the bayonet is pushed at their breasts. . . . An unaccountable kind of stupidity in the lower class of these people . . . prevails but too generally among the officers . . . and adds not a little to my difficulties. . . . There is no such thing as getting officers . . . to exert themselves in carrying orders into execution. . . . To curry favor with the men (by whom they were chosen and on whose smiles possibly they may think they may again rely) seems to be one of the principle objects of their attention.[16]

Washington went on to ask Lee to convince Congress to give him, as commander-in-chief, the power to appoint all officers below the rank of general. Until then the general of each state militia held powers over officer promotions and tended to promote higher-level subordinate officers from that state—all too often relatives, relatives of friends, or men of high standing in the state. The troops themselves elected lower-level officers—again, always men from their own state.

"Gentlemen," he said, "will stand an equal chance of being promoted according to merit if appointed by the Commander in Chief," Washington wrote. His suggestion originated the practice of awarding battlefield commissions, which would become official military policy in 1845 at the outbreak of the Mexican War.

"I made a pretty good slam among such kind of officers as the Massachusetts government abound in since I came to this camp," Washington boasted to Richard Henry Lee, "having broken one colonel and two captains for cowardly behavior in the action on Bunker's Hill. Besides these, I have at this time one colonel, one major, one captain, and two subalterns under arrest for trial."[17]

To the dismay of reconciliationists in Congress, King George refused to receive the Olive Branch Petition, just as he had rejected a previous appeal for reconciliation from the First Continental Congress. In addition, he issued a royal proclamation closing the colonies to all commerce and ordered a build-up of British arms. At Richard Henry Lee's behest, Congress responded by authorizing development of a full-fledged navy, converting sturdy fishing vessels into armed ships, seizing two British naval vessels, and fitting out four ships with ten guns each.

Richard Henry Lee wrote to General Washington that he had also ordered fourteen tons of powder sent to the army and asked the committee of secret correspondence to establish ties with "friends of the colonies in Great Britain, Ireland, and in other parts of the world."

He said the committee would try to "ascertain the feelings and views of the courts of France and Spain . . . and how far they would assist . . . in arms, ammunition, and money."[18] It would also appoint secret agents abroad, with Richard Henry Lee winning official appointment of his brother Arthur as America's principal agent in London.

In London British authorities apparently learned that Wilkes and his aides were feeding the Lees confidential information on government military plans and began disseminating false information.

"We are here as much in the dark about news from England as you are," Richard Henry Lee reported to Washington. "The indistinct accounts we have tell us of great confusion all over England and a prodigious fall of the stocks. I heartily wish it may be true, but if it is not, I have no doubt of its shortly being the case."[19]

One letter Arthur sent his brother stated that "General [Lord Jeffery] Amherst had recommended (& 'twas said it will be executed) to remove the army this winter from Boston to Long Island in order to get amply supplied by ravaging N. Jersey, N. York, and Rhode Island."[20] To which Richard Henry added his hope that Washington would give the departing British "a genteel parting salute."[21]

With carte blanche from London to combat Virginia's rebellion, Royal Governor Lord Dunmore ordered marines to seize Norfolk, Virginia's largest town. With sentries posted at every corner, he proclaimed martial law and offered residents a choice of swearing allegiance to the king or losing their homes and properties. He ordered all able-bodied men to report for duty in the British military or risk forfeiting their properties and possibly their lives as deserters. He offered all slaves, indentured servants, and criminals their freedom if they turned on their masters and joined the British army. "I hope it will oblige the rebels to disperse to take care of their properties," Dunmore gloated.

Virginia's militia commander turned to Richard Henry Lee, who, in turn, appealed to Washington, asking, "what number and what strength of armed vessels could possibly be procured from the ports where you are to be in Delaware Bay . . . by the middle or last of December. Two or three vessels of tolerable force . . . may effect a stroke or two of great consequence. We have 4,000 weight of powder, and a very considerable quantity of Oznaburgs [army coats made of a heavy linen fabric] arrived in Virginia from Statia* for the use of our little army . . . of about 2,000 men now at Williamsburg and Hampton."[22]

After lengthy strategy discussions, 1,200 Virginia militiamen marched out of Williamsburg to repel the British landing at Norfolk. Before attacking, however, the Virginia commander sent one of his servants into the British camp pretending to be a runaway with information that the Virginia troop strength was far smaller than it actually was. On that intelligence the British charged into battle with only 200 regulars and 300 blacks and Tories. The result was a slaughter that left even the most battle-hardened frontiersmen retching at the blood bath. Lord Dunmore and the survivors fled to the safety of British frigates, with Dunmore plotting swift revenge.

---

*A diminutive name for Sint Eustatius, northwest of St. Kitts.

In mid-November Arthur Lee, now spying for America, sent a coded message to Richard Henry, who informed George Washington but took care not to reveal Arthur's identity in case the message was intercepted. "'Tis from a well-informed, sensible friend and may be relied on," Lee wrote to Washington, confirming "the fixed determination of the King and Court to leave undone nothing they can do to compel obedience in America."[23]

Washington replied. Citing his lack of "armed vessels . . . of any tolerable force" to defend American shores. "For God's sake, hurry the signers of money that our wants may be supplied."[24]

Richard Henry wrote to Arthur, urging him to step up efforts to find financial and military aid from friendly European nations. Vergennes and French king Louis had examined Beaumarchais's *La paix ou la guerre* by then but feared that French intervention might provoke Britain to send an army across the English Channel and attack France. France had yet to recover from the Seven Years' War and could not withstand a direct assault on her homeland. Vergennes nonetheless sought to ascertain the strength and determination of the American rebels to see whether the surreptitious aid to the Americans Beaumarchais proposed might weaken Britain enough for France to win a future confrontation. He sent the French army's most accomplished intelligence officer to America to find out.

Disguised as a French businessman, Achard de Bonvouloir reached Philadelphia just before Christmas 1775 to meet with members of Congress. Clinging carefully to his disguise as a merchant, Bonvouloir told Richard Henry and other members of the Congressional Committee of Secret Correspondence that he personally could promise no French military aid but that he understood the French court to be "well-disposed" toward the Americans. Indeed, he said he saw "no obstacles" to American merchants buying arms and other supplies from French merchants in exchange for produce—tobacco, rice, and the like.

By then so many secret messages were floating back and forth across the ocean that Richard Henry urged Congress to limit the number of members on the committee of secret correspondence. "The Congress consists of too many members to keep secrets," Benjamin Franklin agreed. Congress agreed to reduce committee membership to five. Besides Lee, they included the powerful Pennsylvania delegate Robert Morris, a brilliant merchant-banker who speculated in commodities and land with his partner, Thomas Willing.

From the first, however, Lee suspected Morris of using his seat in Congress to enhance the value of his investments, including western lands he and his partner had bought through the Grand Ohio Company—a rival of Lee's (and Washington's) Ohio Land Company. At the time there was nothing illegal or unethical about using a political seat to enhance one's private fortune—if it did not undermine government interests. It was a common practice.

On January 1, 1776, as Bonvouloir set sail for France to report to Vergennes, Lord Dunmore ordered his ships to fire on the Norfolk waterfront while marines landed and set the town ablaze. The conflagration left 6,000 people homeless in the dead of winter—some of them loyal Tories. With Dunmore's ships patrolling the coast, every other town along Virginia's shoreline feared the same fate. "Lord Dunmore . . . committed every outrage at Norfolk," Richard Henry fumed as he sent a report of the action to Washington.

Washington, however, faced problems of his own. "The money . . . came seasonably but not in *quantum sufficit*," he wrote to Richard Henry Lee regarding funds for the troops. "Our demands at this time being peculiarly great for pay and advance for the troops—pay for their arms, blanketing, etc.; independent of the demands of the commissary and quartermaster general."[25]

Adding to Washington's money problems was the nuisance of having to pay postage for letters to and from Congress carried by the continental post. Several states displayed their independence by charging out-of-state mail carriers to cross their borders and requiring that all mail be transferred to and handled by local mail carriers within their borders. It was America's first bureaucratic nightmare.

"When will the express be established between Philadelphia and this post?" Washington cried out in despair.[26]

Washington went on to tell Richard Henry that Lord Dunmore's letters to General Howe " . . . which fell into my hands . . . will let you pretty fully into his diabolical schemes. If, my dear sir, that man is not crushed before spring, he will become the most formidable enemy America has . . . nothing less than depriving him of life or liberty will secure peace to Virginia."[27]

Compounding American anti-British anger over Dunmore's "outrage at Norfolk" was the mid-January appearance of a pamphlet called "Common Sense." Written by one Thomas Paine, a hitherto unknown Scottish editor/polemicist, it claimed that "the ideas I present here are so new that many people will reject them." He asked readers to "clear their minds of long-held notions, apply common sense, and adopt the cause of America as the 'cause of all mankind.' How we respond to tyranny today will matter for all time," Paine claimed, adding that the monarchy was not, as it claimed to be, a protector of Americans and that it had brought nothing but misery to its subjects. He called the idea of monarchy "absurd."

> Why should someone rule over us simply because he is someone else's child? So evil is monarchy by its very nature that God condemns it in the Bible. . . . It's folly to think we should maintain loyalty to a distant tyrant. For us, right here, right now, reconciliation means ruin. America must separate from Britain. Can we win this war? Absolutely. . . . Let us declare independence. If we delay, it will be that much harder to win.[28]

Shortly thereafter Patriot forces scored monumental victories repelling British attempts to land in North Carolina and Charleston, South Carolina. As news of the Patriot victories reached Philadelphia, word arrived from Boston that Washington's chief of artillery Henry Knox had engineered a triumph of equal proportion with an impossible feat: the transport of nearly four dozen cannons through more than 200 miles of deep snows from Fort Ticonderoga, New York, to the heights overlooking Boston, where they now menaced British occupying forces with annihilation. Faced with sniper fire on their troops and destruction of their fleet by cannon fire, the British command chose flight. Evacuating the city in March 1776, the British occupiers sailed across Boston Bay into the Atlantic, effectively ceding Massachusetts and most of New England to the Americans.

"I congratulate you sincerely on the several advantages your troops have lately gained over the enemy," Richard Henry rejoiced in a letter to Washington. "'Tis amazing with what force and infamous perseverance the devils of despotism . . . pursue the purpose of enslaving this great continent. They mean to keep their own people in Great Britain quiet and the other powers of Europe still for this campaign by an infinite number of falsehoods . . . and encourage with hope their deluded people."[29]

In London Arthur Lee—now an accomplished spy with eyes and ears in every sector of the British government—learned details of an imminent British plan to send more troops to America. He described them in a letter, which he slipped into an envelope that he then put into a second envelope and handed to an intermediary. He left the outer envelope blank but told the carrier to deliver it "only to R.H.L. of Virginia, and he will guess from whence it comes." To hide his own identity and that of Richard Henry Lee if the British intercepted the double package, he addressed the inner envelope and the letter itself to Cadwallader Colden, the Tory lieutenant governor of New York, and signed it with the fictional name John Horsfall. It was a clever ploy that proved successful for a good while. If intercepted, it did not disclose any information to Colden that British officials did not already know. If, however, it got through safely to his brother's hands, the Patriots would receive valuable intelligence.

The letter read in part:

> You will be curious to know what are the ministerial intentions and their force for the next campaign: Hessians, 12,000; Brunswickers, Wolkenbutlers, and Waldeckers, 5,000; six regiments under Lord Cornwallis, 3,000; eight more to sail in the spring, 4,000; Highlanders, 2,000; now in America, 8,000.[30]

Lee went on to expose their destinations, specifying Virginia as the destination of Lord Cornwallis, who was about to sail from Cork, Ireland. "Upon the whole, the ministry, if everything favors them, may have thirty thousand men in America by the latter end of June."[31]

The letter told "Colden" the English would have "no horse but two light dragoons that are now there." He appeared to warn Colden that if the Americans had a cavalry well trained for dodging in and out in the woods unpredictably, they would succeed in harassing the British and putting them on the defensive. "It will harass such an army infinitely . . . cut off their convoys, and if ever they hazard an engagement, it is imagined here that no general on earth can make the campaign decisive."[32]

"Horsfall" wrote that the British ministry had found it impossible to recruit soldiers in England, Ireland, or Scotland to fight the Americans, many of whom were their own relatives—often distant but nonetheless kinsmen. In a separate note to Richard Henry, Arthur told his brother "the intelligence . . . should be communicated to every part of America," and Richard Henry Lee did just that, shocking Patriots and Loyalists alike.

The Lees' motives were three-fold: first, to expose and reveal to all Americans the British ministry's military plans and frighten Americans into realizing they faced annihilation if they did not embrace independence and, where possible, enlist to fight the British. Secondly, the Lees hoped to force ordinary Americans—farmers and the like—to prepare themselves for war and its inevitable hardships. And lastly, they wanted to embarrass New York's Tory governor, his government, and the state's large numbers of Tories by revealing that they—the Lees and the Patriots—knew every move the British government planned before the Tories knew it: that Patriot friends and spies were everywhere in Britain as well as America.

By then the French spy Achard de Bonvouloir had returned to Paris and reported to Vergennes. The foreign minister, in turn, sent the king a thoughtful report he called *Reflexions*—a historic paper assuring the king that the goal of colonial rebels was "no longer a redress of grievances, but a determined effort to cut ties to England." He warned the king that without foreign aid, the rebels would lose, allowing England to prevent her colonies from trading with other nations "while accumulating all the benefits of exclusive trade with those colonies." Vergennes called it "imperative" for France to intervene. "England is France's natural enemy . . . her cherished, long-standing goal is, if not the destruction of France, at least our emasculation, humiliation, and ruin."[33]

Although George Washington and Richard Henry Lee had no way of knowing it, a nobleman and king in the Palais de Versailles near Paris and a scheming French playwright lurking in a palace antechamber were plotting the fate of the American Revolution and whether the American people were to become a free and independent people.

Flush with his improbable victory in Boston, George Washington moved his forces to New York to seize control of New York and its huge deep-water harbor. Richard Henry Lee believed the time had come for Americans to declare independence from Britain and wrote to Patrick Henry, Virginia's unquestioned leader who was all but certain to win election at the imminent state convention to become Virginia's first governor.

"Virginia has hitherto taken the lead in great affairs," Lee wrote, "and many now look to her with anxious expectation, hoping that the spirit, wisdom, and energy of her councils will rouse America . . . and above all set an example which North Carolina, Maryland, Pennsylvania, and New York will most assuredly, in my opinion follow. . . .

Parliament has to every legal intent and purpose dissolved our government and placed us on the high road to anarchy. . . . This proves the indispensable necessity of our taking up government immediately."[34]

Lee warned Henry that the revolution against Britain could not continue without developing and expanding the nation's trade, "but no state in Europe will either treat or trade with us so long as we consider ourselves subject to Great Britain. Honor, dignity, and the customs of states forbid them until we take rank as an independent people. . . . I hope your powers will be fully exerted into securing the peace and happiness of our country by adoption of a wise and free government."[35]

Richard Henry Lee had now come to the firm conclusion:

> It is not choice . . . but necessity that calls for independence as the only means by which foreign alliance can be obtained and a proper confederation by which internal peace and union may be secured.[36]

Although British forces had repelled the American invasion of Canada, North Carolina's Patriot militia had prevented a British landing near Wilmington and crushed a Loyalist militia at Moore's Creek Bridge. On April 12 the North Carolina Assembly authorized its delegates in Congress to vote for independence from Britain.

Unfazed by the setbacks, two British fleets set sail from Britain with 40,000 troops—British, Scot, Hessian, and Hanoverian. As Arthur Lee had indicated, one fleet had indeed left for New York, the other fleet for the South—probably Charleston. Richard Henry immediately ordered twenty tons of powder and as many brass field pieces as he could locate sent to Washington in New York.

On May 15 Patrick Henry responded to Richard Henry Lee's call for Virginia to declare independence and, backed by the formidable Lee family bloc, won the Virginia Assembly's unanimous support. A week later Richard Henry reported that thirteen of the new American navy's "gundolas" had intercepted two British battle ships "coming up the Delaware. After two engagements of three hours each on the two following days, the [British] ships returned down river well bored with large cannon shot."[37]

In Versailles, meanwhile, King Louis XV approved the ingenious scheme devised by playwright Beaumarchais to keep France out of war while helping the Americans and earning the king—and Beaumarchais himself—substantial profits. Using a loan from the king of 1 million livres (about $4 million today) Beaumarchais was to establish a private company with an invented Spanish name to disguise all connections with France. His company was to use the king's funds to buy surplus French-army arms and ammunition to resell to the Americans in exchange for tobacco, cotton, lumber, and whale oil for resale in French markets. "This exchange," Vergennes explained to the king, "could be made without the [French] government appearing involved in any way."[38]

At the time French military depots were bulging with obsolete arms and ammunition from the Seven Years' War. Although technological advances had rendered much of the artillery obsolete for European warfare, it was more than adequate for American rebels in the wilderness. The French military had about 400 cannons dating back to the seventeenth century bearing the back-to-back double L's of Louis XIV. In effect, the king would lend Beaumarchais money from one royal pocket to buy royal weaponry from the royal army, which would put the money back into the royal pocket. The transaction would cost the king nothing and rid French army warehouses of useless weaponry. Beaumarchais would then sell the weaponry to the Americans for boatloads of tobacco, grains, furs, and other precious American commodities for sale in French markets. After deducting his own commission from the proceeds of such sales, Beaumarchais would return the rest of those proceeds to the king. Both the playwright and the king stood to derive enormous profits from the American Revolution—without firing a single shot. It was a plot only the author of *The Barber of Seville* could have devised.

"The respectful esteem that I bear towards that brave people who so well defend their liberty," Beaumarchais wrote to Richard Henry Lee "has induced me to form a plan . . . to supply you with necessaries of every sort . . . clothes, linens, powder, ammunition, muskets, cannon, and even gold for the payment of your troops, and in general everything that can be useful for the honorable war in which you are engaged. Your deputies . . . will find in me a sure friend, and asylum in my house, money in my coffers."[39]

On May 21 "a gentleman just from New York" reported seeing seventy transports with 10,000 troops under sail off Sandy Hook, in northern New Jersey, across the bay from New York. "Contrary to our earnest, early, and repeated petitions for peace, liberty, and safety," Richard Henry Lee responded angrily, "our enemies press us with war, threaten us with danger and slavery. And this, not with her single force, but with the aid of foreigners."[40]

With that—and the knowledge of the Beaumarchais scheme to provide French aid—Richard Henry Lee stood in Congress on June 7, 1776, and with John Adams ready to second him, he called on each of the colonies to formulate constitutions and establish independent state governments. Knowing he was now inviting death on the gallows for treason, Lee rose a second time, his crippled hand throbbing as it always did in stressful situations, and read from a paper he held in his good hand:

Resolved:

That these United Colonies are, and of right ought to be, free and independent States, that they are absolved from all allegiance to the British crown, and that all political connection between them and the State of Great Britain is, and ought to be totally dissolved.

That it is expedient forthwith to take the most effectual measures for forming Alliances.

That a plan for confederation be prepared and transmitted to the respective Colonies for their consideration.[41]

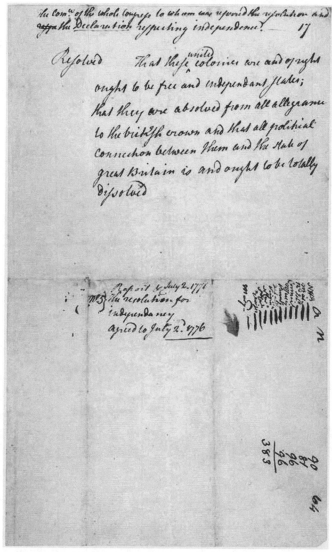

20. *Richard Henry Lee's original handwritten declaration of American independence, which Congress approved on July 2, 1776, making that date the true Independence Day.*

Lee looked up, expecting a standing ovation and a chorus of huzzahs. To his dismay, there was nothing but silence.

CHAPTER 6

The Enemy of Everything Good

THE SILENCE IN PHILADELPHIA'S CARPENTERS' HALL STUNNED Richard Henry Lee. He had just sounded the most important words of his life, indeed, the most important words in American history—perhaps world history.

In response delegates in the Continental Congress only muttered, shuffled papers, and shifted in their seats uneasily, looking to their neighbors in all directions to assess reactions.

Washington was in the field with thousands of troops risking their lives to fight for independence, believing that their home colonies supported them. The North Carolina and Virginia legislatures had already opted for independence, as had Rhode Island. But now, with a call to all other colonies to follow suit . . . nothing.

"Why then, Sir, do we longer delay?" Lee called out in stentorian tones. "Why still deliberate? Let this happy day give birth to an American republic. Let her arise, not to devastate and to conquer, but to reestablish the reign of peace and of law."[1]

"All was silence," John Adams noted in his diary afterward. "No one would speak." All eyes had turned to Adams as the senior member and acknowledged sage. "The subject had been in contemplation

21. John Adams of Massachusetts was first to stand in support of Rich-
ard Henry Lee's original resolution for independence in the Continen-
tal Congress. With Lee, Adams established a north-south coalition that
helped unite the thirteen colonies during the Revolutionary War.

for more than year," Adams recalled, "and frequent discussions had
been had concerning it. At one time and another, all the arguments
for it and against it had been exhausted and [had] become familiar.
I expected no more would be said in public but that the question
would be put and decided."[2]

Still, no one spoke, and South Carolina delegate Edward Rutledge approached Adams: "Nobody will speak but you on this
subject. You have all the topics so ready that you must satisfy the
gentlemen."

Adams laughed a laugh of embarrassment. "I was ashamed to re-peat what I had said twenty times before. The gentlemen, however, insisted on hearing at least a recapitulation of the arguments and no other gentlemen being willing to speak, I summed up the reasons, objections, and answers . . . till at length . . . they were fully satisfied and ready for the question, which was then put and determined in the affirmative."[3]

History has left only two descriptions of the responses of Con-tinental Congress members to Lee's historic resolution. One is the diary of John Adams; the other the "Notes of the Proceedings in the Continental Congress" by the enthusiastic thirty-three-year-old Thomas Jefferson, then a relative neophyte to politics. Aware that they and the other delegates were flirting with treason and summary execution, neither took notes while sitting in Congress nor did Con-gress keep any word-for-word transcripts. There is no way to know when Adams and Jefferson actually compiled their notes or how ac-curate they were. Although Philadelphia delegate Charles Thomson had won appointment as secretary of Congress, he made only these cursory notes:

> Friday, June 7, 1776: The Delegates from Virginia moved in obe-dience to instructions from their constituents that the Congress should declare that these United colonies are & of right ought to be free & independent states, that they are absolved from all allegiance to the British crown, and that all political connection between them and the state of Great Britain is & ought to be totally dissolved; that measures should be immediately taken for procuring the assistance of foreign powers, and a Confederation be formed to bind the colo-nies more closely together.
>
> The house being obliged to attend at that time to some other business, the proposition was referred to the next day when the members were ordered to attend punctually at ten o'clock.
>
> Saturday, June 8. They proceeded to take it into consideration and referred it to a committee of the whole, into which they immediately

resolved themselves, and passed that day & Monday the 10th in debating on the subject.[4]

The outlook for colonial unity in the struggle for independence looked glum following Lee's resolve, however. Although all the delegates in Philadelphia shared a degree of antagonism toward Britain's Parliament for taxing and otherwise expanding its authority over the colonies, the colonies disagreed over whether to declare independence. The larger, wealthier colonies such as Virginia insisted independence was the only solution, while the smaller, poorer, and largely defenseless colonies such as Delaware were reluctant to cede membership in and the collective protection of the British Empire—regardless of the outcome of the tax disputes. And then there were the devout Anglicans, who opened their Sunday church services singing *God Save the King* and often repeated that exhortation before the recessional. All were wealthy landowners angered by arbitrary taxation of their properties by Parliament, where they had no direct representation.

But when they had stated all their grievances, the fact remained that they were all Englishmen! Englishmen in their minds, Englishmen in their hearts, Englishmen in their souls. Even those who had never set foot in Britain called it "home," and even as some took up arms against parliamentary taxation, most were determined to remain Englishmen—and wealthy enough to pay taxes if forced to do so.

In the debate that followed, Pennsylvania, New York, and South Carolina delegates agreed that reconciliation with Parliament seemed all but impossible for the moment, but they opposed a break with the homeland until they returned to their legislatures, which they said represented "the voice of the people" and "were our power. . . . Without them our declarations cannot be carried into effect."[5]

South Carolina's Edward Rutledge stated his continuing hope for "an accommodation with Great Britain," and Maryland, Delaware, and New Jersey delegates echoed his sentiments.[6] Tiny Delaware was too terrified by the presence of British warships along its undulating coastline to consider independence, while Maryland's Roman Catholics feared separation from the Motherland might set off a religious war in that colony. Georgia delegates sat silently, remaining inscrutably noncommittal.

In a shock to Lee and the rest of the assemblage, Massachusetts, whose leaders had sparked the entire revolution during the Stamp Act controversy a decade earlier, abstained. The Adamses, of course, stood solidly behind Richard Henry Lee and independence, but other Massachusetts delegates insisted that too many towns outside Boston's influence were not in favor of separation from the mother country.

Connecticut and New Hampshire were enthusiastically in favor of Lee's motion for independence, while delegates from other states argued that their legislatures had expressly forbidden them to consent to independence. Still others said they lacked instructions of any kind, and without authority to vote, they refused to risk mounting the gibbet without orders to do so.

There were many other issues, with some states banding together in agreement on some, only to step away from each other in disagreement and bond with delegates with whom they had just argued bitterly. Though heartfelt—often deeply so—their arguments remained free of personal animosity, with none of the clever barbed sarcasm nor angry retorts associated with fictional depictions of the Congress on stage and screen. Dueling was too frequent a consequence of thoughtless remarks for the dandies in Congress to risk a careless remark. In any case, many had fraternal bonds formed at Eton, Oxford, or the University of Edinburgh, and they remained "Gentlemen." Indeed, they were more than that—they were *English* gentlemen.

Lee's supporters tried bolstering enthusiasm for independence with assurances of forthcoming French military aide. Others, however, questioned whether France and her ally Spain would not fear an independent America that might threaten their North American colonies. Several delegates warned that if some states voted for independence and others did not, foreign powers might take advantage of the division by agreeing "to partition our territories. . . . France and Spain have reason to be jealous of that rising power which would one day certainly strip them of all their American possessions."[7]

As the debate dragged on, Richard Henry Lee and John Adams stepped in to demand that delegates return to the original proposal before the Congress: whether to separate from Britain. "No gentleman has argued against the policy or the right of separation from Britain," Richard Henry Lee pointed out, "nor supposed it possible we should ever renew our connection. They have only opposed its being now declared. The question is not whether, by a declaration of independence, we should make ourselves what we are not, but whether we should declare a fact that already exists: The ties to the king [were] dissolved by his assent to the late act of Parliament by which he declares us out of his protection and by his levying war on us."[8]

"Mr. Lee was by far the most elegant scholar in the house," Maryland's William Wirt remarked. "He possessed a rich store of historical and political knowledge, with an activity of observation and a certainty of judgment that turned that knowledge to the very best account. Such was his promptitude that he required no preparation for debate. He was ready for any subject as soon as it was announced."[9]

"The eyes of Europe are fixed upon us," Lee proclaimed as he continued his call for independence.

> She demands of us a living example of freedom that may exhibit a contrast in the felicity of the citizen to the ever increasing tyranny which desolates her polluted shores. She invites us to prepare an asylum where the unhappy may find solace and the persecuted repose.

She entreats us to cultivate a propitious soil, where that generous plant, which first sprang and grew in England but is now withered by the poisonous blasts of tyranny, may revive and flourish, sheltering . . . all the human race. If we are not this day wanting in our duty to our country, the names of the American legislators of '76 will be placed at the side of Theseus, of Lycurgus, of Romulus, of the three Williamses of Nassau, and of all those whose memory has been and forever will be dear to virtuous men and good citizens.[10]

The effects of his rhetoric were almost magical. "His eloquence was free from those stiff and technical restraints which habits of forensic speaking are apt to generate," Wirt commented. "His gesture was so graceful and highly finished . . . his speech was so copious, so rich, so mellifluous, set off with such bewitching cadence of voice and such captivating grace of action that, while you listened to him, you desired to hear nothing superior, and indeed thought him perfect."[11]

John Adams seconded Richard Henry Lee, all but repeating Lee's argument word for word. "We have always been independent of Parliament, their restraints on our trade deriving efficacy from our acquiescence only and not from any rights they possessed of imposing them. . . . Our connection . . . was now dissolved by the commencement of hostilities. As to the king . . . his assent to the late act of parliament . . . declares us out of his protection. . . . Allegiance and protection are reciprocal, the one ceasing when the other is withdrawn."[12]

Despite the emotional effects of his rhetoric and that of John Adams, Lee recognized that if he forced a vote on his resolution, he might lose. Only five states—Virginia, North Carolina, Connecticut, Rhode Island, and New Hampshire—had expressed unconditional support for independence; five—South Carolina, Georgia, Maryland, Pennsylvania, and Delaware—were opposed, with the remaining three undecided and ready to abstain if Richard Henry pressed for a vote. Although he rallied nine states to his side—enough to pass his resolution under the rules then in place—he believed unanimity essential to ultimate victory and opted to postpone the debate for two weeks until July 2. He would use the interim to launch a campaign of personal diplomacy to win reluctant delegates. He had one advantage—his sister Alice's lavishly stocked table and wine cellar. Alice Lee had married Dr. William Shippen, one of Philadelphia's most renowned physicians and famed anatomist, whom Washington had just named Director of Hospitals—the equivalent of today's surgeon general.

While cajoling delegates to embrace unity while dining on savory game and fine wines at the Shippen dinner table, Lee also fed intelligence to Washington and rounded up money and supplies for Washington's army, including 5,000 shoes and blankets and $300,000 to pay the troops. He also worked out a plan for Cotton Tufts, a Boston-area physician and dedicated Patriot, to oversee construction of a foundry to supply Patriot forces with cannons.

By July 2 Richard Henry Lee had finished winning over most of the delegates at the Shippen dinner table—and the Continental Congress. Meanwhile pro-independence members of the Maryland, New Jersey, and Pennsylvania assemblies staged revolutions of their own, walking out of the established assemblies and creating new rump assemblies. The extralegal bodies then instructed their representatives to the Continental Congress to vote for Richard Henry Lee's resolution.

When Congress finally voted, twelve states voted for American independence, with one state—New York—abstaining until its delegates received instructions from their state legislature.

Banner newspaper headlines confirmed the vote, heralding Richard Henry Lee as Father of American Independence. John Adams, who had seconded Lee's resolution, wrote to his wife, Abigail, that July 2, 1776, would become "the most memorable epoch in the history of America . . . solemnized with Pomp and Parade . . . from one end of this Continent . . . forever more." History and the American people, he predicted, would remember and eternally embrace Richard Henry Lee as Father of American Independence.

Lee had unquestionably engineered one of the most significant events in American—indeed, world—history, giving an entire people the right and power of self-determination for the first time since man had shed his gills and, at the same time, putting the lie to and signaling the end of any man's divine right to rule over others. To add luster to Lee's concise declaration, however, Congress appointed a committee of five members with literary gifts to embellish it with the reasoning that spawned it. Because Lee had planned to return to Virginia immediately after the vote, Congress named John Adams, Benjamin Franklin, Thomas Jefferson, Robert R. Livingston of New York, and Roger Sherman of Connecticut to the committee, but the older members were so exhausted that they assigned the chore to Jefferson.

As the Continental Congress voted to adopt Richard Henry Lee's resolution for American independence, what seemed like certain victory after the British evacuated Boston suddenly turned into almost certain defeat. Instead of retreating from Boston Bay to Halifax, Canada, British general William Howe had shifted course and sailed toward New York. On July 2, as Richard Henry Lee rode away to his Virginia home, elated over his triumph in Congress, 150 British transports sailed unimpeded into New York Bay, carrying 20,000 troops, including 9,000 Hessian mercenaries, to complement Howe's 10,000-man army.

Some historians explain Lee's inexplicable departure from Philadelphia as pique over being left off the committee appointed to draw up the showpiece Declaration of Independence, but pique was not a Lee characteristic. He was no prima donna—and never had been. He was fully aware of his accomplishments in the Continental Congress and in the war for independence. If others wanted to capture fame poeticizing his words with resplendent calligraphy on costly parchment, he was perfectly willing to cede them that glory.

Nothing in his voluminous correspondence—some of it exception-
ally personal—indicates any resentment at that time toward Jefferson or anyone else associated with the document that became the
official Declaration of Independence.

What is indisputable, however, is that as he voted on July 2, he
found himself inundated with demands for his presence elsewhere—
at home at Chantilly and in the Virginia state capital at Williamsburg. His brother Thomas had written from Virginia that Richard
Henry's wife, Ann, was ailing and needed him—and that the state
legislature needed him to help resolve disputes over the form of independent state government to adopt. And still more pressing was
news of depredations by British raiders along the shores of Chesapeake Bay and the rivers feeding into it.

Determined to pillage tobacco warehouses, disrupt trade, and
bankrupt Virginia's great plantations, Lord Dunmore had established a military base on the southern tip of the Northern Neck,
from which he sent troops to raid plantations on the Maryland coast
and replicate the savagery at the four Lee plantations and that of
George Washington, among others, on the Virginia side of the river.

News of the British depredations sent Lee riding south as fast
as he could to Alexandria, Virginia, where he joined George Mason, among others, in organizing a Virginia navy to ward off Dunmore's incursions. Donning his Westmoreland County militia
colonel's uniform, Lee ordered the removal of all supply depots to
inland locations out of reach of British landing parties. He then
contacted Maryland authorities, who agreed to build a joint naval
force of fourteen ships—eight Virginia ships armed with thirty-two
cannons each and six Maryland ships carrying twenty-four cannons
each. Although militia leaders had planned to build forts along the
river bluffs, Lee convinced them that stationary forts openly re-
vealed defender strengths and weaknesses. He urged them to organize their men in "movable batteries," or "flying squads," which he
said would leave the enemy uncertain of the safest, most strategic
landing areas. He then positioned the squads along the forty-mile

length of the Westmoreland County cliffs overlooking the Potomac and waited for the enemy to approach. He did not have to wait long.

The British had already landed sixty agents "for the purpose of plunder," Lee wrote to Samuel Adams. They had landed where no militia had been stationed to oppose them, he said, and burned warehouses with between 200 and 300 hogsheads of tobacco, each weighing about a thousand pounds.

"These wretches have it in their power to create us great expense and much trouble, pierced as we are in every part with waters deep and broad, without marine force sufficient to oppose this contemptible collection of pirates."[13]

Congress, meanwhile, had become too immersed in debate over the Declaration of Independence to concern itself with Richard Henry Lee's tobacco warehouses. After Lee had left Philadelphia on July 3 Thomas Jefferson hurried to finish embellishing Lee's declaration of independence, relying in part on John Locke's *Second Treatise of Government*. "Men are by nature . . . all free, equal and independent," Locke had written. "No one can be put out of this estate, and subjected to the political power of another, without his own consent.

> And that all men may be restrained from invading others rights, and from doing hurt to one another, and the law of nature be observed, which willeth the peace and preservation of all mankind, the execution of the law of nature is, in that state, put into every man's hands. . . . Being all equal and independent, no one ought to harm another in his life, health, liberty, or possessions.[14]

A poet at heart, Thomas Jefferson transposed Locke's somewhat clumsy, early-eighteenth-century phrasing into the beautiful preamble of the American Declaration of Independence:

> We hold these truths to be self-evident, that all men are created equal, that they are endowed, by their Creator, with certain

unalienable Rights, that among these are Life, Liberty, and the pursuit of Happiness.

He then listed more than a dozen grievances against the British monarch before composing a coda that recapitulated the words of Richard Henry Lee (shown below in italics) and, intentionally or not, usurped Lee's claim to immortality as author of the Declaration of Independence.

We, therefore, the representatives of the United States of America, in General Congress assembled, appealing to the Supreme Judge of the world for the rectitude of our intentions, do, in the name, and by the authority of the good people of these colonies, solemnly publish and declare, *that these united colonies are, and of right ought to be free and independent states; that they are absolved from all allegiance to the British Crown, and that all political connection between them and the state of Great Britain, is and ought to be totally dissolved;* and that as free and independent states, they have full power to levy war, conclude peace, contract alliances, establish commerce, and to do all other acts and things which independent states may of right do. And for the support of this declaration, with a firm reliance on the protection of Divine Providence, we mutually pledge to each other our lives, our fortunes and our sacred honor.[15]

After submitting the document to Congress, Jefferson reported arguments erupting among some delegates "that we had friends in England worth keeping terms with. . . . For this reason those passages which conveyed censures on the people of England were struck out, lest they should give them offence.

The clause, too, reprobating the enslaving of the inhabitants of Africa was struck out in complaisance to South Carolina and Georgia, who had never attempted to restrain the importation of slaves, and

22. Thomas Jefferson's extensive embellishment of Richard Henry Lee's original resolution for American independence created the document Americans celebrate annually at Independence Day.

who on the contrary still wished to continue it. Our northern brethren I believe felt a little tender . . . under those censures; for tho' their people have very few slaves themselves yet they had been pretty considerable carriers of them to others.[16]

On July 4 Congress voted twelve to zero in favor of the new document, with New York's delegates again stating they would abstain until they received express instructions from their state legislature.

After New York's legislature voted in favor on July 12, Congress sent copies to each of the states for ratification at special popularly elected conventions called in each state for that purpose.

As delegates left the Pennsylvania State House, however, they realized they had made an enormous blunder: "The United States of America" were not legally "united." Indeed, Richard Henry's "declaration of independence" of July 2—unlike Thomas Jefferson's version of July 4—had included the essential condition that "a plan for confederation be prepared and transmitted to the respective Colonies for their consideration."[17]

Accordingly, on July 12 Congress appointed a committee headed by John Dickinson to do just that, and it spent the next month debating issues that remain controversial to this day. A handful of southern representatives refused to cede an iota of state sovereignty to a central—or federal—authority, for example, and in the end Congress voted to postpone consideration of confederation until all the states had ratified the Declaration of Independence and were indeed free to confederate—or not.

By mid-July Virginia royal governor Lord Dunmore had expanded his forces on Chesapeake Bay and sent troops fanning out to ravage nearby plantations, raid tobacco warehouses, and confiscate tobacco supplies for shipment back to England. On July 20 Richard Henry Lee looked out over the Potomac from his second-floor window at Chantilly and saw British sails looming on the horizon down river. Assuming they were preparing to land troops, he rounded up hands on his own property to defend against a British landing and sent messengers to warn neighboring plantations. Despite his mangled hand, he led "a party of militia expecting visits from four of the enemies' ships and three tenders that appeared off this house at sunset."[18]

"The enemy of everything good has at length turned his wicked steps to this river, on the north side of which [Maryland] we can every day see the smoke occasioned by his conflagrations," Richard

Henry wrote to Landon Carter, whose plantation lay on the southern shore of the Northern Neck along the Rappahannock River.

> We learn that the people of Maryland are not quiet spectators of his proceedings, but that they have attacked and killed some of his people and obliged his whole fleet to move its station. They are continually blasting away at each other. We understand that they [the British] are in great want both of water and provisions.[19]

As the British ships approached the shore beneath Chantilly Lee ordered his makeshift band of fighters to fire a volley of musket shots and so surprised the approaching Redcoats that they jumped back in their boats and rowed back to their mother ship, which turned about and headed upstream. "They are gone up the river," he reported, "upon what errand I know not, unless to get water where the river is fresh or to burn Alexandria."[20]

As Lee defended the shoreline at Chantilly, frightening news arrived from New York. Even as General George Washington was reading the Declaration of Independence to his troops, a British armada of 400 ships had filled New York Bay near Manhattan Island and disgorged 20,000 battle-hardened troops onto Staten Island. Adding to the bad news from New York came word that the British had invaded upper New York and routed American forces, forcing their retreat southward past Lake Champlain toward Albany, New York.

And there was still more bad news—frightening, really. To his horror, Richard Henry received word that "a very extensive conspiracy . . . has been detected at New York" to bring about an abrupt end to the war by assassinating America's commander-in-chief. "Washington was to have been assassinated," Lee explained, "the magazines blown up, the cannons spiked. Many are now in jail for this nefarious business."[21] Newspapers cited New York mayor David Matthews as the suspected leader of the plot. A pro-Patriot newspaper ran a front-page headline offering a $50 reward for his capture—the equivalent of about $3,000 today. Charging Matthews with "high crimes," the newspaper described him as "well made, about 6 feet high, short brown hair, about 39 years old, and had a very plausible way of deceiving people. . . . Many are now in jail in this nefarious plot."*[22]

By the end of July the legislatures of all thirteen former British colonies had ratified the Declaration of Independence, and on August 2, 1776, forty-two solemn-faced delegates to Congress returned to Philadelphia, shuffling in groups of twos and threes into the Assembly Hall of the Pennsylvania State House. Only silence filled the hall as they took their seats and the president of the Continental Congress called out each name. One by one each delegate stood, then stepped to the front of the room to sign the document pledging his life, his fortune, and his sacred honor to declare his province independent of Britain. Well aware by then of the British army presence on Staten Island, each signer knew he was committing treason as he penned his name, inviting summary death if captured by the British.

Only Benjamin Harrison, the fat and jolly Virginia delegate who had married Martha Washington's niece, provided a note of levity, lowing to the rail-thin Elbridge Gerry of Massachusetts, "When the hanging scene comes, I shall have all the advantage over you. It will be over with me in a minute, but you will be kicking in the air half an hour after I'm gone."[23]

Although Francis Lightfoot Lee signed with the others, Richard Henry Lee did not arrive until a few days later, as did thirteen other delegates who signed the document.

---

*Matthews escaped behind British lines in New York, and when the British recaptured the entire island of Manhattan, he reassumed his post as mayor late in 1776. Although sentenced to death by the New York provincial government, Matthews remained mayor of New York under the British until Evacuation Day in 1783, when he sailed to Nova Scotia, Canada, with other Tories and then to Prince Edward Island. He died in 1800.

23. *The signing of the Declaration of Independence in the summer of 1776, as imagined here by artist John Trumbull in 1818. All fifty-six signers never convened as a group, however, and the painting, now in the rotunda of the Capitol, shows only forty-two of the fifty-six, as well as six who never signed. Richard Henry Lee sits, his legs (in white stockings) crossed, on the far left of the front row in the rear grouping. Samuel Adams sits beside him to his left. Francis Lightfoot Lee is missing. (See Appendix B, page 270, for a key to identify figures in the painting.)*

Ironically, only the president of Congress, John Hancock of Massachusetts, had signed the Declaration on July 4, the date now celebrated as Independence Day. Although memoirs written years later by John Adams, Thomas Jefferson, and a few others claim that they too signed the document on that date, witnesses insist they did not sign until July 19. Still other signers such as Philadelphia's Benjamin Rush, MD, had not even been elected to Congress by July 4 and did not sign until August 2.

By early August 1776, however, more than forty delegates from all thirteen states had indeed signed "A Declaration by the Representatives of the United States of America . . . that these united

colonies are, and of right ought to be free and independent states."
The secretary of Congress, Charles Thomson, who alone had wit-
nessed John Hancock's signature, would add his signature later.

At Chantilly Richard Henry Lee received this letter from Thomas
Jefferson:

> I enclose you a copy of the declaration of independence as agreed to
> by the House, and also, as originally framed. You will judge whether
> it is the better or worse for the Critics. I shall return to Virginia after
> the 11th of August. I wish my successor [in the Continental Con-
> gress] may be certain to come before that time, in that case, I shall
> hope to see you . . . in Convention, that the business of Govern-
> ment, which is of everlasting Concern, may receive your aid. Adieu,
> and believe me to be your friend & Servant, Thomas Jefferson[24]

Ironically, Thomas Jefferson would not spend a moment in battle
or fire a single shot at the enemy, let alone risk his life, fortune, or
sacred honor as pledged at the end of the document he signed and
submitted to Congress as the Declaration of Independence.

After Richard Henry Lee had tended to his wife's illness and embraced his children innumerable times, he traveled to Williamsburg
"to assist my countrymen in finishing our form of government." By
countrymen, of course, Lee still meant Virginians. Despite calling
their country the "United States of America" in the Declaration of
Independence, the signers (and all other Americans) still meant their
states of residence when they used the term "my country."

When Richard Henry Lee entered the Virginia Convention the
most difficult task he and other members faced was disposing of
lands in the Ohio Territory. Independence from Britain, of course,
had negated the Quebec Act and left much of the Ohio Territory in
dispute between the original Washington-Lee Ohio Company and
the old Loyal Land Company, now called the Grand Ohio Land
Company. With the Lee bloc in control, however, the Virginia convention voided all titles not obtained under the original 1612 royal

land grant, in effect restoring the Washington-Lee claims and voiding almost all rival claims.

After deciding who owned which lands and where, the Virginia Convention turned to fashioning a new government. All eyes turned to Richard Henry Lee, who signaled his choice of Patrick Henry as governor. The other delegates agreed.

"The mighty work is now done," he enthused after the convention had voted.

After helping Virginia's Convention design the world's first democratic government, Lee returned to Chantilly to check on his wife, then rode back to Philadelphia to finish the work of the Continental Congress. Almost all delegates recognized that their states would have to go to war to win concessions from Britain's Parliament, and most realized they would lose the war if they did not unite with other states. Any union, however, would force them to devise a central authority to coordinate the war—the very type of authority they were seeking to dislodge.

Although Congress had rejected John Dickinson's proposed articles of confederation, Richard Henry Lee tried developing a more acceptable set of articles after the states had approved the Declaration of Independence. He turned to his four-volume set of Sir William Blackstone's *Commentaries on the Laws of England*, which John Adams had recommended to him. One major argument against the Dickinson articles centered on voting. Small states demanded one vote for each state, while large states wanted voting based on population, arguing that giving each state only one vote would allow states with a tiny combined population to group together and dictate to the vast majority of the American people. The small states countered that voting by population would allow two or three states with large populations to combine to dictate to ten or eleven other states.

After days of tiresome, inconclusive arguments, news of the British landings on Staten Island in New York forced delegates to deal with more immediate issues. In mid-August 1776 they tabled the Articles of Confederation indefinitely and ended efforts to form a union—perfect or imperfect. The thirteen states remained independent nations, so divided in their loyalties that George Washington and Richard Henry Lee would now have the impossible task of dealing with thirteen different state legislatures if they were to pursue the war against Britain. And even if, in the end, Washington's Continental Army emerged victorious, each state would have to negotiate its own peace with Great Britain or resume war on its own. The vision of a united America that Washington and Lee had shared now seemed far out of reach.

CHAPTER 7

A Most Bloody Battle

AT THE END OF AUGUST THE BRITISH EXPEDITIONARY FORCE ON Staten Island sailed across New York Bay and stormed ashore in Brooklyn. They overran 5,000 American defenders, killing 1,500, seizing the American army's meat supply, and capturing two army field commanders, Generals John Sullivan and Israel Putnam. Only a thick fog had allowed American survivors to escape in the dark of night across the East River to New York Island (Manhattan) on August 29.

Crestfallen by the overwhelming defeat on Long Island, Congress ignored Richard Henry Lee's objections and sent Benjamin Franklin, John Adams, and Edmund Rutledge to talk peace at British headquarters on Staten Island. Once there they found the British commanding general Lord Howe unwilling to talk of a cease-fire until Congress ordered troops to lay down their arms, renewed allegiance to Britain, and revoked the Declaration of Independence. Infuriated by Howe's arrogance, Franklin and the others stomped out of Howe's tent and returned to Philadelphia, where they acknowledged their error in having ignored Richard Henry Lee's objections to their quest for peace. Four days later the British army renewed its assault on Washington's troops.

Washington posted the Connecticut militia to guard against a British landing at Kips Bay on the eastern shore of New York Island and moved the main body of troops to Harlem Heights, about six miles to the north.* On the morning of September 15 five British ships pounded American emplacements at Kips Bay with cannon fire. Within hours 6,000 of the 8,000 Connecticut troops—enlisted men and officers alike—had fled, terrified, sprinting to the rear without firing a shot, leaving Washington and his aides exposed to possible capture.

"Good God," Washington cried out. "Are these the men with which I am to defend America?"[1] As the British landed, Washington and his aides galloped off to safety, with British buglers sounding the call of hunters on a fox chase to mock the fleeing Americans.

"I never felt such a sensation before," said a Washington aide. "It seemed to crown our disgrace."[2]

"The conduct of the [state] militia has been so insufferably bad," Richard Henry Lee fumed to Patrick Henry after hearing from Washington, "that we find it impossible to support the war by their means and therefore a powerful army of regular troops must be obtained or all will be lost." Lee had again turned to Henry after Washington's humiliation. As governor of America's largest, wealthiest, and most heavily populated state, Henry had more political influence and resources than Congress. Lee now believed Henry alone could turn Washington's humiliation into a victory.

"It seems to be the opinion that each state should furnish a number of battalions proportionate to its strength," he wrote to Henry, "and the whole be paid by the continent." Richard Henry then

---

*Kips Bay is near present-day 34th Street on the east side of Manhattan Island; Harlem Heights stretched from present-day 110th Street to 125th Street, on the west side of Manhattan, where Columbia University now stands.

24. *Benjamin Franklin, in the fall of 1776, was sent to France by Congress to negotiate military aid and support for the flagging Continental Army, then in full-scale flight across New Jersey after a stunning defeat by the British in New York.*

shared intelligence from his brother Arthur that "letters from Bordeaux . . . inform us of the greatest preparations for war in France and Spain . . . and the strongest assurance and acts of friendship imaginable shown to North America."[3]

On October 1 Arthur Lee sent word to Richard Henry that the French government "could not think of entering a war with England" but would assist America with secret shipments of £200,000 sterling worth of arms. Arthur reported that the French court itself refused to deal directly or indirectly with him regarding officially recognizing American rebels. Instead, they demanded a meeting with an official representative of the Congress—someone with international standing.

There was but one such American, of course: Benjamin Franklin.

Richard Henry wrote to Samuel Adams urging the immediate dispatch of American ambassadors to foreign courts—especially to

France. The interest of the French government, he argued, "is clearly to support the new Confederacy. When the Court of France has received our ambassador . . . most of the other European powers will, I apprehend, quickly follow the example."[4]

As Washington's troops licked their wounds after the disaster in Brooklyn, Connecticut's militiamen continued disappearing, reducing one regiment to only fourteen men, another to fewer than thirty. With his troop strength disintegrating, Washington withdrew from Manhattan Island to White Plains, on the mainland to the north in Westchester County.

A few days later, however, the main body of British troops overwhelmed the Americans again, scattering them in several directions. While two regiments fled northward into the Hudson River highlands, Washington led a contingent of about 5,000 across the Hudson River to New Jersey. With winter approaching earlier than usual and the British in close pursuit, Washington's men staggered westward through sheets of icy autumn rains, eventually crossing the Delaware River into Pennsylvania by early December. Besides the dead or captured troops, desertions had reduced his army to little more than 3,000. Sickness left half unfit for duty; of seventeen officers, only five stood ready to fight. Only Washington's foresight in ordering his men to seize all river craft halted the British pursuit at the Delaware River's edge.

"The retreat across New Jersey," Virginia lieutenant James Monroe recalled later, "will be forever celebrated in the annals of our country for the patient suffering, the unshaken firmness, and gallantry of this small band . . . and the great and good qualities of its commander. . . . [Washington] was always near the enemy, and his countenance and manner made an impression on me which time can never efface. A deportment so firm, so dignified, so exalted, but yet so modest and composed, I have never seen in any other person."[5]

Lee tried to bolster Washington's spirits: "I congratulate you sincerely on the several advantages your troops have lately gained over the enemy. . . . May the great Dispenser of Justice to Mankind put it in your power before this campaign ends to give these foes to human kind the stroke their wicked intentions entitles them to.

> I have the pleasure to assure you . . . that we have the fairest prospect of being soon supplied, and copiously too, with military stores of all kinds and with clothing fit for the soldiers. Immediately, to be sure, we are much pressed for want of the latter, but if we can brush through this crisis, we shall be secure. The French court has given us so many unequivocal proofs of their friendship that I can entertain no doubt of their full exertions in our favor, and . . . that a war between them and Great Britain is not far distant.[6]

Without boats to cross the Delaware River, the British commander ordered his 3,000 Hessian mercenaries to remain on the river's eastern shore at Trenton, New Jersey, to watch the Americans on the opposite bank. He then led British troops to more comfortable quarters at nearby Princeton to wait for the river to freeze and cross on foot to wipe out Washington's crippled army and end the Revolution.

The British advance left most of New Jersey in British hands, and with Redcoats almost within sight of Philadelphia, Congress fled to Baltimore on December 12 and began debating terms of capitulation. Only Richard Henry Lee objected, outraged by the thought of surrender, refusing to cede an inch of American territory to the British. Only Lee sought to move ahead, sensing how to achieve victory. Like Washington, he intended maintaining a constant barrage of correspondence with state leaders such as Virginia governor Patrick Henry to keep them apprised of wartime progress and the needs of the military to achieve victory. In effect Richard Henry Lee had emerged as the civilian leader of the Revolution in concert with the military leader, George Washington.

Shortly after reaching Baltimore Richard Henry Lee received a coded message from Arthur warning that the British planned to sail into Chesapeake Bay with a large landing force. "The eastern shore is the first object or place of landing," Richard Henry relayed his brother's message to Washington and Patrick Henry.

"The movements of the enemy's army in the Jerseys, by which the neighborhood of Philadelphia had become the seat of war, determined Congress to adjourn from thence to this town," Richard Henry Lee explained in a note to Henry. He maintained his belief that American victory rested on keeping Virginia's Patrick Henry involved in day-to-day military developments. Although the largest, richest, and most heavily populated state, Virginia had yet to host open warfare with British forces, and Governor Patrick Henry had not participated in the decisions of Congress affecting the war. Richard Henry knew, however, that without the support of Patrick Henry and Virginia, Washington would lose the war.

"At this place," Richard Henry explained to Patrick Henry, "the public business can be conducted with more deliberation and undisturbed attention than could be the case in a city subject to perpetual alarm.

> So long as the American army kept together, the enemy's progress was extremely limited, but they knew and seized the opportunity of coming forward, which was occasioned by the greater part of the [American] army dispersing in consequence of short enlistments. . . . When a new army is assembled, the enemy must again narrow their bounds, and this demonstrates the necessity of every state exerting every means to bring the new levies into the field with all possible expedition.[7]

Even Washington, however, had grown discouraged by then. "It is impossible," he wrote to his brother, "to give you any idea . . . of my difficulties—and the constant perplexities and mortification I constantly meet with."[8] Washington seemed ready to concede defeat in the war unless he could stage a remarkable counterattack.

Still writing from Baltimore, Richard Henry Lee appealed a second time to Patrick Henry to reinforce Washington's army: "The

British army," he pleaded, "is at present stationed along the Delaware from above Trenton on the Jersey side, to Burlington, about
20 miles above Philadelphia. General Washington . . . is on the river
opposite to Trenton. . . . If the country reinforces the general with a
few thousand, so as to enable him to press the enemy's front, it may
turn out a happy circumstance."[9]

Washington, however, had devised a plan to engineer his own
"happy circumstance"—without help from Patrick Henry or anyone
else. In the most daring military strike of the Revolutionary War,
Washington led some 2,400 troops onto a flotilla of small boats on
the night of December 25 and ordered them to row through the
blinding snowstorm across the ice-choked Delaware River. At eight
o'clock the next morning, they reached the east bank near Trenton,
New Jersey, and found the 1,400-man Hessian garrison still abed,
dissuaded by the storm from posting their usual patrol. Shocked
awake by the reality of their plight, the terrified Germans raced into
the snow in night clothes to fire at the approaching Americans. But
they were too late. Washington's troops had battled their way up
King Street through the center of Trenton and forced the Hessians
to surrender.

Cheers echoed across the American landscape as news of Washington's triumph spread from King Street, Trenton, to Philadelphia,
then to the congressional meeting house in Baltimore, northward to
Boston, and southward to Charleston harbor. Washington's startling
roundup of more than 1,000 Hessian troops—in their underwear, no
less—amazed the world. A small, undisciplined mob of ragtag farmers and hunters with muskets had overwhelmed two battalions of the
Western world's best-trained, best-equipped mercenaries.

The triumph provoked laughter in the halls of Versailles, where
King Louis grew convinced an alliance with Washington's American
rebels might help him defeat England and restore Canada to French
rule.

Paris and all France had welcomed Benjamin Franklin a month earlier, fêting him day and night as the great thinker-philosopher-scientist

that he was, but the French court had refused to entertain him as a diplomat without assurances that the American military would prove an effective ally if France went to war with Britain.

"The number of Hessian prisoners does not fall much short of 1,100," Richard Henry Lee enthused in a letter to Patrick Henry. He went on to describe Washington's subsequent march to Princeton, where he routed the British a second time—this time using a ruse that humiliated the British army and provoked even more laughter at Versailles and admiration for the American commander-in-chief.

With intelligence that British general Howe was on the march, Washington ordered large fires built to simulate an encampment. When Howe's troops attacked the empty camp, Washington's men surrounded them and, according to Richard Henry Lee, "routed his troops, taking from 600 to 800 prisoners. Pursuing the fugitive, we entered Princeton, where a number of [British] officers, six or seven field pieces, and the 40th regiment were taken."[10] Washington had adopted a new type of warfare developed by American Indians on America's forested hills but unknown to military strategists in Europe and Britain who fought on large open spaces laid bare by overcultivation.

Confident his victory at Princeton would encourage the French to provide military aid, Washington ordered his troops to drive British forces eastward to Brunswick, where he hoped to capture a huge British arms depot while leaving western New Jersey in Patriot hands and allowing Congress to return to Philadelphia.

"We wait in hourly expectation of receiving authentic intelligence of the total rout of the enemy's army in Jersey and their disgraceful evacuation of that state," Richard Henry Lee continued his regular reports to Patrick Henry. He wrote that Washington had encamped at Morristown, about twenty miles west of Brunswick, "where the enemy keep their headquarters. . . . A gentleman who arrived here yesterday and who passed through our army . . . says the men were in high spirits. . . . They were 12,000 strong . . . under marching orders and . . . going towards Elizabeth Town, which is between the main body of the enemy and New York."[11]

Lee then sent orders to Maryland officials on behalf of the Maritime Committee of Congress "that the State of Maryland be directed to proceed immediately to provide timber for building two thirty-six gun frigates."[12] By mid-February Richard Henry was able to boast to his brother Arthur, "We shall have a number of exceeding fine frigates at sea very soon, from 24 to 36 guns."

Facing increased personal dangers in Britain after the battle at Trenton, Arthur and William Lee had already started making secret preparations to flee with Richard Henry Lee's two boys. "I am exceedingly uneasy about my poor boys," Richard Henry admitted to Arthur, "and beg of you to get them to me in the quickest and safest manner."[13]

To that end Richard Henry prodded Congress to appoint Arthur Lee a commissioner in Paris with Benjamin Franklin and Silas Deane. The appointment would allow him to exit Britain with his family without interference by British authorities. For the same reasons he obtained a congressional appointment for William Lee as US commercial agent at the busy French port of Nantes, where he could oversee secret shipments of arms, ammunition, and military supplies to America. Later Congress would expand responsibilities of the Lee brothers by sending Arthur to seek loans and military assistance in Spain, while William went to Vienna and Berlin on similar missions.

When Richard Henry Lee returned to his sister's house in Philadelphia, a letter awaited that eased his worst fears: his brothers had escorted Richard Henry's children out of England without incident.

"I heard with great pleasure that my dear children were safely arrived in France," he wrote to his sons Thomas and Ludwell. (He had a curious habit of addressing them in the third person in his joint letters to them.) "I had suffered from apprehensions both for them and their worthy uncles in a country where every consideration of virtue and justice is sacrificed to wicked resentment and views of tyranny."

Lee told his boys the war had made him change his ambitions for them. "Instead of the Church, I would now have [Thom] . . . in commerce. For this purpose if his good Uncle William should reside in France, my son will be employed by him as clerk or agent in some capacity, by which a temporary support may be gained and a lasting knowledge of business at the same time. . . . I want Thom to . . . learn the French language so that when he returns to his own country he might be qualified to undertake any foreign business that may be entrusted to his care."[14]

In a second letter he stated his ambitions for his younger son:

> I wish Ludwell to go deep into the study of natural and civil law and eloquence, as well as to obtain the military improvement. . . . My desire being that he may be able to turn either to the law or sword here, as his genius or his interest and the service of his country might point out.[15]

Returning to Congress the next day, Richard Henry encountered a barrage of complaints from Washington and other Army leaders about the droves of French officers who had been appearing unexpectedly at Washington's headquarters demanding high-level commands they insisted Silas Deane had promised them in Paris.

Two top aides to Washington—Major Generals Nathanael Green and Henry Knox—threatened to resign, along with a score of junior officers. Washington sent an angry letter to Congress, protesting "the distress I am . . . laid under by the application of French officers for commission in our service.

> This evil . . . is a growing one . . . they are coming in swarms from old France and the Islands. . . . They seldom bring more than a commission and a passport, which, we know, may belong to a bad as well as a good officer. Their ignorance of our language and their inability

to recruit men are insurmountable obstacles to their being engrafted into our Continental battalions. Our [American] officers, who . . . have served through the war upon pay that has hitherto not borne their expenses, would be disgusted if foreigners were put over their heads.[16]

When Congress failed to respond, Washington sent another angry note—this one to Richard Henry Lee, who had only just returned to Congress. "Under the privilege of friendship," Washington wrote, "I take the liberty to ask you what Congress expects I am to do with the many foreigners . . . promoted to the rank of field officers and . . . two to colonels. . . . These men have no attachment nor ties to the country . . . and are ignorant of the language they are to receive and give orders in . . . and our officers think it exceedingly hard . . . to have strangers put over them, whose merit perhaps is not equal to their own, but whose effrontery will take no denial." Washington told Richard Henry he was "disgusted" by the practice of "giving rank to people of no reputation or service."[17]

In a long rambling letter Lee tried to explain the inexplicable, saying, "I beg you, sir, to be convinced that no desire to get rid of importunity has occasioned these appointments, but motives military and political." He went on to divide "these adventurers" into three groups—the unemployed without recommendations but hopeful of profiting from their service; a second similar group with recommendations from the French military command on the Caribbean island of Martinique; and a third group from France, carrying enlistment agreements "with our commissioners [in Paris], or one of them at least.

"I really believe there are many worthless men, and I heartily wish we were rid of them," Richard Henry Lee told Washington.

The desire to obtain engineers and artillerists was the principle cause of our being so overburdened. Many of the last class are, I believe men of real merit, and if they will learn to express themselves

25. Silas Deane, a member of Congress from Connecticut, was appointed by Congress commissioner to France to assist Franklin in seeking military aid from the French government and to recruit artillery and engineering specialists for the Continental Army.

tolerably in English may be of service to the army. When General Conway was appointed, I did hope that as he knew most of them and spoke both French and English well, he might relieve you from the greater part of this difficulty. . . . We have further written to France and Martinique to stop the further flow of these gentlemen here.[18]

Unwilling to add to Washington's antagonism, Lee stood in Congress to demand that it stop granting military commissions to foreigners unless Washington himself requested it. Lee also asked his brothers William and Arthur to probe as discreetly as possible into Silas Deane's motivation for issuing so many commissions in Paris.

It was not long before Arthur Lee learned that Deane had promised French officers not only commissions in the American army—with pay and postwar retirement pensions—but also options to buy land in Ohio from the Grand Ohio Company that Lee's Ohio Land Company had long claimed. Indeed, Deane specified the land he sold as "land at the mouth of the Ohio, between that and the Mississippi, equal to two hundred miles square." In addition to pocketing money from "land sales" to French officers, he borrowed £2 million for his personal use, offering as collateral the same lands he had already sold. Infuriated by his brother's intelligence, Richard Henry Lee moved that Congress recall Deane to America and replace him as envoy to France with John Adams.

As Lee tried stemming the flow of unwanted officers from France, Washington appealed for more American enlisted men. "Recruiting . . . seems to be at end," Washington wrote. "The regiments of Pennsylvania indeed appear to be growing worse, and unless some coercive method can be hit upon to complete the battalions, I see no chance of doing it."[19]

When Congress recessed, Richard Henry Lee returned to Virginia, only to learn that a group of disgruntled state assemblymen—largely less-literate, up-country farmers who resented the power wielded by the Lee family—had taken personal affront to Richard Henry Lee's deportment at the previous session of the Assembly. They had resented his elegant dress, his language, and what they deemed his arrogant references to political concepts alien to them but, according to Richard Henry, "common knowledge" to the rest of the world. His continual use of the phrase "as you all know" irritated them—especially delivered with his quasi-English accent.

They did not know! Nor did they want to know. They had not attended British schools and resented his assumption that they had. None had heard of—let alone read—Montesquieu, and when the Lees had left the Assembly in May 1777 to celebrate having shaped the new state government, those they left behind unleashed their resentment by denying Richard Henry Lee reelection to the Continental Congress.

His political enemies accused him of exploiting his tenant farmers, profiting from shortages of specie, and undermining the value of paper money printed by the Continental Congress—and there was a grain of truth to their accusations. But no more than a grain.

When the Revolution had started, Congress printed its own paper money to replace British currency. With no gold or British reserves to back it, however, the new currency quickly lost its value, giving rise to the expression, "Not worth a continental." As the value of continentals plunged, Richard Henry urged his tenant farmers to keep their continentals and pay their rent in tobacco or other commodities instead—a common practice at the time. But the practice led to further devaluation of continentals, thus giving his political enemies grounds for charging him with enriching himself at the expense of poor tenant farmers and undermining the national economy.

The rest of the Lee clan rallied around Richard Henry, with his younger brother Francis Lightfoot Lee even resigning his seat in Congress to stand by his brother in Williamsburg. With oratory his best defense, Richard Henry displayed it in its full glory, saying that his tenants had lacked the cash to pay him, that he had actually benefited them by giving them options other than cash to pay their rent.

Lee demanded an impartial investigation by both the Assembly and Governor Patrick Henry, who exonerated Lee of any wrongdoing.

"If I have contributed in any degree to your satisfaction or enabled you to combat false news intended to injure the cause of America, I am happy," Lee wrote to Patrick Henry. "I love that cause and I have faithfully exerted myself to serve it well."[20]

The subsequent Assembly investigation not only proved the charges against Lee to have been false, it yielded "a most triumphant and flattering acquittal [and] a humble vote of thanks for his patriotic services,"[21] according to the future US Attorney General William

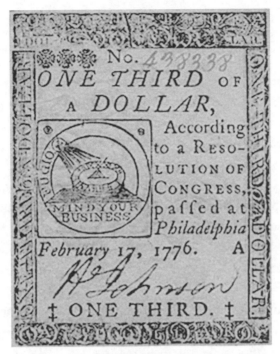

No. 438338
ONE THIRD OF A DOLLAR,
According to a RESOLUTION OF CONGRESS, passed at Philadelphia February 17, 1776.   A
‡ ONE THIRD. ‡

26. A one-third-dollar paper "continental," the currency Congress ordered printed after declaring independence from Britain. Without gold backing, it plunged in value and gave rise to the all-but-universal expression "not worth a continental."

Wirt. "His orations were warmer . . . could unlock the sources of the strong or tender passions," and the same delegates who had dislodged him from Congress now restored him to his old seat—with apologies. He and his brother Frank would ride back to Philadelphia to reclaim their places and positions in Congress.

Before leaving, Richard Henry took steps to bolster Virginia's defenses. Although confident France would soon intervene, he nonetheless called on Patrick Henry and Virginia's legislature to act. "When we consider the water accessibility of our country [Virginia], it is most clear that no defense can avail us so much as a marine one, and of all sea forces . . . that of gallies.*

> I wish therefore that . . . the General Assembly may early direct the immediate building of 10 or 12 large sea gallies . . . to carry two 32 pounders in the bow, two in the stern, and 10 six pounders on the side, to row with 40 oars and be manned with an hundred men.[22]

The galleys, he said, would keep Virginia's trade routes open and secure the state's shores "better than 50,000 men. Besides the great security these vessels will yield, they will be a fine nursery for seamen so much wanted by us. If the forge and foundry on James River be well attended to, we may easily and quickly be furnished with plenty of cannon."[23]

Before Arthur Lee had left England for Paris, he had obtained intelligence of British government preparations to extend the front in America. "Chesapeake Bay will be the seat. . . . The Eastern Shore is the first object, or place of landing." Lee learned of a "grand plan of joining their Canadian [army] with [General Lord] Howe's army." Later, after he had landed in Bordeaux on his way to Paris, Lee forwarded another message that "ten thousand Germans are already engaged, and ships sent to convey them. . . . Boston is certainly to be attacked in the spring. Burgoyne is to command. Howe will probably turn against Philadelphia."[24] Once in Paris Arthur warned his brother that the British were preparing to print counterfeit American currency that Congress had printed—the so-called continentals. By flooding the market, they hoped to render it worthless and bankrupt Congress.

Richard Henry sent Arthur's message to Washington, who reacted angrily: "That Great Britain will exert every nerve to carry her

---

*A low-slung boat with a variable number of guns but propelled by oars and highly maneuverable in narrow waterways.

tyrannical designs into execution, I have not the smallest doubt," Washington replied. "For should America rise triumphant in her struggle for independence, she must fall. It is not to be wondered therefore, after she had departed from that line of justice which ought to characterize a virtuous people that she should descend to such low arts and dirty tricks. None of which have they practiced . . . with more dangerous consequences to our cause than their endeavors to depreciate the continental bills."[25]

In still another message Arthur Lee suggested that Washington prepare a surprise counterattack on British and German troops as they attempt to land in the Philadelphia area. When Richard Henry forwarded the message, Washington—exhausted from several days with little sleep—replied almost incoherently that Arthur's suggestion "is certainly well founded if our own circumstances will admit of it," but that Arthur "little apprehended that we ourselves should have an army at this late hour to raise of men equally raw and officers probably more so."[26]

Although the first of William Lee's ships carrying Beaumarchais arms had left Nantes and crossed the Atlantic safely, British frigates intercepted it as it approached the Delaware capes. "The captain," Richard Henry Lee learned, "after bravely defending himself for some time in vain, blew up his ship rather than let her fall into the enemy's hands. He lost his life, the rest of the crew was saved, and, what is remarkable . . . a considerable part of the cargo was driven safely ashore by the exploding powder, and persons are now securing it."[27]

Humiliated before the world by Washington's victories in New Jersey, the British government recalled its commanding generals to London, leaving Congress hoping peace might be at hand. King George quickly dashed their hopes in his annual New Year's speech to Parliament, calling for higher taxes to prosecute the war "with unrelenting vigor." Richard Henry Lee responded by prodding Congress to promote Washington's best-performing officers—only to find himself scolded by the commander-in-chief.

"I am anxious to know," Washington sent an angry note to Lee, "whether General Arnold's non-promotion was owing to accident or design—and the cause of it! Surely a more active, more spirited, and sensible officer fills no department in your army. Not seeing him in the list of major generals and no mention made of him has given me uneasiness, as it is not to be presumed (being the oldest brigadier) that he will continue in service under such a slight. I imagine you will lose two or three other very good officers by promoting [others] . . . over them. . . . My anxiety to be informed of the reason of Arnold's non-promotion gives you the trouble of this letter."[28]

Lee said he would inform Congress of Washington's views but promised nothing else. Arnold had already resigned by then—a usual response of all high-level officers passed over for promotion. After refusing to accept Arnold's resignation, Washington soothed Arnold's feelings by explaining that Congress allocated all promotions by state and that it had filled the quota for Connecticut. He successfully convinced Arnold to return to active duty, but Arnold, who had fought heroically and suffered wounds in the failed American invasion of Canada, would never forgive Congress for what he considered a cruel insult.[29]

In April 1777 Richard Henry Lee prodded delegates into resuming their debate over the Articles of Confederation, only to have new differences surface. Rather than allow Congress to table the issue again, Richard Henry Lee coaxed them to continue the debate at least two days a week, only to have a North Carolina delegate—the fiery Irish-born physician Thomas Burke—all but crush hopes for an effective confederation. A gifted orator with a hypnotizing lilt in his voice, Burke charged that small states were conspiring to create a strong central government only to seize and redistribute lands of large states and create thirteen equal-sized states. His baseless accusation frightened delegates into leaving all sovereign power in the states and limiting central government powers to those obtained only by a unanimous vote of the states—an all-but-impossible outcome that would render the confederation impotent.

While Congress ceded all governing authority to the states, the British high command in New York took full advantage by launching military campaigns on two fronts in the north and south. As Arthur Lee had warned, General Lord Howe in New York led one-third of the troops southward toward the rebel capital of Philadelphia. On a second front British troops initiated a three-pronged attack to isolate New England from the rest of the colonies by overrunning the Hudson River Valley and the waterways to the Canadian frontier. While troops sailed up the Hudson River from New York toward Albany, a second force under General John Burgoyne was to invade upstate New York from Canada, march southward along Lake Champlain and Lake George to join the troops from New York and establish lines around the north, east, and south flanks of American troops at Albany. Meanwhile a third British force from western New York would march eastward toward Albany to close the vise.

Burgoyne's campaign started well, as his 8,000 British troops and an assortment of Indian warriors captured Lake Champlain and overran Fort Ticonderoga at Lake George. Hopelessly outmanned and outgunned, the Patriot troops deserted by scores, all but ceding the Revolution to the Redcoats and provoking a harsh evaluation by Richard Henry Lee, who called the northern campaign "disgraceful."

Lee told Virginia lieutenant governor John Page that Congress had responded by putting the popular British-born general Horatio Gates in command of the American Northern Army. "The militia is turning out to join that army," he added, "and now that they have the general they love and can confide in, I hope our affairs will soon wear a better countenance." Because of Gates's extensive battlefield experience, Congress had almost chosen him over George Washington when it considered candidates to lead the Continental Army in 1775. On John Adams's insistence, however, it decided against entrusting a Briton with command of America's incipient rebellion against Britain.

On August 11 a small band of grizzled farmers appeared on the outskirts of Bennington, Vermont, about forty miles east of Albany,

New York, where British troops were threatening to overrun a force of badly outnumbered American Patriots. Each of the farmers carried as many muskets as he could in one arm, firing at random toward the enemy with his free arm, and shouting incomprehensibly to their countrymen about a ship—a French ship. The 300-ton *Mercure*, the first of three Beaumarchais ships that would sail into the harbor at Portsmouth, New Hampshire, had arrived. It carried 12,000 muskets, fifty brass cannons, and all the powder and ammunition they needed. In addition, the ship carried 1,000 tents and enough clothes for 10,000 men. As sailors ran the French flag up the mast, townsmen cheered, danced for joy, and jumped aboard to embrace the sailors.

Within a week their euphoria metamorphosed into a carefully organized, 2,000-man wagon train that rolled 150 miles to Bennington, Vermont, where 500 militiamen with the American Northern Army had run out of powder and faced annihilation by a British force twice their size. With their powder horns refilled, the Americans in Bennington slaughtered 200 Redcoats and captured 700 in what proved the first in a series of crushing defeats that the steady arrival of Beaumarchais's ships would inflict on Burgoyne and his Redcoats in the summer and fall of 1777.

Few Beaumarchais ships risked sailing into major ports fully loaded with arms, however. Using a flow of coded messages to his brother Richard Henry, William Lee arranged for most Beaumarchais ships to sail to one or another of the French sugar islands, where small American vessels would pick up the arms and carry them to one of the many coves along the Atlantic coast for delivery to Patriot troops. Many never reached American shores.

"You would be greatly surprised at the number and value of the French vessels taken and destroyed by the English on our coasts this last winter and spring," Richard Henry lamented to John Adams.[30]

As the Northern Army under Gates was repelling Burgoyne's advance in upper New York, Washington's Continental Army in New Jersey prepared to defend Philadelphia from assault by Lord Howe.

"General Washington's forces are so placed as to be ready to meet Mr. Howe's visitation if it happens," Richard Henry Lee told Virginia Lieutenant-Governor John Page,[31] and to Thomas Jefferson, Lee boasted, "The General [Washington] and his Army . . . made a fine appearance. . . . Should General Howe venture to enter the country against this force, I think his ruin will be sure."[32] To build support for the Revolution in Virginia, Lee constantly teased state leaders with hints of victory to come, but only if they continued supplying Washington with arms, ammunition, and troops.

Despite Arthur Lee's advance intelligence and Richard Henry Lee's warning, Washington was unprepared not because of negligence but because of impotence—his own and that of Congress. He could not restore troop strength unless each state government recruited troops and sent them to him. He could not procure arms and ammunition unless Congress provided them, and Congress could not pay for such materiel unless each of the states appropriated the money to do so. Richard Henry Lee did his best, but it was seldom enough, and General Lord Howe knew it. The British had spies in America every bit as effective as Arthur and William Lee had been in Britain.

On July 23, 1777, Howe took full advantage of Washington's vulnerability, ordering 15,000 troops onto ships bound for Chesapeake Bay, where they sailed to the northernmost rim and streamed ashore unopposed at Head of Elk (now Elkton, Maryland). Once on land they all but strolled toward Brandywine Creek, the last natural barrier on the way to the national capital at Philadelphia. They saw no American troops until Washington and a force of just over 10,000 appeared on the opposite, Philadelphia side of Brandywine Creek.

Washington badly miscalculated the strength and intentions of his enemy, however, by concentrating his troops and fire power at the center of the British line at Chadd's Ford. As the battle raged with ever-greater intensity, British general Lord Cornwallis quietly slipped away to the northwest with 8,000 British and Hessian troops. They crossed Brandywine Creek at its narrowest point, far from the battle at Chadd's Ford, and looped around and behind the American army's right flank, threatening to encircle Washington's entire force.

As paralyzing British fire swept across American lines from three directions, Washington's troops turned about and fled in panic, leaving half an army of dead and dying men and boys, screaming in pain, their tatters soaked in blood, sweat, and dirt. British troops closed in from three sides—south, west, and north—to claim victory.

"We had a most bloody battle with General Howe, which ended [with] our army retiring," a crestfallen Richard Henry Lee, admitted to Patrick Henry. As the member of Congress most responsible for reinforcing Washington's army, however, Lee shone as bright a light on the disaster as he could: "Every account . . . says the enemy's loss in killed and wounded must be between 2,000 and 3,000. . . . Our loss in killed and wounded comes up to 500."[33] In fact, American losses were about 1,000 killed and wounded, and the losses for the British were 576.

On September 19 Richard Henry Lee and the rest of Congress fled Philadelphia, with members scattering in different directions to return to their homes while Lee and his brother Francis Lightfoot Lee rallied a handful of colleagues to follow them to Lancaster, eighty miles to the west.

"At 3 this morning, [I] was waked . . . and told that the members of Congress were gone, some of them a little after midnight," a startled John Adams scribbled in his diary later. He and another delegate sent for their horses "and rode off after the others," finding delegates from New York and New Jersey gathered at a tavern in Trenton, New Jersey. "So many disasters," he seemed to moan as he penned his recollections of the day.

"Oh, Heaven! Grant us one great soul! One leading mind would extricate the best cause from that ruin which seems to await it for the want of it. We have as good a cause as ever was fought for."[34] Rather than rejoin Congress, John Adams decided to return home, leaving Richard Henry Lee without his closest friend and ally in Congress.

"It was my intention to decline the next election and return to the bar," Adams explained.

> I had been four years in Congress . . . I was daily losing the fruits of seventeen years industry. . . . My children were growing up without my care in their education. All my emoluments [pay] as a member of Congress . . . had not been sufficient to pay a laboring man upon my farm. Young gentlemen who had been clerks in my office . . . were growing rich. I thought, therefore, that four years drudgery and sacrifice . . . were sufficient . . . that another might take my place.[35]

On September 26 Howe's army marched into Philadelphia unopposed.

Washington was to suffer still more humiliations. To try to prevent further advances by Howe's army, Washington staged what devolved into a suicidal counterattack near Germantown, just outside Philadelphia. He sent two separate columns along what a schematic diagram showed as parallel roads to Germantown for a two-pronged pincer attack on the British. In fact, one road followed a longer serpentine course, allowing the column on the straighter, shorter road to reach Germantown before its twin column.

Faced with an impenetrable wall of British fire and no support from the second column, the first column retreated. As night fell a dense fog enveloped the area, and the retreating column collided with the second American column, which was still advancing. Mistaking them for enemy soldiers, they fired at their American comrades. Caught between American and British fire, the trapped column lost 700 men, with 400 more taken prisoner as they retreated into British lines. The British had crushed the American army and put the American government to flight. For all intents and purposes, the American Revolution was over. North America would remain British.

Richard Henry Lee, however, refused to concede defeat.

CHAPTER 8

To Discard General Washington

As British commanders doubled over with laughter in Germantown, the two Lee brothers—Richard Henry and Francis Lightfoot—led the remnants of the American government, barely twenty delegates, thirty miles farther west from Lancaster to York, Pennsylvania. Richard Henry Lee nonetheless sought to paint as fine a picture as he could to sustain Patrick Henry's support for the war.

"We have had another general engagement with the enemy," Lee wrote of the Germantown disaster. "We attacked their army. The plan was well executed, and . . . a brilliant victory was on the moment of being obtained, when accident alone removed it from us." After describing how the Patriots had "quitted a glorious victory absolutely in their power," Lee assured Henry that the army had "retired in order . . . is now upon the ground they left before the battle in high spirits, and satisfied they can beat the enemy."[1]

If Patrick Henry was by now able to read between the lines of Richard Henry Lee's embellished versions of Washington's disastrous encounters, the unadorned news of Gates's stunning victory over Burgoyne at Saratoga cheered him—and thousands of other Americans. Under the terms of surrender Burgoyne agreed to march his 5,700 Redcoats back to Boston, where they were to sail to Britain, barred from ever returning to America or serving in battle against Americans.

The victory at Saratoga electrified the Western world—Europeans as well as Americans. Patriot morale soared. Believing victory near, if not at hand, the withering Congress put aside interstate disputes to renew work on creating the "Articles of Confederation and Perpetual Union," with Richard Henry Lee again named chairman of the committee to develop a final draft. In Europe political leaders routinely spoke of "the new nation," while monarchs shuddered at the epochal character of Saratoga: an army of farmers and woodsmen with no military training had humiliated a well-disciplined, accomplished professional army; a peasant rebellion had crushed the military might of a divinely ordained, absolute monarch. If it happened in America . . .

In Versailles Vergennes ignored the possible social contagion and pushed the king closer to war with Britain, using as a lure the immeasurable wealth awaiting the nation that dominated trade with the new American nation. The costs of war, he told the king, were simply an investment to assure that wealth. Blinded by the prospects of immeasurable profits, the king ignored the warnings of some who feared that a commoner rebellion against an absolute monarch in one country might spark similar political conflagrations elsewhere—perhaps even in France.

As the extent of the American victory became clearer, a few European newspapers not only embellished the British-Hessian humiliation, they invented other American victories and British disasters and elevated the Anglo-American conflict to an Arthurian romance.

In York, Congress, or what was left of it, sensed victory and independence near at hand—and the need to establish a nation with officials empowered to sign a peace treaty with Britain and trade agreements with other nations on behalf of all the states. Still fearful of the taxing powers and other emasculating tactics of a strong central government, delegates decided to perpetuate state sovereignty in virtually every area of government except foreign affairs. In one of the last obstacles to national unity, a majority of states balked at allowing Virginia to retain control over the huge "northwest territory," which encompassed present-day Ohio, Indiana, Illinois, Michigan, Wisconsin, and part of Minnesota. When Virginia expressed willingness to cede public but not private lands in the territory to the Confederation, Congress agreed, thus safeguarding Washington and Lee's ownership of hundreds of thousands of acres in the Ohio territory. With that, Congress adopted America's first constitution on November 15, 1777, and sent copies to each of the states for ratification by their legislatures.

Map 2. Northwest Territory. Once part of Virginia, the Northwest Territory encompassed present-day Ohio, Indiana, Illinois, Michigan, Wisconsin, and part of Minnesota. Virginia's cession of the territory to the Confederation ensured passage of the Articles of Confederation, the first "constitution" of the United States. In creating the first federally own lands in America, the transfer ensured a permanent ban on slavery in any states created in the territory.

To ensure agreement by all states Richard Henry Lee composed Articles of Confederation that created an all-but-impotent Confederation Congress. A combined executive and legislative body, it would be unable to take any action without unanimous consent of the states. Under Article Two, moreover, each state would retain its sovereignty. Although Congress would be able to appoint Confederation emissaries to foreign capitals, they would have no negotiating authority without unanimous consent of the states. The Articles created "a firm league of friendship" that "bound" states to the common defense but made no provision for ensuring they would have to act for the common defense by providing money or troops. Nor did the Articles give Congress powers to raise or fund an army or tax states to procure arms and ammunition. Until then the lack of congressional taxing powers had so frustrated Richard Henry Lee's every attempt to supply Washington's army that he invested all his energy into trying to convince delegates to give Congress at least limited taxing powers.

One by one the states succumbed to the logic of his persistent appeals, and in the end twelve states agreed. But New York delegates stood firm in opposition and left Congress with no way to pay for the rest of the Revolutionary War except by borrowing from foreign countries.

As Congress debated the Articles of Confederation, Washington and his army limped away from its humiliation in Germantown and set up winter quarters on an elevated plateau above Valley Forge, about twenty-five miles northwest of Philadelphia. At first glance the site gave Washington's army the advantage of elevation on the east if it had to defend itself against British troops advancing from Philadelphia. A gentle slope to the west gave his men a route for an orderly retreat, while steep walls to the north and south made the camp impregnable to a pincer attack from the sides.

In what proved to be a poor political decision, however, Washington downplayed the extent of his losses at Germantown in a letter to Congress: "Upon the whole," he wrote, "it may be said the day was more unfortunate than injurious. . . . The enemy are nothing better by the event."[2] Within a week, however, he confessed that his "military chest is nearly exhausted. . . . Our distress for want of shoes and stockings is amazingly great."[3] Making matters worse, there were no springs on the plateau. The stream and the forge that gave the site its name were at the foot of the hill.

Washington ordered his men at Valley Forge to raise a city of huts with branches and twigs that might have been tolerable even in the bitter winter that followed had the quartermaster general provided clothes, blankets, foods, and other supplies that Washington had ordered.

"The soldiers lived in misery," according to the Marquis de Lafayette, who had come from France to volunteer in the American army. "They lacked for clothes, hats, shirts, shoes, their legs and feet black from frostbite—we often had to amputate. . . . The army often went whole days without provisions. . . . The misery prevented new enlistments."[4]

By Christmas desertions, disease, exposure to subzero temperatures, starvation, and thirst had reduced Washington's Continental Army, once 11,000 men, to 5,000. Some froze to death; most of those who survived were too weak to fight. With Congress disabled and impotent in York, Washington pleaded in vain to Richard Henry Lee for supplies, then to Quartermaster General Thomas Mifflin. When Mifflin failed to respond, Washington turned to state governors for help.

In York, meanwhile, Richard Henry Lee and Congress lived in conditions only slightly better than those at Valley Forge. Although Lee's sister Alice and her husband, Dr. William Shippen, managed to ship twenty-five gallons of fine French wine to him in York, the wine did nothing to soothe fraying tempers of Congress—or what was left of it. More than annoyed by the repeated British humiliations of Washington's army—which stood in stark contrast to Gates's Saratoga victory—Congress started questioning Washington's military skills. To weaken Lee's influence in Congress—and

Ohio Land Company control of western territory—Robert Morris stirred dissent, whispering that Richard Henry Lee himself was dissatisfied with Washington's leadership but refused to show his dissatisfaction because of his friendship with the general.

A barrage of anonymous letters to Congress and articles in the press denounced Washington's loss of the national capital while praising Gates's success at Saratoga. Washington was furious at the comparison, confiding in Henry that "I was left to fight two battles . . . to save Philadelphia with less numbers than composed the army of my antagonist, whilst the world has given us at least double.

> This impression, though mortifying in some points of view, I have been obliged to encourage, because, next to being strong, it is best to be thought so by the enemy. . . . How different the case in the northern department! There the states of New York and New England resolving to crush Burgoyne, continued pouring in their troops till the surrender of that army; at which time not less than fourteen thousand militia . . . were actually in Gates's camp . . . in many instances supplied with provisions of their own carrying.[5]

With encouragement from Robert Morris and Quartermaster General Thomas Mifflin, Congress effectively demoted Washington by creating a Board of War with supreme powers over him and the military. Ignoring protests from Richard Henry Lee, it named General Gates Board president, giving him overall authority over the war. It also promoted Gates's aide, Colonel Thomas Conway, to inspector general, with authority to investigate misconduct by army officers—including George Washington.

Washington let loose a blast of his legendary temper at Richard Henry: "If there is any truth in the report . . . that Congress has appointed Brigadier Conway to be major general in this army, it will be as unfortunate a measure as ever was adopted. I may add (and I think with truth) that it will give a fatal blow to the existence of this army.

The duty I owe my country, the ardent desire I have to promote its true interests, and justice . . . require [that] I speak plain."[6]

Washington said he would not object to Conway's promotion "if there was a degree of . . . merit in General Conway unpossessed by his seniors." But this was not the case, he insisted. "General Conway's merit . . . as an officer and his importance in this army exists more in his own imagination that in reality, for it is a maxim with him to leave no service of his own untold." Washington warned Lee that once other officers of greater merit learned of Conway's promotion, they would resign in droves. "These gentlemen have feelings as officers, and though they do not dispute the authority of Congress to make appointments, they will judge of the propriety of acting under them.

> In a word, the service is so difficult and every necessary so expensive that almost all your officers are tired out. Do not, therefore, afford them good pretexts for retiring. Within the last six days, twenty commissions have been tendered to me. I must therefore conjure you to conjure Congress to consider this matter well, and not by a real act of injustice compel some good officers to leave your service and incur a train of evils unforeseen and irremediable.[7]

By implication Washington himself seemed ready to quit. "I have been a slave to the service," he fumed at Lee. "I have undergone more than most men are aware of to harmonize so many discordant parts, but it will be impossible for me to be of any further service if such insuperable difficulties are thrown in my way." He said he hoped Lee would bring the Conway controversy "to a speedy and happy issue," then reminded Lee that "half of our men are rendered unfit for service for want of . . . clothing."[8]

Lee found himself trapped between his loyalty and friendship of many years to his friend (and sometimes business partner) and the overwhelming sentiment of a shrunken Congress that favored subordinating Washington to the victor at Saratoga and his aide. Lee told Washington that he—Lee—was helpless to prevent "a speedy erecting and judicious filling of the new board" and the appointment of Conway as inspector general.

Lee was aware of rumors that he too had been dissatisfied with Washington's performance as commander of the army. Adding to the rumors was the appearance in a Boston newspaper of letters apparently signed by Washington deploring the rebellion against British rule, criticizing Congress, and calling for rapprochement with Britain.

"The enclosed came to my hand only a few days past," Richard Henry wrote of the pamphlet to Washington to try to console and display his loyalty to his friend. "The arts of the enemies of America are endless, but all wicked as they are various; among other tricks, they have forged a pamphlet of letters . . . the design of the forger is evident and no doubt gained him a good beef steak from his masters."[9]

The pamphlet contained seven letters supposedly written by Washington—one each to his wife and stepson and five to his cousin Lund Washington, whom he had appointed caretaker of the Mount Vernon plantation in the general's absence.

"How cruelly are my hopes in one sad moment blasted and destroyed!" Washington was accused of having written in the forged letter to Lund Washington. "I am positively ordered to wait for the enemy in our lines and, lest I should be mad enough not to obey their mandates, not a single tittle of anything I had asked for is granted. Thus has a second opportunity of rendering my country an essential service . . . been unwisely and in the most mortifying manner been denied me. I hardly know how to bear it."[10]

Washington responded quickly after receiving the pamphlet, opining to Lee that "the enemy are governed by no principles that ought to actuate honest men. No wonder then that forgery should be amongst their other crimes. I have seen a letter published in a handbill in New York and extracts of it republished in the Philadelphia paper, said to be from me to Mrs. Washington, not one word of which did I ever write."[11]

"My dearest love and life," he was said to have written to Martha Washington. "You have hurt me. I know not how much by the insinuation in your last that my letters to you have lately been less frequent because I have felt less concern for you." It was signed, "Your most faithful and tender husband."[12] Not only did Washington not use such terms in writing to his wife, Martha Washington was actually with her husband on the date shown at the top of the letter. The author of the letters remains unknown. Printed in London, they appeared in Loyalist newspapers in New York and Philadelphia in 1777 and 1778 and reappeared from time to time in anti-Washington newspapers during his presidency.

Despite concerted efforts by Washington and his friends, the author or authors managed to remain anonymous, although it is certainly possible that, given his other machinations in the twisted plot of his misadventures in America, Conway or one of his subordinates produced them.

"These letters," Washington mused to Richard Henry, "are written with a great deal of art—the intermixture of so many family circumstances (which by the by wanted foundation in truth) gives an air of plausibility, which renders the villainy greater, as the whole is a contrivance to answer the most diabolical purposes. Who the author is I know not. From information or an acquaintance, he must have had some knowledge of the component parts of my family, but has most egregiously mistaken fact in several instances."[13]

Conway's bitterness over Washington's opposition to his appointment as inspector general never lost its edge, and he used his newfound authority in 1778 to plot Washington's ouster. While disparaging Washington and his generals with anonymous letters to Congress, he enlisted Gates into the plot by appealing to the Englishman's ambitions and heaping scorn on Washington. "Heaven has been determined to save your country," Conway flattered Gates, "or a weak general and bad counselors would have ruined it."[14]

An anonymous letter writer tried to enlist Patrick Henry in Conway's plot:

"The northern army has shown us what Americans are capable of doing with a general at their head," the anonymous critic wrote to Henry. Calling himself "one of your Philadelphia friends," he charged that "a Gates or a Conway would, in a few weeks, render them an irresistible body of men." Warning Henry that "the letter must be thrown in the fire," he nonetheless urged Henry that "some of his comments ought to be made public, in order to awaken, enlighten, and alarm our country."[15]

In what may have been one of the most significant and least-known decisions in his life and, indeed, of the Revolutionary War, Virginia governor Patrick Henry sent the letter by express rider to try to bolster the morale of his friends Washington and Lee. Lee was still sitting with the remnants of an impotent Congress at York, while Washington shivered at Valley Forge with the remnants of his equally impotent army. "I am sorry there should be one man who counts himself my friend who is not yours," Henry wrote to Washington.

> The censures aimed at you are unjust. . . . But there may possibly be some scheme or party forming to your prejudice. . . . Believe me, sir, I have too high a sense of the obligations America has to you to abet or countenance so unworthy a proceeding. . . . I really cannot tell who is the writer of this letter. . . . The handwriting is altogether strange to me. . . . But I will not conceal anything from you by which you may be affected; for I really think your personal welfare and the happiness of America are intimately connected.[16]

And to Lee, Henry wrote, "You are traduced by a certain set who have drawn in others who say you are engaged in a scheme to discard General Washington. I know you too well, but it is your fate to suffer the constant attacks of disguised Tories who take this measure to lessen you."[17]

Washington responded to Henry with thanks "in language of the most undissembled gratitude, for your friendship. All I can say is that [America] has ever had, and I trust she will ever have, my honest exertions to promote her interest. I cannot hope that my services have been the best; but my heart tells me they have been the best I can render."[18]

Washington told both Patrick Henry and Richard Henry Lee that he had been aware of "the intrigues of a faction . . . formed against me. . . . General Gates was to be exalted on the ruin of my reputation and influence . . . and General Conway, I know, was a very active and malignant partisan, but I have reason to believe that their machinations have recoiled most sensibly upon themselves."[19]

Washington thanked Lee as well for both his loyalty and friendship—and for his efforts to recruit more volunteers in Virginia. But he asked Lee to convince state legislatures to fill their regiments by drafting eligible single men. "If all the states would do this and fall upon ways and means to supply their troops with comfortable clothing . . . and make the commissions of officers of some value to them, everything would probably go well." He also called on Lee to effect reforms in army departments. "Nothing [is] standing in greater need of it than the quartermasters and no army has ever suffered more by their neglect."[20]

Washington then reiterated his concern for his men at Valley Forge, hoping Lee and Henry would respond appropriately. "It is not easy to give you a just and accurate idea of the sufferings of the troops," he wrote. "On the 23rd [of December], I had in camp not less than 2,898 men unfit for duty by reason of their being bare foot and otherwise naked. . . . I cannot but hope that every measure will be pursued . . . to keep them supplied from time to time. No pains, no efforts can be too great for this purpose. The articles of shoes, stockings, blankets demand the most particular attention."

Lee was soon able to write that the Virginia Assembly had voted "two thousand men to be drafted from the single men to fill up the regiments. They have adopted a very extensive taxation, which will produce a large sum of money."[21]

Henry, in turn, confiscated nine privately owned wagonloads of clothing and blankets for the troops at Valley Forge. He promised Washington more of the same and pledged that "nothing possible for me to effect will be left undone in getting whatever the troops are in want of."[22]

Richard Henry Lee's brother Arthur sent good news from Europe as well, writing, "I have pleasure to inform you that our friends in Spain have promised to supply us with three millions of livres in the course of this year. . . . My last advices from Bilbao assure me they are shipping the blankets and stockings I ordered."[23]

In the weeks that followed, however, officers at Valley Forge informed Patrick Henry that the food and clothing he had sent to Quartermaster General Thomas Mifflin for delivery to the camp were being sold in markets in nearby towns. Henry wrote to Richard Henry Lee: "I am really shocked at the management of Congress," he declared. "Good God! Our fate committed to a man [Mifflin] utterly unable to perform the task assigned to him! . . . I grieve at it. Congress will lose respect."[24]

Washington seconded Henry's complaints with an angry note: "It is a matter of no small amount to the well-being of the Army," he wrote to Lee, "that the several departments of it should be filled with men of ability, integrity, and application." He said the previous choices of adjutant and quartermaster generals had "embarrassed the movements of this army exceedingly.

> We seldom have more than a day or two's provisions beforehand and often behind, both of meat and bread. It can be no difficult matter . . . for you or any other gentleman to conceive how much the movements of an army are clogged and retarded. Whilst I am upon this subject, let me add that I am convinced that the salt provision necessary for the next year . . . will not be provided, as the season

is now far advanced, and I have heard of no proper measures being taken to lay them in.[25]

Richard Henry apologized to Washington and ordered an immediate investigation: "It is greatly to be regretted that the situation of your army unfits it for vigorous action, because it is very obvious that the enemy's possession of Philadelphia this winter and the ensuing spring may produce consequences extensively injurious." Lee said that loyalties in both Pennsylvania and Delaware were divided and he feared that "by supplying the wants fanciful and real with all kinds of European goods . . . it will be no surprise if we were to find a total revolution in Pennsylvania and Delaware."[26]

Lee told Washington he had appointed a committee "to confer with the commissary general and see what can be done. . . . That there should be a want of flour amazes me and proves great want of attention in the commissary general, because I know that any quantity might have been got in Virginia at a reasonable price." Like Washington, however, Lee was exhausted and warned Washington that "my ill state of health will compel me to return home in a few days."[27]

The investigation by Lee's committee found that aides to Mifflin, a Philadelphia merchant before the Revolution, had been diverting some of the supplies bound for Valley Forge into Mifflin's warehouses, which resold them to area merchants at handsome profits. When confronted, he confessed to participating in the Conway Cabal and resigned.

With Mifflin's revelations, Richard Henry Lee demanded that Congress dissolve the Board of War. It agreed and exiled Conway to a Hudson River backwater. It sent Gates back into battle and gave Washington all-but-dictatorial powers to conduct the entire war as he saw fit. He immediately persuaded his friend Rhode Island major general Nathanael Greene—also a merchant in private life—to accept the quartermaster general's post. Within days Greene had the camp overflowing with supplies—cattle, vegetables, water, and rum—and enough uniforms and shoes to clothe twice the number of men encamped there. A new inspector general from Germany, "Baron" von Steuben, had the men marching in step and drilling like a crack European elite guard, their arms snapping confidently, their tough bronzed faces radiating invincibility.

By early March nine states had ratified the Articles of Confederation but had ordered their delegates to Congress to propose amendments before signing it, thus forcing a renewal of the seemingly endless debate. Seven states proposed amendments, and one by one Congress rejected them. By July 9 ten states had ratified the document—enough to form a republican confederation. Congress asked Richard Henry Lee to write to leaders of the other three states, urging them to ratify the Articles.

Meanwhile, on April 22, 1778, Conway had offered his resignation, and Congress immediately accepted it. Shortly thereafter the embittered cabalist again slandered Washington, inciting General John Cadwallader, a fierce Washington loyalist, to challenge the Irishman to a duel. Cadwallader wounded Conway badly. Believing he was about to die, Conway sent Washington a letter of apology. Although Conway recovered from his wound, he later left North America in disgrace.

With Washington restored to full command of the war, Arthur Lee in Paris urged the French court to declare war against Britain. He told Foreign Minister Vergennes that "the interests of France and those of the United States [were] upon an equal footing . . . that Great Britain cannot make head for a year against the united . . . force of the house of Bourbon and the United States of America." He told Vergennes that the time had come for France and the United States "to make common cause" against Britain.

On May 1 a messenger rode into Washington's headquarters with a letter signed by Benjamin Franklin, Silas Deane, and Arthur Lee in Paris. They had been officially received in the Palais de Versailles by

His Majesty Louis XVI, who then named a minister to the United States and signed two treaties with the new nation.

"We have now the great satisfaction of acquainting you and the Congress," they exulted, "that the Treaties with France are at length completed and signed. The first is a treaty of amity and commerce . . . the other is a treaty of alliance, in which it is stipulated that in case England declares war against France . . . we should then make common cause of it and join our forces and councils, etc. The great aim of this treaty is declared to be 'to establish the liberty, sovereignty, and independency, absolute and unlimited, of the United States, as well in matters of government as commerce'; and this is guaranteed to us by France. . . . The preparations for war are carried on with immense activity and it is soon expected."[28] Indeed, the French were putting together a fleet and planning to send an expeditionary force to fight alongside the Americans in the struggle to expel British forces from American soil.

On May 6 Washington issued a general order: "It having pleased the Almighty Ruler of the Universe to defend the cause of the United American States, and finally to raise us up a powerful friend among the princes of the earth, to establish our liberty and independency upon a lasting foundation; it becomes us to set apart a day for gratefully acknowledging the divine goodness and celebrating the important event, which we owe to his divine interposition."

Washington went on to proclaim an official day of "public celebration," beginning with morning religious services and followed by "military parades, marchings, the firings of cannon and musketry."[29] One officer described the event in his diary: "The appearance was brilliant and the effect imposing. Several times the cannons discharged thirteen rounds." The ceremony . . . closed with an entertainment, patriotic toasts, music, and other demonstrations of joy."[30]

Steuben's training had imbued the troops with confidence. They swaggered as they marched, firing the traditional *feu de joie*, or "fire of joy," with precision, with each musketeer in a long line of musketeers firing a single shot in rapid succession, to produce a long, continuous, and thunderous sound. Washington responded accordingly: "The Commander-in-Chief takes great pleasure in acquainting the army that its conduct afforded him the highest satisfaction. The exactness and order with which all its movements were formed, is a pleasing evidence of the progress it has made in military improvement, and of the perfection to which it may arrive by a continuance of that laudable zeal which now so happily prevails."[31]

Richard Henry Lee's joy over the news from France came to an abrupt end, however, with news that "my very dear brother Thomas Ludwell Lee expired . . . after a severe and very long illness of six weeks and three days." Three years older than Richard Henry, Thomas had studied in England as a boy and earned his law degree there but had been a firm, if quiet, supporter of the American Revolution. Unlike Richard Henry, however, Thomas had eschewed fame and settled happily on the land he had inherited from their father in Stafford County, upriver from the palatial family estate at Stratford Hall.

Elected to the House of Burgesses, Thomas had joined Frank and the other Lees in the House to support Richard Henry's every legislative battle for individual rights and independence. Beloved by his colleagues in the Virginia legislature for his warmth and understanding of all political points of view, he won appointment as one of four lawyers to rewrite Virginia's laws after independence, then won election to one of the five seats on Virginia's first supreme court. His death left Richard Henry charged with caring for a widow and seven children, two of them youngsters—a ten-year-old boy and seven-year-old girl—for whom Richard Henry became a second father.

News that a French fleet might sail to America with an invasion force convinced the British to consolidate their northern armies at their main base in New York City. Accordingly, British troops evacuated Philadelphia on June 18, 1778, and began the march northward through New Jersey to New York at the head of a long wagon train of arms, ammunition, and provisions.

"I cannot help congratulating you, Sir, on the enemy's abandoning Philadelphia," Lee, still languishing in York, wrote to Washington at Valley Forge. "Let their motives be what they may, this step evidently proves their prospect of conquest here is vanished. . . . Should Great Britain be engaged in war with the [French royal] Bourbon family, it will furnish us an opportunity of pushing the former quite off this northern continent, which will secure to us peace for a century."[32]

With the British evacuation of Philadelphia, Washington had hoped to harass the British rear, but he and his men remained put.

"Our situation here on account of the sick and stores is embarrassing," he lamented to Richard Henry Lee. "I dare not detach [troops] to harass the enemy in . . . the Jerseys before they have actually crossed the Delaware, and then it will be too late as their distance to South Amboy [and the narrow crossing onto Staten Island] will be much less than ours. . . . Were it not for the number of our sick (upwards of 3,000 in camp) and security of stores . . . I could take such a post in Jersey as would make their passage through that state very difficult."[33]

By the end of May, however, the supplies and troops that Patrick Henry had sent from Virginia and that Richard Henry Lee had requisitioned from other states arrived at Valley Forge. Once resupplied, Washington ordered his men off the Valley Forge plateau to chase the retreating Redcoats. After a week the Americans caught up with their British foes. Exhausted by the daily tramp in the blistering New Jersey heat, the British encamped for what they hoped would be a long, restful sleep at Monmouth Courthouse in central New Jersey.

At dawn the next morning, however, Washington ordered his troops to attack, triggering a day of exhausting heroics by both sides, but the fighting proved indecisive. As darkness set in, Washington's troops bedded down for the night, and as they slept, the British quietly slipped away to Sandy Hook, a spit of land on the northern New Jersey shore at the entrance to New York Bay. Transport ships waited to carry them away to New York, ceding New Jersey to the Americans. Washington claimed victory in a letter to his brother John, calling the battle at Monmouth Courthouse "a glorious and happy day." It had cost the British "at least 2000 of their best troops," he declared. "We had 60 men killed."[34]

After Lee congratulated him, Washington effused, "I thank you very much for your congratulations. The prospect we have before us is certainly pleasing, and such as promises a glorious and happy issue to all our struggles."[35]

A few days later Lee and Washington received more good news to celebrate: "All our intelligence announces the utmost confusion in Great Britain," Arthur Lee had written to Richard Henry from Paris. "Their councils are so fluctuating in consequence of . . . their [military] distress that advices cannot be given with great certainty." He said the ministry had agreed to an exchange of 200 prisoners.[36]

Although the British withdrawal from New Jersey ended the threat to the American capital in Philadelphia, Richard Henry Lee still faced an exhausting political battle when Silas Deane returned to America and promptly accused the Lees—Richard Henry in America and Arthur and William in France—of having surreptitiously aided the British. All the Lees, he charged, had consorted with an admitted British spy. In fact, they had, but far from delivering any state secrets, they had simply given the British spy details of the price the American government would demand from the British to end the war. Deane also charged that Arthur and William Lee had only received their overseas appointments because of the influence of Richard Henry, Francis Lightfoot, and several Lee cousins in Congress. Although the charges contained some truth, no Americans in Britain at the time had been in a position to be more effective spies than Arthur and William Lee.

As Arthur and William continued investigating Deane's activities in France, they found he had stolen "large sums of the public's money."[37] Richard Henry Lee confronted Deane, saying Congress had ordered him to purchase "two quick sailing cutters . . . with stores, . . .

"And how did you do it?

> Were they ever sent? Were they not made a mixed business of public and private concern? Were not 100,000 livres at least of the public money employed in fitting and refitting them? Were not they sent first on the coast of England, against the desires of France and the orders of Congress, instead of bringing stores here [America] for the army? . . . Were not those prizes consigned to private hands . . . instead of being delivered to the agents of the U.S.? Have they not finally been sold, without public authority, to private use, and has the money been brought to the public credit?[38]

Bit by bit Lee's brothers in Europe fed him more information on Deane's activities, including evidence that Deane had pocketed commissions from funds Congress had sent for purchasing military supplies. In what may be one of America's earliest money-laundering schemes, some of the funds Deane pocketed found their way into the coffers of Robert Morris's firm of Willing and Morris, whose land speculations had attracted Deane as a silent partner. While probing into Deane's conduct as an American diplomat, the Lees also exposed Deane's close friend and private secretary, Edward Bancroft, as having been a British spy.

Even Franklin was implicated, albeit indirectly. His landlord in Paris, the French merchant Jacques-Donetien Leray de Chaumont, had given Franklin and Deane elegant apartments rent-free in his lavish chateau in Passy, just outside Paris on the road to Versailles. Instead of rent, Chaumont had accepted "a gift" of more than 100,000 acres in northern New York. In the end Deane and Robert

Morris reaped huge profits from Deane's activities in Paris. Called to account by Congress, Deane immediately attacked the Lees, insisting he could account for every penny of public funds, but had left his account books in Paris and would need to return there to recover them and bring them back to Philadelphia to show Congress. He sailed for France in 1780 and never returned. Deane died in London in 1789.

CHAPTER 9

President Richard Henry Lee

EXHAUSTED BY THE DEANE CONFLICT BUT SATISFIED WITH THE outlook for the nation's new government and its constitutional foundation, Richard Henry Lee and his brother Francis Lightfoot Lee announced they would resign from the Continental Congress at the end of its spring session in May 1779.

Richard Henry's last act as a Washington representative in Congress was to try to feed more troops into the southern sector, but as he had found so many times before, it proved impossible to provide "the force you had a right to expect from Virginia for reinforcing the main army. We have no reason to suppose that [more] than 1,400 militia—perhaps not more than 1,000 will go . . . and of the 1,000 ordered . . . not more than 350 have been obtained."[1] As before, few men—regardless of their political leanings—were willing or able to enlist. More than 90 percent of American men were farmers, whose properties—and families—depended on year-round ministrations. At most they could enlist for three months in midsummer after the spring plantings to earn some extra money, but the sums were not enough to forego soldiering as fall harvest approached.

"The situation of affairs . . . has an aspect truly alarming," Washington warned Lee. With North Carolina's troop quota in the field far below what state officials had pledged, British troops were threatening to overrun the South. Washington all but ordered Lee to draft North Carolina troops if necessary, forgetting that the Articles of Confederation left the state sovereign and gave Congress—and Lee—no power to draft anyone.

"I am at a loss what additional measures to advise," Washington lashed out, his temper frayed, his military strategy constantly frustrated—not by the enemy but by the lack of authority in Congress to force states to provide him with the means of victory. Although he knew Lee was helpless to respond, he demanded tougher laws to help him win the war.

"Troops from this [Continental] army cannot possibly be sent [to the South]," he explained to Lee. "It seems however necessary that troops of a better consistence than militia, whose time of service expires almost as soon as they arrive at their destination, should be provided. This can only be done by laws in the neighboring states for drawing out a body for a longer term."[2]

Washington's last words to Lee did not lighten Lee's homeward journey: "The want of arms is a melancholy circumstance," he told Lee, "and it is the more distressing after so long a war—and after the most conclusive proofs that nothing would be left untried on the part of the enemy to carry their points against us."[3]

Lee, however, now admitted there was little he could do to force states to do Washington's bidding, and he decided not to reply to Washington's letter. Washington by then knew what the answer would be without Lee having to write it.

As Richard Henry and Francis Lightfoot Lee left Philadelphia, their younger brothers Arthur and William Lee both resigned their diplomatic posts in Europe and set sail for America, leaving Washington without the benefit of either foreign or domestic intelligence reports from the Lees. Arthur, by then, had reported from Berlin,

Vienna, and Madrid as well as Paris. Although he had been unable to maintain direct contacts with his sources in London, Paris was a crossroads for European diplomats, and Arthur by then was a trained hand in the lighthearted banter at receptions and salons that often elicited important intelligence.

And in Congress it was not the outspoken Richard Henry but the quiet, unassuming Francis Lightfoot Lee who extracted intelligence from various state representatives. More than any of his brothers, Francis Lightfoot was quiet, thoughtful—"calmness and philosophy itself," said brother Arthur. Frank's calm demeanor and evident interest in the words of others provided comfort to those bursting with troubling political secrets. But Frank had, nonetheless, disliked the savage political infighting that marked life in the Continental Congress, and he often complained to Richard Henry, "When all our attention [and] every effort should be to oppose the enemy, we are disputing government and independence."[4]

After leaving Philadelphia, Francis Lightfoot Lee returned to the peace of his Richmond County plantation and the arms of his wife, Rebecca ("Becky"), meddling only occasionally in regional politics from the seat he accepted in the Virginia Senate. Deeply devoted to each other, he and Becky had no children of their own but would virtually adopt and raise the two young daughters of his brother William after William's wife died in 1785. William had returned to America with brother Arthur in 1781, crippled by excruciatingly painful arthritis and virtually blind. He and his son—almost a man by then—settled on William's farm, where the boy cared for his father and learned to run their property.

In contrast to the quiet life of brother Frank on the south coast of the Northern Neck, Richard Henry Lee spent the summer of 1779 covered with dust, loping along the bluffs of the Northern Neck coast but nonetheless resplendent in his colonel's uniform, inspecting defenses and leading militiamen into skirmishes with British troops attempting to land. Without fingers on one hand, he guided his horse with his legs, shifting his weight slightly to direct the animal in one or another direction. Despite the dangers he faced, life out of doors exhilarated him, relieved him of the tensions and insoluble problems of congressional life. During the summer of that year his wife, Anne, gave birth to a boy they named Cassius—their eighth child and Richard Henry's third son. In addition to caring for his own tribe, Richard Henry rode back and forth between plantations to tend to the needs of the widows and children of his deceased brothers Philip and Thomas.

By 1780 the conflict in Chesapeake Bay gained enough breadth and momentum that Richard Henry Lee felt bound to rejoin Virginia's Assembly, which immediately elected him speaker and then sent him back to Congress. He immediately wrote to the new governor, Thomas Jefferson, to bolster the state's defenses along the more than 1,000 miles of inland waterways. Jefferson had replaced Patrick Henry at the end of Henry's third consecutive term—Virginia's constitutional maximum. Richard Henry's letter to Jefferson coincided with one from George Washington urging Jefferson to expand Virginia's navy and implant *chevaux de fries*—spiked logs—into the river beds at the entrance to the state's waterways to prevent enemy ships from carrying British troops upstream toward Richmond.

Unlike the American North, winter weather in the milder climate of the South did not force British forces to retire to winter quarters as early or as long, and British troops from Florida had pushed northward and captured most of Georgia by mid-March. By April they had overrun the entire state and reached the outskirts of Charleston. To the horror of farmers and plantation owners, the British freed indentured servants and slaves who were willing to swear allegiance to Britain and, if able, fight the Patriots.

On May 10 a British fleet sailed into Hampton Roads and set fire to Portsmouth and what was left of Norfolk and captured a supply depot at nearby Suffolk, burning more than 100 American ships and capturing 30,000 hogsheads of tobacco. The threat of further British incursions sent Virginia's government fleeing inland to Richmond.

On May 12, 1780, Americans suffered their worst defeat in the war when the southern army surrendered unconditionally to the British in Charleston, South Carolina. Fourteen thousand British troops had attacked, surrounding and capturing the entire 5,400-man American force and its commanding general, Benjamin Lincoln. Among the captured troops were 1,400 Virginians.

In January 1781 Governor Thomas Jefferson paid the price of ignoring the military advice of George Washington and Richard Henry Lee. With no underwater barriers to block it, a fleet of six British frigates, eight brigs, and ten other vessels with 2,200 troops aboard sailed into Chesapeake Bay toward the mouth of the James River. The expedition commander, Brigadier General Benedict Arnold, was brother-in-law of Richard Henry Lee's sister Alice. He had defected from the American army the previous September in exchange for £6,315 (about $750,000 today) and a commission as a brigade commander in the British army.

Now chairman of the Assembly's Maritime Committee, Richard Henry had no sooner learned of Arnold's incursion when word arrived that a second fleet had sailed into the bay under the command of the renowned Captain Thomas Graves, an admiral's nephew and soon to become an admiral himself. Graves headed north toward the mouth of the Potomac, putting Chantilly in danger of assault and Richard Henry's family under threat of capture.

After calling on the Assembly to fund immediate construction of six more cruisers to patrol the bay, Richard Henry left Richmond and rode home, arriving just as Graves's fleet entered the mouth of the Potomac. Two days later it attacked Stratford Landing, but by then Richard Henry and his militia were positioned to repel the British, and he proved himself a skilled field commander.

"In a late engagement," Richard Henry wrote gleefully to his friend Samuel Adams in Boston, "the enemy landed under cover of a heavy cannonade from three vessels of war . . . a small body of our militia [were] well posted. After a small engagement, we had the pleasure to see the enemy, though superior in number, run to their boats and precipitously re-embark, having sustained a small loss of killed and wounded."[5]

Fearing Graves's return and possible capture, Richard Henry bundled his family into a set of carriages and fled inland to Epping Forest, a 500-acre plantation that had been the home of George Washington's mother. From there he ventured in and out, organizing a militia of more than 400 with which he hoped to defend the Northern Neck against British incursions by land and water.

On March 1, 1781, after the last of the thirteen state legislatures had agreed to the Articles of Confederation, Congress ratified the document, creating a new nation and the first republic in the Americas. Congress assumed a new title, "The United States in Congress assembled," or, more simply, the Confederation Congress. In the South, meanwhile, American forces under the supreme command of General Nathanael Greene had halted the northward advance of British troops and, indeed, had pushed the British back to the seacoast. American privateers, meanwhile, had disrupted British supply lines with the capture of 600 British ships, while the fledging American navy had captured or destroyed nearly 200 British warships.

Britain was now willing to talk peace.

The Confederation Congress responded by naming a commission of four to begin negotiations in Paris—John Adams, Benjamin Franklin, Thomas Jefferson, and Henry Laurens of South Carolina. Jefferson, however, decided against serving, and Laurens was captured by the British on his way to Europe. New York's John Jay sailed to France and took the third seat at the negotiations.[*]

The British army commander in North Carolina, Earl Charles Cornwallis, was in no mood to seek peace, however. Seething with anger from the humiliations his army had suffered at the hands of

---

[*] Laurens was later released by the British in exchange for Lord Cornwallis and was able to sit in as an observer during the final days of peace negotiations.

semiliterate woodsmen, he believed he could crush the American Revolution by increasing the size of his army and overrunning the plantations of the principal leaders of the Revolution in Virginia—Washington, Mason, the Lees, and others. Accordingly, he led his 1,500-man force out of Wilmington, North Carolina, into Virginia, joined Arnold's 4,000 troops at Petersburg, Virginia, then added a third force of 2,000 horsemen—dragoons trained in terrorizing defenseless rural families and commanded by the fearsome Banastre Tarleton—"Bloody Ban, the Butcher," as some called him.

Richard Henry Lee blanched when he learned that Washington had countered by sending a force of only 1,200 men to defend Richmond under the leadership of the untried young French commander Marquis de Lafayette—a mere "boy," in the estimation of Cornwallis. On May 23, 1781, the British seized the Virginia capital, setting it ablaze as Lafayette and his little band fled northward while Governor Thomas Jefferson and members of the Assembly fled westward toward the mountains. Although Tarleton and his dragoons chased after them, Jefferson managed to reach Charlottesville and the mountaintop home he called Monticello outside of town. He arrived with just enough time to alert his wife and send her and their two daughters to safety in another town, then barely escaped capture himself by riding off through the woods.

As Tarleton terrorized local farmers and their families, Richard Henry Lee wrote in desperation from Epping Forest to his "dear brother" Arthur Lee, then still hunkered down at Chantilly. "The enemy are within 30 miles of Fredericksburg," he warned, "and our army a little above them but too weak to approach.

> We shall receive all the injury possible before aid is sent to us. What will become of these lower parts, heaven knows. We and our property here are now within the power of the enemy. . . . The enemy affect to leave harmless the poor and they take everything from those they call the rich. Tis said that 2000 or 3000 negroes march in their

train, that every kind of stock which they cannot remove they destroy. . . . They have burned a great number of warehouses full of
tobacco, and they are now pressing on to the larger ones . . . and the
valuable iron works in our northern parts.[6]

To his brother William, who had fled to safety with his son, he
lamented that "your neighbors lost every slave they had in the world,
[but] your loss is much less than that of the others. . . . The enemy
have not injured your crops . . . which are at present very good. In
their first visit, they took 60 head of cattle away. The enemy's generals here appear to carry on the war much more upon views of private
plunder and enriching individuals than upon any plan of national
advantage."[7]

Though frightened for his family, Richard Henry Lee was flush
with anger at Jefferson for his inept handling of the state's defenses
and at other states for their failure to send aid. As Cornwallis pushed
Lafayette's little force northward to within sight of the Rappahannock River and the southern shore of Lee's Northern Neck, he wrote
an angry letter he never thought he would ever have to write to Congress, urging delegates "not to slumber a moment":

> Decision, dispatch, and much wisdom are indispensably necessary,
> or . . . we shall soon be lost. . . . The enemy . . . are now in the center
> of Virginia with an army of regular infantry greater than that . . .
> commanded by the Marquis [de Lafayette]. . . . This country is in
> its greatest danger, without government, abandoned to the arts and
> arms of the enemy. Congress alone can furnish the preventative: Let
> General Washington be sent to Virginia . . . possessed of dictatorial
> powers. . . . The time is short, the danger presses, and commensurate
> remedies are indispensable.[8]

Richard Henry told Congress that he had used all his oratori-
cal powers to rally Virginians, "but the people of this country are

dispersed over a great extent of land" and the British had destroyed the last remaining newspaper press in Charlottesville, where Jefferson and the remnants of the state Assembly had taken refuge.

Lee did not write to Congress without notifying Washington, of course, saying, "I verily believe there is not a good citizen or friend to the liberty of America . . . who does not wish that this plan be immediately adopted.

> It would be a thing for angels to weep over if the goodly fabric of human freedom which you have so well labored to rear should in one unlucky moment be levelled with the dust. There is nothing more certain than that your personal call would bring into immediate exertion the force and resource of this state and its neighboring ones.[9]

As it turned out, the sudden arrival of General "Mad" Anthony Wayne and 1,300 Pennsylvanians in Fredericksburg halted the British advance through Virginia. After Wayne replenished, reclothed, and rearmed Lafayette's little army, their combined force crossed the Rappahannock to attack. Cornwallis had no choice but pull back. Far from his sources of supplies, his men exhausted by the searing Virginia heat and choking humidity, he ordered a measured retreat to Chesapeake Bay and the safety of his ships.

As Cornwallis retreated, Lee wrote to Washington to learn his plan of action. Well aware of the ongoing Virginia campaign, Washington nonetheless seemed unsure of how to proceed. "The designs of the enemy" he wrote to Lee, "are mysterious, indeed totally incomprehensible. That they are preparing for some grand manoeuver does not admit of a doubt. . . . I believe they are waiting for orders." While the British awaited orders, Washington strengthened his posts in the Hudson River Highlands and prepared his army to "move on in different columns by different routes . . . to the eastward."[10]

Thomas Jefferson, meanwhile, realized he was out of his depth in dealing with military matters and had turned his office over "to abler hands." He told Washington he believed that "a military chief" would bring "more energy, promptitude and effect for the defense of the state."[11] By June 22 Cornwallis's retreat toward the sea left Richmond back in American hands, and Virginia's Assembly elected General Thomas Nelson, the owner of a large Tidewater plantation, to replace Jefferson, satisfying Richard Henry Lee's demands for the restoration of state government.

Patrick Henry was as unhappy as Richard Henry Lee with Jefferson's conduct in office and, with Lee's support, moved that the Assembly open "an inquiry . . . into the conduct of the executive of this state for the last twelve months." Henry accused Jefferson of failing to make "some exertions which he might have made for the defense of the county"—in effect, treason.[12] Outraged by the proposed inquiry, Jefferson would never forgive Patrick Henry or Richard Henry Lee.

With Cornwallis retreating toward his supply ships in Chesapeake Bay, Lafayette's force followed hard on the English rear guard, sniping first at one flank, then the other, and pouncing on foraging parties. At Richmond 1,600 militiamen had joined his force, and as volunteers from plantations pillaged by Tarleton's dragoons swarmed into camp, Lafayette's army swelled to more than 5,000 men, gradually forcing the English onto the cape between the York and James Rivers. With sharpshooters guarding the opposite banks of the rivers on either side of the cape, Lafayette's vanguard gradually pushed Cornwallis to Yorktown at the end of the cape overlooking Chesapeake Bay.

In the north, meanwhile, an army of nearly 7,000 French troops had joined Washington's 8,000-man Continental Army near New York and were on the march southward. On August 30 a French fleet of warships entered Chesapeake Bay and surrounded the cape at Yorktown to prevent any British escape by water. Two weeks later the combined allied force marched into Williamsburg, and four weeks later the American Continental Army charged through enemy redoubts at Yorktown. As shell bursts reduced British fortifications

27. *The surrender at Yorktown. A British officer surrenders on behalf of commanding general Lord Cornwallis and the British army at Yorktown, Virginia, on October 19, 1781. He is portrayed here preparing to hand his sword to French commanding general Comte de Rochambeau, as General George Washington looks on, with the French Marquis de Lafayette standing just behind.*

to rubble, Redcoats made a valiant but vain counterattack. On October 17 Cornwallis sent a message to Washington proposing "a cessation of hostilities." Two days later a Cornwallis aide signed the articles of capitulation with Washington and French general Rochambeau.*

In the euphoria that followed, the Virginia Assembly not only laid aside its Jefferson inquiry, it passed a resolution of "sincere thanks . . . to our former Governor . . . for his impartial, upright and attentive administration whilst in office . . . and mean, by thus publicly avowing their opinion, to obviate and remove all unmerited censure."[13]

Formal peace talks between the British and Americans got under way in the spring of 1782, concluding in November of that year

---

*"Yorktown Day" remains an official state holiday in Virginia.

and setting January 20, 1783, as the effective date of the Articles of
Peace, which Congress ratified on April 15. By then all the states
had passed confiscation acts, seizing the properties and possessions
of Tory Loyalists, and on April 26 7,000 Loyalists sailed from New
York bound for either Halifax, Canada, or Britain—the last of
100,000 Tories who had refused to repudiate their ties and loyalty to
George III and Britain.

With little else to accomplish in Congress or the Virginia Assembly after Yorktown, Richard Henry Lee spent his time putting his
own house in order and settling the affairs of still another sibling, his
widowed sister Hannah. His wife, Anne, gave birth to their second
son—his fourth—whom they named Francis.

On June 13, 1783, Congress voted to disband the Continental
Army, only to flee Philadelphia eleven days later when more than
200 mutinous soldiers stormed the State House demanding long-
overdue back pay. Congress fled to Princeton, New Jersey, meeting
there in tight quarters for a month before moving to the more spa-
cious Maryland State House in Annapolis.

On December 23, 1783, the new nation's commander-in-chief,
General George Washington, appeared before Congress to surrender his commission before a gallery packed with former officers,
public servants, relatives, and friends.

"Mr. President," Washington declared, "I have now the honor of
offering my sincere congratulations to Congress and of presenting
myself before them to surrender into their hands the trust committed to me, and to claim the indulgence of retiring from the service of
my country." As he recalled the "services and distinguished merits"
of his officers and "the Gentlemen who have been attached to my
person during the War . . . "—he choked with emotion and paused.
Spectators held back their tears.

Having now finished the work assigned me, I retire from the great
theater of action; and bidding an affectionate farewell to this august

body under whose orders I have so long acted, I here offer my commission, and take my leave of all employments of public life.[14]

It was a startling scene, a drama not seen or imagined in the Western world in more than 1,200 years. In 458 BC the Romans had given the consul Lucius Quinctius Cincinnatus dictatorial powers, which he relinquished, as Washington would now do. With the defeat of their enemies, both men returned to lives as simple farmers.

Richard Henry Lee did not rejoin Congress until 1784, when it moved to a temporary capital in Trenton, New Jersey. By then his brother Arthur had also won a seat, allowing the two brothers to serve in Congress together for the first time. Two weeks elapsed before enough delegates arrived to form a quorum, however, allowing northern cronies of Robert Morris to dominate and vote to move the federal capital to New York City. The new location would force southerners to travel such long distances that many would stay home or arrive too late to prevent Morris and the northerners from taking control of Congress and emasculating Richard Henry Lee and the Virginians politically.

Lee had one major defense against Morris, however: the three-year limitation on service in Congress established by the Articles of Confederation, and when Morris left, a new majority elected Richard Henry Lee "President of the United States in Congress assembled." Richard Henry Lee was now the nation's chief executive in name, if not authority. Indeed, the "president" did nothing but "preside" over the Congress—like the chair at any meeting—but with no authority. He could and did perform ceremonial duties as the representative of Congress and occasionally signed measures on behalf of Congress, but it was, in the end, an honorific passed from one state leader to the next.

Lee was the sixth such Confederation President, following Samuel Huntington of Connecticut, Thomas McKean of Delaware, John Hanson of Maryland, Elias Boudinot of New Jersey, and Thomas

Mifflin of Pennsylvania.* More than any of his predecessors, Richard Henry reveled in the role, wearing the finest clothes and ordering the finest foods and wines for his presidential table. With Congress paying his residential expenses, he moved into a stunning mansion on New York's most elegant street. Uniformed guards stood at attention at the door, while servants darted about the interior with silver trays and such in their hands, carrying messages, cups of tea, and other miscellany.

He entertained like a sultan, twenty to twenty-five guests at a time, as often as three times a week, according to his nephew Thomas Shippen, Alice's son from Philadelphia. They dined on "black fish, sheep's head and sea bass," accompanied by "champagne, claret, madeira, and muscat." Chamber music groups entertained during and after dinner. Shippen called his uncle's presidential home "a palace" and said Richard Henry "does the honors of it . . . as if he had been crowned with a royal diadem."[15]

Richard Henry did not, however, wear his figurative "diadem" to satisfy his own epicurean whims. In fact, his primary purpose was to impress European emissaries with the status of the United States of America as equal to Old World nations in pomp, grandeur, and power—both economic and military. In effect, his stately surroundings and personal appearance were simply diplomatic restatements of Virginia's Revolutionary War slogan, warning other nations, "Don't tread on me." A secondary purpose was to display to members of

---

*Four more Confederation presidents—John Hancock and Nathaniel Gorham, both of Massachusetts, Arthur St. Clair of Pennsylvania, and Cyrus Griffin of Virginia—would succeed Lee before ratification of the Constitution and the election of George Washington as first President of the federated republic. Prior to ratification of the Articles of Confederation, eight men had served as "presidents" of the Continental Congresses—again, presiding officers with no executive authority: Peyton Randolph of Virginia (twice), Henry Middleton of South Carolina (acting), John Hancock of Massachusetts, Charles Thomson of Pennsylvania (acting), Henry Laurens of South Carolina, John Jay of New York, and Samuel Huntington of Connecticut.

Congress and the rest of the American political world the conduct the world would expect of the nation's future leaders.

Although his foreign visitors could not discern it from his luxurious living quarters, Richard Henry Lee had assumed the nation's "presidency" at a particularly difficult time. The nation was on the verge of bankruptcy and desperately needed funds—not only in the form of loans from European nations but also in expanded foreign trade for the growing number of farms west of the Appalachians.

"The Court of Spain has appointed Mr. Gardoqui their chargé d'affaires to the United States," President Lee wrote to George Washington, who remained America's behind-the-scenes "commander in chief," if not on center stage in Congress. "Time and wise negotiation . . . I hope may secure to the U.S. . . . the great advantages . . . from a free navigation of that [Mississippi] river."[16]

Also of vital importance to the "President" at the time was his close political ally, three-time governor Patrick Henry, who had won reelection to Virginia's governorship after waiting the constitutionally prescribed four years out of office. Lee hoped that by involving Henry in national affairs, Virginia would provide the central government with needed funds.

"The courts with which we are most immediately concerned are Spain, England, France and Holland," Lee wrote to Henry. The nation owed millions to France and Holland for loans during the Revolutionary War, while Spain controlled navigation rights to the Mississippi River but was "extremely jealous of our approximation to her South American territory . . . and fearing our . . . ascendency upon that territory."[17]

With Lee and Washington still holding title to tens of thousands of acres in Ohio and Henry the owner of farmlands in western Virginia, all three hoped negotiations with Spain would open the Mississippi River to western farmers and transform the nation into a rich provider of agricultural and natural resources to the world.

The nation also faced problems with Britain—problems greater even than those with Spain. "She remains sullen after defeat and seeming to wish for just provocation to renew the combat," Lee told Patrick Henry.

> Both countries have been to blame . . . so that while we charged them with removing the slaves from New York, they pointed to the violence with which their [Loyalist] friends were everywhere treated. . . . This again is followed by their detention of our western posts . . . and by their unfriendly interruption of our commerce. . . . If temper and wisdom are not employed on both sides, it is not difficult to foresee a renewed rupture ere long.[18]

Lee said he hoped the nation would not give Britain any further cause for offense and, at the same time, adopt the wisdom of Switzerland, as inscribed above the arsenal in their capital city, "that people are happy who during peace prepare the necessary stores for war."[19]

To that end he told Henry of his need for funds, saying that "our friends"—that is, France and Holland—had sent "strong intimations that we must be exact in the payment of our interest upon the foreign debt and . . . be punctual in [our] payments, that those who have answered us in the day of our distress may not suffer for their generosity."[20]

Sitting in the chief executive's chair, he faced the same problems he had faced during the Revolutionary War, unable under the constitution of the Confederation to pay down the national debt because of member states' refusal to fund the central government.

When he proposed the sale of unsettled western lands, Lee encountered "excessive rage" among the states, whose bankers and land speculators had filed individual claims as absentee owners to land actually owned by Congress. Lee argued that "Congress must sell quickly or . . . render doubtful this fund for extinguishing the public debt."[21] Failure to do so, Lee warned, would plunge the nation into bankruptcy and disorder.

CHAPTER 10

Riots and Mobbish Proceedings

MAJOR OBSTACLES BLOCKED IMPLEMENTATION OF RICHARD Henry Lee's ambition to expand America's boundaries to the Mississippi River and open Ohio—and the thousands of acres he owned in Ohio—to settlers. With enough troops he might have overcome hostile Indian tribes, hostile British troops, and a hostile Spanish government, but he had no troops and no money to pay them, and Congress had no power to raise any. It had tried to enact a federal tax, but without the unanimous consent of the states, it could not do so. New York had vetoed the plan and left each of the states responsible for paying—or not paying—for all governmental functions, including back pay for tens of thousands of troops for their service during the Revolutionary War.

With Congress impotent and New York City so distant, delegates to the Confederation Congress from far-off states appeared only intermittently. A few states even stopped appointing delegates. When Congress did meet, its members—no longer the revolutionaries of the early 1770s—often had little in common and barely fathomed each other's thinking. Without money Congress stopped repaying principal and interest on foreign debts, disbanded the American navy, and reduced the army to a mere eighty privates.[1]

Richard Henry Lee sent agents to negotiate peace with western tribes, but the Shawnee chiefs, whose lands covered much of present-day Kentucky, were intractable, and as settlers and land speculators streamed across the Appalachian Mountains into Indian territory, Lee feared an outbreak of an Indian war.

Nor did British troops abandon their forts in western Pennsylvania and other areas of the American frontier south of the Canadian border—despite negotiation efforts by John Adams. Although Britain had ceded the territory to the United States in the 1783 treaty ending the Revolutionary War, she refused to remove her troops until Americans fulfilled their obligations under the same treaty to pay all their pre–Revolutionary War debts to British merchants. As for the Spanish, they had closed the lower Mississippi River to Americans in 1784 to prevent the growing American population in the West from spilling into Spanish territory and gaining control of Mexican silver mines.

In May 1785 Don Diego de Gardoqui, the first Spanish ambassador to the United States, arrived with instructions not to cede navigation rights to the Mississippi River to the United States—and he did as instructed, despite a year of negotiations with New York's John Jay. Exasperated by Jay's failure, Richard Henry took command of the talks, only to realize that the Spanish were willing to risk war rather than cede access to the big river.

George Washington met with Lee and suggested a possible solution: a network of canals, waterways, and portages to tie Potomac River headwaters on the east slope of the Appalachians to Monongahela River headwaters on the western slope, where it flows to the mouth of the Allegheny River to form the Ohio River. The connection would allow grain, furs, and pelts from the west to flow to East Coast ports and trade routes to Europe. The new waterway would shortcut the long trip down the Mississippi River and across the

Gulf of Mexico, yielding its investors enormous profits and spurring an economic boom in the West, where Washington and Lee still owned upward of 100,000 acres in Ohio. In addition to the profits he envisioned for himself and his partners, Washington believed the waterway would create an economic boom that would unite the nation with unbreakable economic, geophysical, and political bonds and end interstate border disputes that threatened to erupt into civil war. Together with Richard Henry Lee and others with stakes in the Ohio Land Company, Washington formed the Potomac River Company. Subsequently they formed the James River Company to build a second network of canals tying the waterways from Williamsburg and Richmond to the West.

"Extend the inland navigation of the Eastern waters with those that run to the westward," Washington enthused, "open these to the Ohio and Lake Erie, we shall not only draw the produce of western settlers, but the fur and peltry trade to our ports, to the amazing increase of our exports, while we bind those people to us by a chain that can never be broken."[2]

Knowing that states bordering the waterways stood to prosper most, Washington invited Richard Henry Lee and other political leaders from Maryland and Virginia to confer in Alexandria, Virginia, in March 1785. The two states had long feuded over control of the Potomac River, with each claiming its border reached across the river to the opposite shoreline, thus giving it the exclusive right to collect fees and duties from ships traveling the waterway. A few weeks later, with Richard Henry Lee's strong support, the two states agreed to join in funding the project and adopt uniform commercial regulations and a uniform currency—in effect, establishing a commercial union. In but a few months Washington and Lee had succeeded in organizing the greatest public works project in North American history and, more importantly, uniting two states that had been ready to war with each other over rights to the very waterway they would now develop together.

But Washington's vision was wider: "We are either a united people or we are not," he asserted to James Madison, for three years a Virginia delegate in the Confederation Congress. "If the former, let us, in all matters of general concern act as a nation which has national objects to promote and a national character to support. If we are not, let us no longer act a farce by pretending to it."[3] Elated by the agreement with Maryland, Washington and Lee decided to host an interstate convention in Annapolis in September to tie other states to the commercial union Virginia and Maryland had formed.

By then, however, the long, tiresome negotiations had taken its toll on Richard Henry Lee, and when Virginia's House of Delegates elected him to another term in Congress, he refused, citing his health as too "precarious" to return.

Without the press of public affairs to distract him, he doted over his wife and children for the first time in years and spent time managing his plantation. His two oldest boys, Thomas, twenty-eight, and Ludwell, twenty-six, had taken jobs elsewhere, but his seven other children were still at home—Nancy, twenty-two, and Hannah, twenty, from his first marriage, and Ann, sixteen; Henrietta, thirteen; Sarah, eleven; Cassius, seven; and Francis, three.

With three-year-old Francis old enough to cede the downstairs nursery, Richard Henry moved the child into a bedroom upstairs and had carpenters transform the nursery into a library. There, for the first time in years, he could relax, rereading his favorite volumes of history, political philosophy, and poetry. Three-year-old Francis, however, often captured his full attention as he watched, transfixed, for long periods by the little boy's antics. He also busied himself with entertaining household matters such as writing to a cousin for fresh grapes and berries, only to have them arrive "so damaged as to be fit for very little."[4]

With nine children, he had necessarily grown concerned with education and its costs. He joined the twelve-member board of a private school in nearby Fredericksburg, raising funds for the school and, occasionally, helping to hire teachers. The high costs of educating his children, however, made him a strong advocate of free public education.

"A popular government cannot flourish without virtue in the people,* and . . . knowledge is a principle source of virtue," he asserted in supporting a group that was organizing Virginia's first public school. "These facts," he told them, "render the establishment of schools for the instruction of youth a fundamental concern in all free communities.

> I wish that it had been made a primary duty of the legislature by our [Virginia] constitution. Such establishments will be the surest means of perpetuating our free forms of government, for when men . . . know . . . the great inherent rights of human nature, they will not suffer the hands of vice, of violence, or of ignorance to rob them of such inestimable blessings.[5]

With that, Richard Henry Lee agreed to transfer two acres of land "for the sole use of a public school."[6]

Lee's decision not to return to Congress proved a wise one. Before delegates could convene, chaos had erupted in Massachusetts and spread into neighboring New Hampshire, then, like a wild fire, it seemed to engulf the entire nation. The failure of Congress to levy a federal tax had left each state responsible for paying its own war debts—and having to impose property taxes to do so. Making tax payments difficult—indeed, impossible for less affluent Americans— was the near-absence of money. The national government and state governments, along with most merchants, had exhausted their supplies of specie, or "hard" money—silver and gold coins, ingots, and

---

*"Virtue," at the time of the American Revolution, meant, among other things, selfless public service with no compensation and a commitment to uproot and eliminate corruption in government.

so forth—during the war. State governments had spent much of it buying arms and ammunition and the rest buying badly needed imports immediately after.

With little specie in circulation, barter became the principal means of commerce, giving rise to a new intermediary in the American business world—the merchant-banker, who combined the functions of both occupations, buying and selling goods like a storekeeper *and* selling goods on credit like a banker—seeds or tools to a farmer, for example, against his future crop. Without money in the marketplace, farmers had no choice but to trade their perishable produce or livestock for whatever merchant-bankers were willing to pay on market day.

A poor harvest could leave farmers with too small a crop to realize enough to pay their property taxes, let alone repay merchants. A bumper crop could produce market surpluses and prices too low to cover farmer expenses. As creditors went to court to collect their due, sheriffs swept across the country with court orders to seize farmer properties. Thousands of veterans, many still unpaid for wartime services, saw their lands and homes confiscated, their livestock, tools, and personal possessions auctioned at prices too low to clear their debts. Hysterical wives and terrified children watched helplessly as sheriffs' deputies dragged farmers off to debtors' prisons, where they languished indefinitely—unable to earn money to pay their debts and without the tools to do so even if they obtained their release.

In western Massachusetts former captain Daniel Shays, a destitute farmer struggling to hold onto his property, organized some 500 armed men—mostly veterans of the Revolution—and marched them to Springfield to force the state supreme court to stop foreclosing on their farms. Shouting "close down the courts!" they sent supreme court justices fleeing, shut down the court, and marched across town to surround the federal arsenal, where a state militia awaited, its cannon loaded to annihilate the rebels. By then, however, Shays's cry had echoed across the state, sending farmers on the march to courthouses in Cambridge, Concord, Worcester, Northampton, Taunton, and Great Barrington—to shut them all down.

Shays's rebellion sent waves of fear into state legislatures across the nation, with Virginia's panicked lawmakers pleading with Richard Henry Lee to return to the Confederation Congress to put the American house in order. "The friends to American honor and happiness here all join in lamenting the riots and mobbish proceedings," Richard Henry Lee wrote to his cousin Henry Lee III, the heroic wartime general "Light-Horse Harry" Lee, who had succeeded Richard Henry in Congress and was a popular favorite to become governor of Virginia.

Although Richard Henry himself finally agreed to return to Congress, he had as little impact on the spreading anarchy as his cousin. Enraged farmers in Virginia and other states emulated Shays and his followers, taking up rifles and pitchforks to protect their properties, firing at sheriffs and others who ventured too near. Reassembling their wartime companies, they set fire to prisons, courthouses, and county clerks' offices. New Hampshire farmers marched to the state capital at Exeter, surrounded the legislature, and demanded forgiveness of all debts, return of all seized properties to former owners, and equitable distribution of property. A mob of Maryland farmers burned down the Charles County Courthouse, while Virginia farmers burned down courthouses in King William and New Kent, northeast of Richmond.

Alarmed by the spreading chaos, Richard Henry Lee urged his cousin, Henry Lee Jr., to appeal to George Washington, then in retirement at his home at Mount Vernon: "I apprehend your solicitude for . . . a nation formed under your auspices will illy relish intelligence ominous of its destruction," Henry Lee then wrote to Washington, "but so circumstanced is the federal government that its death cannot be far distant unless immediate and adequate exertions are made by the several states."

The younger Lee told Washington that the Confederation Congress seemed to agree on but one point: "no money."[7]

Lee said Virginia had printed V£200,000* for its own uses, but like other states, "they are violent enemies to the impost [federal tax], and I fear even the impending dangers to the existence of the Union will not move them."[8]

Washington, of course, had been first to warn of the forthcoming anarchy when he resigned his commission in 1783. At the time he called it "indispensable that there should be lodged somewhere a supreme power to regulate and govern . . . the confederated republic, without which the Union cannot be of long duration.

> There must be a faithful and pointed compliance on the part of every state with the demands of Congress . . . that whatever measures have a tendency to dissolve the Union . . . ought to be considered as hostile to the liberty and independency of America and the authors treated accordingly.[9]

With the chaos that followed Shays's rebellion, Washington pressed state leaders to act to save the nation in peace as they had in war. "There are errors in our national government," he complained to New York's John Jay, who had been secretary for foreign affairs in the Confederation Congress. "Something must be done!"[10]

The national chaos disrupted travel plans of so many delegates who had planned to attend the Annapolis convention on trade and commerce that delegates from only five states showed up on time. Without a quorum to proceed, they had little choice but to postpone their discussions until Congress could fix a new date for deliberations. In February 1787 the Confederation Congress reconvened and broadened the agenda of the next meeting, calling on states to convene for "the sole and express purpose of revising the articles of confederation . . . [and] render the federal constitution adequate to the exigencies of government and the preservation of the union."[11]

---

*One Virginia pound equaled about 75 percent of a British pound, or about $100 in today's currency.

On May 17, 1787, the first delegates appeared in Philadelphia to revise the Articles of the Confederation—a tissue-thin document that had served as a constitution of sorts since the end of the Revolution. Although state legislatures had elected more than seventy delegates to the convention, not enough arrived in Philadelphia to make up a quorum until May 25, when twenty-nine delegates appeared and elected George Washington the convention president.

By then several states were ready to take up arms against each other, spurred by speculation that had sent land values soaring. New York and New Hampshire were ready to war over conflicting claims to lands in Vermont; Virginia and Pennsylvania both claimed sovereignty over lands in western Pennsylvania and Kentucky; Massachusetts claimed all of western New York. Connecticut prepared to send its militia into Pennsylvania after Pennsylvania militiamen fired on Connecticut farmers who had staked out vacant lands in the Wyoming Valley of northeastern Pennsylvania.

In addition to territorial disputes, many of the states were involved in economic disputes over international trade. States with deep-water ports such as Philadelphia, New York, and Boston were bleeding the economies of neighboring states with heavy duties on imports that passed through their harbors on their way to inland destinations. "New Jersey, placed between Philadelphia and New York, is like a cask tapped at both ends," complained Virginia's James Madison, "and North Carolina, between Virginia and South Carolina seems a patient bleeding at both arms."[12]

Virginia governor Edmund Randolph had appointed George Washington, Patrick Henry, and Richard Henry Lee among others as delegates to the Philadelphia convention. By then, however, Virginia's House of Delegates had reappointed Richard Henry Lee to the Confederation Congress in New York, and the prospect of plunging into two political battles—in Philadelphia *and* New York—was too much for the fifty-five-year-old Richard Henry Lee. He turned down the governor's appointment, citing "the circumstances of my health" and adding that, with Washington, Henry, and "so many gentlemen of good hearts and sound heads . . . I feel a disposition to repose in confidence in their determination."[13]

Although Lee did not know it, Patrick Henry, Virginia's first governor and patron saint of state sovereignty, had also refused to go to Philadelphia, but for other reasons. Although Henry agreed that "ruin is inevitable unless something is done to give Congress a compulsory process on delinquent states," he believed the convention, as planned, was a fraud.[14] Most delegates, Henry charged, were the very merchant-bankers who had provoked farmer rioting by profiting from the purchase and resale of foreclosed properties. Henry also believed the failure of Congress to secure navigation rights to the Mississippi River reflected the centralized government's inability to serve the best interests of the states or the American people.

Henry said he would stay home and fight to keep Virginia independent by opposing ratification of whatever changes the Philadelphia convention might make to the Articles of Confederation.

More shocking than the refusals of Richard Henry Lee and Patrick Henry to attend the Philadelphia convention was the refusal of George Washington, whose response stirred an outcry from many of his own influential friends. Most warned that his absence would doom the convention to failure and provoke the very anarchy he sought to prevent.

Secretary at War Henry Knox, a major general in the Revolutionary War and Washington's chief of artillery from their early days in 1775, warned his old friend that "different states have . . . views that sooner or later must involve the Country in all the horrors of civil war.

> A neglect in every state of those principles which lead to union and national greatness—an adoption of local in preference to general measures—appears to actuate the greater part of the state politicians. We are entirely destitute of those traits which should stamp us *one Nation*, and the Constitution of Congress does not promise any alteration.[15]

Knox's letter alerted Washington to the possibility of a bloody civil war and that he was probably the only man in America who might prevent it. Washington finally yielded, admitting that "the disinclination of the individual states to yield competent powers to Congress, their unreasonable jealousy of that body and of one another . . . will, if there is not a change in the system, be our downfall as a nation."[16]

In deciding to attend the Philadelphia convention, Washington expressed his hope that "the good sense of the people will ultimately get the better of their prejudices."[17]

Although Richard Henry Lee was unwilling to participate in the Constitutional Convention, he did not remain aloof from its proceedings and peppered George Mason, who had replaced Lee at the convention, with proposals for shaping the new government. The owner of a plantation near George Washington's Mount Vernon, Mason—like Lee and, indeed, Patrick Henry—was a fervent devotee of state sovereignty and reluctant to give the central government powers that might mimic those of Britain's governing ministry.

"It has given me much pleasure . . . that General Washington and yourself have gone to the convention," Richard Henry Lee wrote to Mason as the convention began. "We may hope . . . that alterations beneficial will take place in our federal constitution. The human mind," he warned, "is too apt to rush from one extreme to another.

> When the confederation was submitted for consideration . . . the universal apprehension was of the too great . . . powers of Congress . . . now the cry is power. Give power to the Congress . . . every free nation that hath ever existed has lost its liberty by the same rash impatience and want of necessary caution.[18]

Lee reminded Mason that the main complaint against the Confederation Congress had been its inability to raise money to pay its debts and support the federal government. He said the states had been so "unpardonably remiss" in providing the necessary funds "as to make impost [a federal tax] necessary for a term of time, with a provisional security that the money arising shall be unchangeably applied to the payment of their public debts."[19]

Lee also proposed giving Congress alone the exclusive right to print paper money.

"Knaves assure—and fools believe—that printing paper money and making it tender is the way to be rich and happy; thus the national mind is kept in constant ferment and the public councils in continuous disturbance by the intrigues of wicked men, for fraudulent purposes, for speculating designs."

Lee also believed the new constitution should bar states from passing any legislation "that shall contravene or oppose the acts of Congress or interfere with the expressed rights of that body."[20] In addition, he urged Mason to ensure inclusion of a bill of rights, adding freedom of speech, freedom of the press, and the right to petition for redress of grievances to those rights already guaranteed by the Articles of Confederation, namely freedom of worship, the right to trial by jury, and public support of education.

Because of the secrecy oath that Constitutional Convention delegates had taken, Mason did not—indeed, could not—reply, leaving Richard Henry Lee no option but to return to the Confederation Congress and await the finished document.

When Lee reached New York in the summer of 1787 he found the Confederation Congress debating the first—and what would be the only—significant piece of legislation in its short history. The fulfillment of his ambitions to expand the nation westward, the Northwest Ordinance, as it was called, would create the first American territory—the Northwest Territory—beyond all state boundaries. The federal government acquired full sovereignty along with authority to create new states and sell land within the territory.* In effect,

---

* Six states would emerge from the Northwest Territory: Ohio (1803), Indiana (1816), Illinois (1818), Michigan (1837), Wisconsin (1848), and part of Minnesota (1858).

the Northwest Ordinance blocked existing states from extending their territories into the western wilderness, prevented them from warring with each other over conflicting claims, and, for the first time in America, provided the federal government with sovereignty over American territory and authority to raise money without state authorization.*

To govern the territory Congress would appoint a governor, a secretary, and three judges. Ultimately Congress was to carve the territory into at least three but as many as five states, each requiring at least 60,000 free residents to become a state and each to be "on an equal footing with the original states in all respects whatsoever."[21]

Once again Richard Henry Lee seized a leadership role by pressing Congress into including a bill of rights that established freedom of worship, trial by jury, and public support of education as rights of all citizens in the new territory. He then convinced the Confederation Congress to pass the most remarkable act in its history—one that fulfilled a moral quest he had started as a twenty-year-old upstart burgess more than thirty years earlier: the prohibition of "involuntary servitude"—that is, slavery—in the Northwest Territory and the states formed within it.

In effect the Northwest Ordinance established the Ohio River as the border between free states and slave states and prepared the geographic stage for the Civil War seventy years in the future. How he accomplished such a radical turnabout in the thinking of Congress is not evident in any of the records of Congress. One factor in his success may have been a change in the complexion of that body with the calling of the Constitutional Convention. Among those elected to both bodies, many of the die-hard southern slave owners and older northerners opted to abandon their seats in the relatively impotent Confederation Congress in favor of creating a new

*The First Congress would replace the Northwest Ordinance of 1787 with an almost identical measure in 1789 transferring sovereignty from the Confederation Congress to the federal government created by the Constitution.

government in the Constitutional Convention. Their absence left northern Quakers—all fervent opponents of slavery—and younger, more advanced-thinking southerners with moral objections to slavery in a position "to put an end to that iniquitous and disgraceful traffic" in the future American states of the northwest.[22]

Passage of the Northwest Ordinance sent wilderness property values north of the Ohio River soaring and promised enormous profits for the Lee and Washington families. "I have the honor," Lee enthused to Washington, "to enclose to you an ordinance that we have just passed in Congress for establishing a temporary government beyond the Ohio, as a measure preparatory to the sale of the lands." Lee told Washington the ordinance had secured their property rights and would protect them against "licentious people," including squatters and overlapping claims by companies such as the Grand Ohio Company (the old Loyal Land Company).[23]

On September 20, 1787, Richard Henry Lee received a copy of the new constitution and spent the next week studying it and writing comments. Lee soon learned that even Washington had mixed feelings about it.

"Every state has some objection," Washington admitted. "That which is most pleasing to one is obnoxious to another and vice versa." But, he added, there were "seeds of discontent in every part of the Union ready to produce disorders" if the convention had not created "a more vigorous and energetic government."[24]

Like the Confederation Congress debate over the Articles of Confederation, the Constitutional Convention had stalemated for a while over the issue of whether congressional voting was to be by state or population size. Both sides had legitimate arguments, with those favoring one vote for each state contending that voting by population size would allow the two or three states with the largest population—Virginia, Massachusetts, and Pennsylvania—to dictate to the other ten states. Rather than a republic that protects the rights of all citizens, it would create a democracy, with absolute rule by the majority. But the large states argued with equal validity that a one-state, one-vote system would allow ten states with a combined population smaller than Virginia's alone, to dictate to the vast majority of the people.

A few delegates walked out and left for home in disgust at what they perceived as an insoluble problem. Two of the three New York delegates quit after New York governor George Clinton called the proceedings an illegal usurpation of power, unauthorized, he said, by the majority of Americans.

Roger Sherman, the mayor of New Haven, Connecticut, calmed the remaining delegates, however, by proposing what he called a relatively fair compromise: "Let voting in the lower house be proportionate to each state's population, and give each state parity . . . in the upper house. Otherwise a few large states will rule. The smaller states would never agree to a plan on any other principle than an equality of suffrage in this branch."[25]

Intent on holding the Union together, a majority of delegates agreed and went on to propose "a national government . . . consisting of a supreme Legislative, Executive and Judiciary," with the national legislature consisting of two branches: a popularly elected lower house and an upper house elected by state legislatures. Each state in the lower house would cast votes proportionate to the total of its free population and three-fifths of its slave population, while each state in the upper house would have two votes, giving small states parity with large states. They gave the national legislature almost all the powers of the British Parliament—namely, to tax the people directly without consent of state legislatures, to raise troops for a federal force, to declare war, and to enact any laws it deemed "necessary and proper." All national laws would "negative" all state laws that contravened the federal constitution.

Much as Richard Henry Lee had proposed to George Mason, the delegates effectively barred states from printing or coining money, giving all such powers to the federal government. To keep the South in the Union, the North agreed to prevent Congress from interfering with the importation of slaves for twenty years.

With Lee and other influential political leaders peppering convention members with demands, it decided on a one-man executive
chosen by electors (the Electoral College) appointed by each of the
state legislatures along with the votes of each state's two US senators.

Although the constitution as written allowed a president to serve
an indefinite number of four-year terms—a condition Lee warned
would open the way for the president to turn tyrant—other conditions of his service left him little more than a figurehead.* It
named him commander-in-chief, for example, but gave Congress
sole powers to declare war, raise troops, and send soldiers into action. Although it charged him with faithfully executing the laws, it
gave him no evident enforcement powers to do so. Confident that
Washington would win election as the nation's first president, the
convention paid token tribute to his stature as a national icon by
giving him a veto over legislation, but empowered the legislature to
override his veto by a two-thirds majority. It allowed him to propose candidates for judgeships and key executive posts, but placed
approval of such appointments in the Senate and gave him no specific authority over appointees once they assumed office—nor could
he dismiss them.

The national judiciary was equally impotent, consisting of "one
supreme tribunal" that would try cases without juries, and giving the
national legislature sole powers to create lower courts—again, empowered to hear cases without jurors. Richard Henry Lee howled
with outrage but with little effect. A proposal that judges be appointed for life on condition of "good behavior" drew a second outcry
by Lee, but Benjamin Franklin stifled any support for Lee's objections by asserting that lifetime appointments of judges had worked
exceedingly well in Scotland.

*The Twenty-Second Amendment passed in 1947 now limits presidents to
two elected terms in office—one term if he assumed the presidency while vice
president and then held the presidency for more than two years.

"The nominations proceeded from the lawyers," he explained, "who always selected the ablest member of their profession" to serve as a judge—"in order to get rid of him and share his practice among themselves."[26] After the roars of laughter subsided, delegates approved lifetime appointments for the Supreme Court. Twenty-nine of the forty-two remaining delegates at the convention were lawyers.

Only thirty-nine of the forty-two delegates signed the constitution, and Pennsylvania delegate Gouverneur Morris's disingenuous statement at the top of the signatures—"Done in Convention by the Unanimous Consent of the States present"—used the unanimity of one-state, one-vote balloting to mask all opposition to the document and the divisions between delegates in many states.

Virginia governor Edmund Randolph, evidently influenced by Richard Henry Lee, "said it would be impossible . . . to put his name" on a document that gave Congress "dangerous power" over the states.[27] George Mason agreed. Having failed to win inclusion of Richard Henry Lee's proposed bill of rights in the constitution, Mason vowed, "I would sooner chop off my right hand than put it to the Constitution as it now stands."[28] Mason contended that while the opening words of the constitution mentioned "we, the people," the secret proceedings gave the people no knowledge of its contents. He called for a second convention to determine the true will of the people and to rewrite the document accordingly.

Elbridge Gerry of Massachusetts agreed, expressing as much outrage as the Virginians at the absence of Richard Henry Lee's bill of rights. Elbridge railed at the powers given to Congress "to make what laws they may please . . . raise armies and money without limit." In addition, he mirrored Richard Henry Lee's objection to creating a supreme court that was "a tribunal without juries."[29]

Even Washington, who was first to sign the document, was less than pleased. "I wish the constitution . . . had been more perfect," he admitted, "but I sincerely believe it is the best that could be obtained at this time. And, as a constitutional door is opened for amendments hereafter, the adoption of it . . . is in my opinion desirable."[30]

Franklin was slightly more enthusiastic. "I confess there are several parts of this constitution which I do not at present approve, but I am not sure I shall ever approve them . . . the older I get, the more apt I am to doubt my own judgment, and to pay more respect to the judgment of others.

> Most men indeed as well as most sects in religion, think themselves in possession of all truth and that wherever others differ from them it is so far error. Steele a Protestant . . . tells the Pope that 'the only difference between our churches in . . . the certainty of their doctrines is the Church of Rome is infallible and the Church of England is never wrong.'[31]

Franklin went on to proclaim his support for the constitution "with all its faults . . . because I think a general government necessary for us, and there is no form of government but what may be a blessing to the people if well administered." He said he doubted whether another convention could write a better constitution. "Thus, I consent . . . to this constitution because I expect no better, and because I am not sure it is not the best."[32]

When the Constitution was read to Congress on September 20, however, Richard Henry Lee grew outraged. On September 27 he stood in Congress and proposed nineteen amendments before reiterating George Mason's call for a second convention. Far from objecting, the members simply ignored Lee. Only thirty-three members had appeared; ten had been delegates to the Constitutional Convention, had voted for and signed the document, and now pressed Congress to approve it without dissent for quick transmission to the states for ratification.

With support from the members of their own states, they did just that. To project an appearance of unanimity, a New Jersey delegate then moved to strike Richard Henry Lee's proposals to amend the constitution from the official record in the *Journals of Congress*—and they did.

"It was with us as with you," Lee remonstrated to George Mason after Congress had adjourned. "This or nothing; and 'this' urged with a most extreme intemperance.

> The greatness of the powers given and the multitude of places cre-
> ated produces a coalition of monarchy men, military men, aristo-
> crats, and drones, whose noise, impudence, and zeal exceeds all
> belief. . . . In this state of things, the patriot voice is raised in vain
> for such changes and securities as reason and experience prove to be
> necessary against the encroachments of power. . . . I availed myself
> of the right to amend. . . . This greatly alarmed the majority . . . for
> the plan is to push the business on with great dispatch with as little
> opposition as possible.[33]

The first ten amendments Richard Henry Lee had proposed were a bill of rights to guarantee "rights of conscience in matters of religion . . . freedom of the press . . . trial by jury . . . safety of life in criminal prosecutions," the last provision having been the first attempt to modify application of the death penalty in America. Lee also called for amendments to guarantee the right of Americans to assemble peacefully to petition the legislature; to ban unreasonable searches or seizures of their papers, houses, persons, or property; and to guarantee the right to be tried "by a jury of the vicinage" and end "the vexatious and oppressive calling of citizens from their own country . . . for trial in far distant courts."

He asked for a total separation of the overlapping powers of the executive (President) and the Senate, and an increase in the number of votes in the House from a bare majority to a two-thirds majority to pass legislation.

"The plan now admitting of a bare majority to make laws," he argued, "it may happen that five states may legislate for thirteen states, though eight of the thirteen are absent."[34] He all but howled his outrage at the prospects of one man—a single vote—determining the outcome of legislation for an entire nation of millions.

He asserted "that standing armies in times of peace are dangerous to liberty" and moved that they not be permitted without approval by a two-thirds majority in both houses of Congress. And in a final amendment, that would not be added to the Constitution until 1917, he moved "to place the right of representation in the Senate on the same ground that it is placed in the House of Delegates [Representatives], thereby securing equality of representation in the legislature so necessary for good government."[35]

The Congress not only refused to record Lee's resolutions in the *Journals of Congress*, it sent the constitution unchanged to the states for ratification with this message, pointedly dismissing Lee and all those seeking to amend the document:

> Congress having received the report of the Convention lately assembled in Philadelphia. . . . Resolved unanimously, That the said report . . . be transmitted to the several legislatures . . . to be submitted to a convention of delegates chosen in each state by the people thereof in conformity to the resolves of the Convention.[36]

Lee protested that the resolution was far from unanimous and aimed only at rallying public opinion in favor of ratification. But, as he had lamented to George Mason, "It was this or nothing."

The harsh—indeed, rude—rebuff infuriated Lee. As old as Washington, he had been president of Congress—by title, President of the United States in Congress Assembled—and, in fact, father of American independence. As the First Founding Father and a staunch Patriot, his age, rank, and family heritage demanded and entitled him to respect, and the cavalier dismissal he suffered pushed him firmly, deeply into the Antifederalist camp. Indeed, he now determined to join Patrick Henry in rallying Antifederalists across the nation to reject the new American Constitution and restore the cry for "Liberty or Death" to the lips of every patriotic American.

CHAPTER 11

The Farmer and the Federalist

WHEN RICHARD HENRY LEE RETURNED TO VIRGINIA HE SET OUT to rally America against the new constitution by detailing objections to the governors of Massachusetts, Delaware, Pennsylvania, North Carolina, and Virginia and to Antifederalist leaders such as Samuel Adams and Elbridge Gerry.

"I incline to think," he wrote to Gerry, "that unless alterations and provisions are interposed for the security of those essential rights of mankind without which liberty cannot exist, we shall soon find that the new plan of government will be far more inconvenient than anything sustained under the present government, and that to avoid Scylla we shall have fallen upon Charybdis."[1]

And to Virginia governor Edmund Randolph, who also favored a bill of rights, he explained, "The human race is too apt to rush from one extreme to another. . . . For now, the cry is power; give Congress power, without reflecting that every free nation that hath ever existed has lost its liberty by the same rash impatience and want of necessary caution."

Lee admitted that the states had been "unpardonably remiss in furnishing their federal quotas" during the Revolutionary War and that federal taxation had become essential to repaying the public debt. But, taking aim at Washington's argument for ratification, Lee added, "To say that a bad government must be established for fear of anarchy is really saying that we should kill ourselves for fear of dying!

> If with infinite ease, a convention was obtained to prepare a system, why may not another convention with equal ease be obtained to make proper and necessary amendments? . . . Bad governments have been generally found the most fixed, so it becomes of . . . importance to frame the first establishment upon grounds the most unexceptionable . . . not trusting to time and future events to correct errors that . . . exist in the present system.[2]

Lee again pointed out the dangerous overlapping powers of executive and legislative branches, allowing the President and Senate to share responsibilities over treaty ratification and, even more dangerous, the appointment of all civil and military officers. "This new constitution is in its first principles, most highly and dangerously oligarchic, and it is agreed that a government of the few is, of all governments, the worst."[3]

Lee repeated his criticism of the constitution for its failure to guarantee individual rights, citing British jurist Sir William Blackstone's volume on individual rights in his *Commentaries on the Laws of England.* "The most transcendent privilege which any subject can enjoy or wish for," Blackstone had written, "is that he cannot be affected either in his property, his liberty, or his person but by the unanimous consent of twelve of his neighbors and equals.

> The impartial administration of justice is the great end of society, but if that is entirely entrusted to . . . a select body of men . . . selected by the *prince or such as enjoy the highest offices of the state* [his italics], their decisions, in spite of their own natural integrity, will have frequently an involuntary bias towards those of their own rank and dignity. It is

not to be expected from human nature that the *few* should be always attentive to the many.[4]

After the *Virginia Gazette* published Lee's letter to Governor Randolph, George Washington bristled, fearing Lee's remarks would have a "bad influence" in Virginia. But Lee was not alone among American leaders who condemned the constitution as written. New York governor George Clinton, a Revolutionary War hero, warned the citizens of his state in an article for the *New York Journal* "to recollect that the wisest and best of men [a reference to Washington] may err, and their errors, if adopted, may be fatal to the community."[5]

And after Patrick Henry called the constitution an "extreme danger to . . . rights, liberty, and happiness," he wrote to Washington, "I cannot bring my mind in accord with the proposed constitution. The concern I feel on this account is greater than I can express."[6]

Instead of producing a groundswell of opposition to ratification, however, Lee's campaign for amendments produced a storm of attacks by Federalists, who tarred him with epithets as an enemy of Washington and the nation. At first Lee countered, pointing out that only *constitutional amendments* could prevent violations of human rights over an extended period. Laws that are passed one year, he argued, can be repealed the next.

Lee also appealed to George Washington, now titular leader of American Federalists: "In consequence of long reflection upon the nature of man and government," Lee explained to his old friend, "I am led to fear the danger that will ensue to civil liberty from the adoption of the new system in its present form." Although he said he agreed to the need for changes in the Articles of Confederation, he insisted that the new constitution gave the federal government too much power. He called a bill of rights essential to secure individual liberties, along with a clause reserving to the states all powers not expressly delegated to the federal government. He called it essential to impose these restrictions *before* ratification rather than after, by which time a new government may well have assumed dictatorial powers.

Eager not to undermine his long relationship with Washington, Lee made a special trip to Mount Vernon to ensure that Washington did not take Lee's criticisms as a personal affront, but he found Washington abrupt and irascible: "The constitution . . . is not free from imperfections," the former general admitted, "but there are few radical defects in it . . . considering the diversity of interests that are to be attended to. As a constitutional door is opened for future amendments . . . I think it would be wise to accept what is offered."[7]

Other Federalists favoring ratification joined Washington in criticizing Lee, with many leveling vicious personal attacks: "Nothing . . . can equal the meanness of the Antifederalist junto in America but the low arts of our enemies during the war," Massachusetts educator Noah Webster opined. "Like them, the Antifederal men are circulating hand bills fraught with sophistry, declamation, and falsehoods to delude the people and excite jealousies."[8] Connecticut Federalist Jeremiah Wadsworth echoed Webster, charging that "a pamphlet is circulating here . . . written with art and . . . calculated to do much harm. It came from New York undercover."[9]

The "pamphlet" was, in fact, the first of two that, together, contained eighteen *Letters from the Federal Farmer to the Republican* (five in the first pamphlet, thirteen in the second). In writing "Farmer's Letters," Richard Henry Lee* hoped to have as much of an impact

---

*Pulitzer Prize–winning historian Gordon Wood contends that Richard Henry Lee was not the author of the *Letters from the Federal Farmer to the Republican*, and a number of respected historians agree, attributing them to Melancton Smith, a New York delegate at the Continental Congress. On the other hand, the highly respected historians Jean Edward Smith and Professor Walter Hartwell Bennett, editor of the *Letters*, among others, are adamant that Richard Henry Lee was *The Federal Farmer*, and I agree—to an extent. Few American political leaders of the 1780s had the formal education, erudition, and command of the English (as opposed to the "American") language to have produced the brilliantly written *Letters*—and the home-schooled Smith was

provoking opposition to the Constitution as John Dickinson's *Letters from a Farmer in Pennsylvania* had had provoking opposition to British rule.

Lee's eighteen letters preceded by three weeks—and, indeed, may have helped provoke—the series of eighty-five essays called, collectively, *The Federalist*, which Alexander Hamilton, James Madison, and John Jay would write under the pseudonym "Publius"—a reference to Publius Valerius Publicola, a Roman consul from 509 to 507 BC. Some reference works credit Publius with having implemented popular, antimonarchical measures in the early Roman Republic. Hamilton used the pseudonym to avoid accusations of violating the Constitutional Convention's rule of secrecy.[10]

As important as Hamilton's *Federalist* in the state-by-state debates over ratification of the Constitution, Lee's *Letters from the Federal Farmer* might well have been called *The Antifederalist*. Together the *Letters* reiterated and expanded upon his long presentation to Edmund Randolph, adding principles from Blackstone's *Commentaries* and Baron de Montesquieu's *De L'Esprit des Lois* (*The Spirit of the Laws*) as well as his own thoughts. The *Letters* appeared from October 8, 1787, through January 23, 1788, and began with his admission that "our federal system is defective and that some of the state governments are not well administered."

---

certainly not one of them. Smith did speak and write profound essays on some of the topics covered by the *Letters*, but not until the spring and summer of 1788, almost a year after Lee's *Letters* appeared in print. After studying the vocabulary, syntax, and other elements of the writing in the *Letters*—including punctuation and rare but consistent punctuation and grammatical errors—and after comparing them with the writings of Lee's political contemporaries, including Melancton Smith, I believe Richard Henry Lee was the primary author of *Letters from the Federal Farmer to the Republican* but that he collaborated with Antifederalist contemporaries—probably Smith among them—and incorporated parts or all of their thoughts in the finished pamphlets. For more on this dispute, see the "Editor's Introduction," xiii–xx, in Walter Hartwell Bennett, ed., *Letters from the Federal Farmer to the Republican* (Tuscaloosa: University of Alabama Press, 1978).

Declaring that "a federal government of some sort is necessary," Lee nonetheless vowed he could not consent to a government "which is not calculated equally to preserve the rights of all orders of men in the community." In reiterating his deep opposition to slavery, Lee added his objections to election laws that limited voting to men of property and allowed appointed electors to override the popular majority in the selection of a president and vice president.[11] Indeed, southerners at the Constitutional Convention had insisted on adding the votes of each US Senator to the electoral college votes for each state. The added votes would give the least populated rural states—at the time, the southern slave states—an advantage in presidential elections over heavily populated urban free states of the north. Indeed, five southern, slave-owning presidents from rural states would win elections for two terms each in ten of the first twelve presidential elections.* In addition, the inequities of the Electoral College would subsequently allow five American presidents into the White House despite their having lost the popular vote: John Quincy Adams (1824); Rutherford B. Hayes (1876); Benjamin Harrison (1888); George W. Bush (2000); and Donald J. Trump (2016).

The *Farmer*'s individual letters had no titles. Beginning with only the salutation, "DEAR SIR," Lee's letters discussed eleven broad topics, sometimes using as many as four letters to elucidate his views on a particularly important topic such as the ratio of representatives to constituents. His other letters discussed what he considered the essentials of free government, the organization of elections, the need for a bill of rights, the division of powers between federal and state governments, and the dangers of a consolidated government. He wrote two letters describing the debates over ratification and two

---

*George Washington, Thomas Jefferson, James Madison, James Monroe, and Andrew Jackson each served two terms, and all owned slaves while in office. Only John Adams and John Quincy Adams, the second and fifth presidents from Massachusetts, did not. Each lost his bid for election to a second term.

letters each on the powers granted to the executive, legislative, and judiciary branches.

In the end Lee laid particular stress on the need to be more specific in stating federal government powers, its means of enforcing those powers, and the safeguards against its use of the military. Its powers to tax, he pointed out, mirrored the taxing powers of Parliament that ignited the Revolutionary War. "Congress," he warned, "will have taxing powers and the people no check. . . . A power to lay and collect taxes at its discretion is in itself of very great importance. By means of taxes, the government may command the whole or any part of the subject's property."[12]

Lee also objected to Article 1, Section 8, which gave Congress powers "to make all laws which shall be necessary and proper for carrying into execution . . . all other powers vested by this constitution in the government of the United States or in any department or officer thereof."[13] It was, he warned, an invitation to tyranny. "In fact, the constitution provides for the states no check . . . upon the measures of Congress. Congress can immediately enlist soldiers and apply to the pockets of the people."[14]

Lee admitted that "a wise and prudent congress will pay respect to the opinions of a free people" but worried that "a congress of a different character will not be bound . . . to pay respect to those principles."[15] As for the President, he warned that the constitution created a chief executive who will have "a strong tendency to aristocracy, or the government of the few.

> The executive is, in fact, the president and the senate in all transactions of any importance. . . . He may always act with the Senate. . . . We may have for the first president . . . a great and good man, governed by superior motives, but these are not events to be calculated upon in the present state of human nature.[16]

Lee argued that the most likely candidates for high office fall into three categories: the "natural aristocracy" with the time and wealth to assume office, "the substantial and respectable part of the democracy who discern and judge well . . . [but] are often overlooked," and the "popular demagogues [who] often have some abilities, [are] without principle, and rise into notice by their noise and arts."[17]

Lee urged that a president be limited to one term in office, saying that a president rendered ineligible for a second term "will be governed by very different considerations."[18]

Lee condemned the constitution's "strong tendency to aristocracy" and "accumulation of powers especially as to the internal police of the country." He said the nature of government would limit representatives to "men of the elevated classes" and that "the great body of the people, the middle and lower classes" will seldom be elected to the federal government. Men from the military, he said, presented an especially great danger to the republic if elected to the legislature or the presidency. "A few men may unite to enact laws," he warned, "and all this may be done constitutionally."

Under the proposed constitution, he explained, the Senate would have twenty-six members, with only fourteen required for a quorum. Thus, a mere eight senators from four states with the smallest voting populations—Delaware, Georgia, Kentucky, and Rhode Island, with 56,000 popular votes—could enact laws affecting 4 million Americans and leave the nation with "very little democracy."[19] He predicted that tiny Delaware, a northern slave state, might combine with one other small northern state and with a handful of plantation owners who controlled votes in the South to pass outrageous laws affecting the vast majority of Americans, including indefinite perpetuation of slavery. Only seven of the original thirteen states—three of them among the most heavily populated—were free states: Connecticut, Massachusetts, Rhode Island, New Hampshire, New Jersey, New York, and Pennsylvania. Together, however, they did not command the 60 percent majority required to control Senate voting.

Nor did the House of Representatives—the so-called People's House—provide a remedy, Lee argued. With but one representative for every 30,000 eligible voters, "there can be but little personal knowledge, or but few communications, between him and the people at large. . . . Mixing only with the respectable men, he will get the best information and ideas from them; he will also receive impressions favorable to their purposes particularly."[20]

"This proves," he declared, "that we cannot form one general government on equal and just principles—and proves that we ought not to lodge in it such extensive powers before we are convinced of the practicality of organizing it on just and equal principles.

> We are not like the people of England, one people compactly settled on a small island, with a great city filled with frugal merchants, serving as a common center of liberty and union. We are dispersed, and it is impracticable for any but the few to assemble in one place. The few must be watched, checked, and often resisted. Tyranny has ever shown a predilection to be in close amity with them. . . . Laws which were to be equal to all are soon warped into the private interests of the administrators and made to defend the usurpations of a few.[21]

Lee argued that the constitution as written might well serve a small republic such as Connecticut, where voters could choose enough representatives familiar with the entire state able to weigh the interests of the state against the interests of any particular community. But a representative from central Georgia could hardly act in the best interests of the people of Connecticut—or Boston, for that matter, or Lancaster, Pennsylvania.

"A man that is known among a few thousand people may be quite unknown among thirty or forty thousand," he explained. "When we call on thirty or forty thousand . . . to unite in giving their votes for one man, it will be uniformly impracticable to unite in any men except those few who have become eminent for their civil or military rank . . . the men who form the natural aristocracy . . . [or] popular demagogues."[22] He equated the power to tax with the power to confiscate private property and the power to muster the army as the power to oppress. Lee called the constitution, as written, a radical departure from republican principles and all but certain to produce rule by oligarchs—if not a single monarch.

> Congress will have taxing powers and the people no check. . . . The constitution provides for the states no check. . . . The House of representatives in fifty or a hundred years will consist of several hundred members. . . . They and their friends will find it for their interests to keep up large armies, navies, salaries, & c., and in laying adequate taxes. . . . We ought, therefore, on every principle now to fix government on proper principles.[23]

Lee called on the states to postpone consideration of the constitution and convene a second convention to improve on it or write an entirely new document that would divide governing responsibilities more equitably between state governments and a strengthened confederation congress.

"It is natural for men who wish to hasten the adoption of a measure," he declared, "to tell us now is the crisis—now is the critical moment which must be seized or all is lost. . . . This has been the custom of tyrants and their dependents in all ages." Scoffing at such arguments, he insisted over and again that what had been written in four months could most certainly be rewritten and improved in another four months. With the nation at peace, facing no threats from beyond its borders, there was no reason not to reconsider the constitution as written. The authors of the constitution had met originally, he argued, to amend the Articles of Confederation. "Not a word was said about destroying the old constitution and making a new one."[24]

"He was not a lawyer by profession," the future Attorney General William Wirt said of Richard Henry Lee, "but he understood thoroughly the Constitution, both of the mother country and of her colonies; and the elements also of civil and municipal law."

Lee, of course, had been as frustrated as Washington by Congress's inability to raise money, troops, arms, ammunition, and supplies for the common cause during the Revolution. Clearly he and other members of the Continental Congress had erred in the design of government under the Articles of Confederation. But in granting the central government more powers, he declared, the Constitutional Convention had made a flagrant error in failing to protect individual liberties. With the publication of his *Federal Farmer*, therefore, Richard Henry Lee became the First of the Founding Fathers to demand incorporation of a comprehensive Bill of Rights in any new constitution. To compensate for what he called "a government where the purse and sword and all important powers are proposed to be lodged," he called for the following guarantees for all citizens:

The right to trial by jury in civil as well as criminal cases;

Security against ex post facto laws;

The benefits of habeas corpus;

The freedom of the press is a fundamental right and ought not to be restrained by any taxes, duties or in any manner whatever.

No man shall be held to answer to any offense till the same be fully described to him, nor to furnish evidence against himself.

Except in the government of the army and navy, no person shall be tried for any offense whereby he may incur loss of life or an infamous punishment until he be first indicted by a grand jury.

Every person shall have a right to produce all proofs that may be favorable to him and to meet witnesses against him face to face.

Every person shall be entitled to obtain right and justice freely and without delay.

All persons shall have a right to be secure from all unreasonable searches and seizures of their persons, houses, papers, or possessions.

No person shall be exiled or molested in his person or effects otherwise than by the judgment of his peers or according to the law of the land.

Lee argued that the "silence" of the Constitution "as to . . . the right to have council, to have witnesses face to face, to be secure against unreasonable search warrants . . . implies they are relinquished or deemed of no importance.

> The essential parts of a free and good government are a full and equal representation of the people in the legislature and the jury trial in the vicinage in the administration of justice. A full and equal representation is that which possesses the same interests, feelings, opinions, and views as the people themselves would were they all assembled. A fair representation, therefore, should be so regulated that every order of men in the community, according to the common course of elections, can have a share in it—in order to allow professional men, merchants, traders, farmers, mechanics, &c. to bring a just proportion of their best informed men respectively into the legislature.[25]

Lee's *Federal Farmer* asserted that all men—professional men, merchants, traders, farmers, mechanics—were, in fact, "created equal with certain unalienable rights" that included the right to govern themselves and their country. Few other Founding Fathers agreed. Even John Adams had stressed the importance of titles that confirmed the inequality of men and ensured deference of the less educated to their betters. But Lee's *Federal Farmer* pointed out that "southern states are composed chiefly of rich planters and slaves . . . and the prevailing influence in them is generally a dissipated aristocracy."[26]

Almost three weeks after the first pamphlet with Lee's *Letters from the Federal Farmer* appeared in the newspapers, Alexander Hamilton's "The Federalist I," the first of his essays defending the Constitution, appeared in New York's *Independent Journal*. John Jay wrote the next four essays, and when Jay fell ill, Hamilton wrote all but two of the next thirty-one. With Virginia's newly elected member of Congress James Madison writing numbers ten and fourteen, the first thirty-six essays of *The Federalist* appeared every week under the pseudonym "Publius" for the rest of 1787.* Four New York City newspapers and twenty-one newspapers in nine other states, including the *Virginia Independent Chronicle*, printed the *Federalist* papers. A reasoned, superbly written, and surprisingly unemotional explanation of the new constitution, *The Federalist* laid bare the differences between "liberty" under a republican government ruled by elected representatives of the people, and "license" in a democracy ruled by a majority with unlimited powers.

The Federalist warned that "a certain class of men in every state" would fight ratification and "union under one government" for fear of losing "the power, emoluments, and consequences of the offices they hold under the state establishments."[27] Although Hamilton admitted that "talents for low intrigue and the little arts of popularity may alone suffice to elevate a man to the first honors in a single state," he insisted it would require "other talents and a different kind of merit" to elevate him to the presidency of all the states.[28]

Lee disagreed, arguing vehemently that the degree of centralization prescribed by the Constitution presaged all the ills that would infect the future United States—a president with unilateral powers to issue executive orders with the force of law and a legislature empowered to confiscate private property by taxation and expand the military into a ruling class. Lee accused the Constitutional Convention of having staged a coup d'état to destroy republican government.

"Our object has been all along to reform our federal system," he argued, "but . . . the plan of government now proposed is calculated totally to change . . . our condition as a people. Instead of being thirteen republics, under a federal head, it is clearly designed to make us one consolidated government."[29]

There was no way for Richard Henry Lee or Hamilton, Jay, and Madison to measure the effects of their writings at first. By

---

*A total of eighty-five *Federalist* essays appeared over six months extending into 1788, with Hamilton writing fifty-one, Madison twenty-nine, and Jay five, according to most authorities.

mid-December 1787 George Washington had read them and was confident *The Federalist* would have "a good effect" in Virginia—until he received this note from his son-in-law: "I am sorry to inform you that the Constitution has lost ground so considerably that it is doubtful whether it has any longer a majority in its favor."[30]

With Richard Henry Lee, George Mason, Patrick Henry, and Edmund Randolph allied in opposition to the proposed constitution, there seemed little hope that Virginia would ratify. Without Virginia, America's richest and largest state, even George Washington realized there could be no effective union even if all twelve other states ratified.

Washington wrote a spirited letter to try to rally Federalist supporters into action, charging, "There are certain characters who are no friends to general government—perhaps I might go further and add, who would have no great objection to the introductions of anarchy and confusion."[31] He accused his friends Patrick Henry and Richard Henry Lee and other opponents of the constitution of using "every art that could inflame the passions or touch the interests of men" to defeat ratification.

"The ignorant are told, that should the proposed government obtain, their lands would be taken from them and their property disposed of, and all ranks are informed that the prohibition of the navigation of the Mississippi (their favorite subject) will be a certain consequence of the adoption of the constitution."[32]

Connecticut's Oliver Ellsworth, who had helped draft the constitution, agreed, setting off a chain of libelous attacks on Richard Henry Lee, exposing him as the "Federal Farmer" and charging that his opposition to the constitution stemmed from personal animosity toward Washington. "In Virginia," Ellsworth declared in an article in the *American Mercury*, "the opposition wholly originated in two principles, the madness of Mason and the enmity of the Lee faction to General Washington."[33]

Ellsworth's venom knew no bounds, going on to poison printer's ink across the nation, inciting newspapers to accuse Lee "with having instigated well-known intrigues" against Washington, including the infamous Conway Cabal. Other Federalists picked up on Ellsworth's libel, heaping more insults and false accusations at Lee—too often and too widespread for Lee to respond. As the attacks increased, Lee grew despondent, and when they touched his family, he abandoned the field, refusing to stand for election to the Virginia ratification convention. What ended his quest was an article in the *Pennsylvania Gazette*, later reprinted in the *Virginia Independent Chronicle*:

> We hear that the eldest son of R. H. L—, Esq., is one of the most zealous and active friends of the federal government in Virginia. In a letter to his father, while in New York, before he knew his sentiments, he unfortunately told him that the constitution had no enemies in Virginia but "fools and knaves."[34]

The attacks temporarily strained Lee's relationship with his two oldest sons, Thomas and Ludwell—both budding lawyers with political ambitions who had publicly endorsed the new constitution. In addition, the newspaper condemnations affected his ties to his younger brothers Arthur and Francis Lightfoot Lee. Francis had publicly embraced the new constitution, while Arthur had sided with Richard Henry at first, but when Richard Henry announced his refusal to serve in the ratification convention, Arthur lashed out at his older brother for political cowardice.

"You will be regarded as having deserted a cause in which you have published your persuasion of its being of the last moment to your country," Arthur snapped at Richard Henry. "Col. Mason laments very much that you do not stand for [Virginia's ratification] convention," Arthur went on. "He is afraid these things will injure your character. . . . I confess, I wish to see you elected whether you serve or not."[35]

Despite Richard Henry's withdrawal from the political fray, his published objections in *Letters from the Federal Farmer*, along with public statements by George Mason and Patrick Henry, had effects far beyond Virginia.

"Beware! Beware!" warned the *Massachusetts Centinel*, parroting Richard Henry Lee's *Letters from the Federal Farmer*. "You are
forging chains for yourself and your children—your liberties are at
stake."[36] Philadelphia's *Independent Gazetteer* predicted that the constitution, if ratified, would create "a permanent aristocracy," while
Freeman's Journal, another Philadelphia newspaper, cited the dangers of congressional powers "to lay and collect taxes."[37]

Although Lee's initial Antifederalist campaign had swayed some
of the general public, his withdrawal from the active political campaign slowed the Antifederalist momentum. Federalists controlled
most state legislatures, and one by one they called ratification conventions in which they dominated the proceedings. By February 6,
1788, conventions in six states had ratified the constitution: Delaware, Pennsylvania, New Jersey, Georgia, Connecticut, and Massachusetts. The three smallest states—Delaware, New Jersey, and
Connecticut—had favored ratification because of the military protection offered by a continental army. Sparsely settled Georgia—
beset by Indian raids from Spanish-held Florida—also needed help
from a strong federal force.

In Pennsylvania and Massachusetts powerful trading interests in
Philadelphia and Boston had controlled the majorities of convention
delegates—despite overwhelming popular opposition to the constitution in both states. To eke out their victory, Massachusetts Federalists pledged to "recommend" a bill of rights to the First Congress.
Pennsylvania Federalists simply stole their victory, with Benjamin
Franklin, of all people, ignoring all principles of self-government by
leading the Pennsylvania delegation out of the Constitutional Convention, up the stairs into the Pennsylvania Assembly hall, and in-
terrupting proceedings. He then bullied state legislators into calling
a state ratification convention immediately—without debate—by
promising that Philadelphia would become the new federal capital if
Pennsylvania were first to ratify the constitution. Like the city's bankers, merchants, and other major property owners, Franklin stood to

reap enormous profits if the new government established the capital in Philadelphia.

Although a huge popular majority of Pennsylvanians—especially rural voters—opposed ratification, Federalist mobs terrorized Philadelphians, throwing stones through homes and lodging houses of visiting Antifederalist delegates and their families. When the ratification convention began, Federalists tried stifling debate, with supporters in the gallery shouting down Antifederalist speakers. When Antifederalists walked out of the hall and left Federalists without a quorum to vote on ratification, convention marshals went to the lodging houses of Antifederalist delegates and carried them bodily back to the hall, where the Federalists ratified the constitution. Mobs in Carlisle and other distant rural communities burned copies of the constitution and threatened to march on Philadelphia, and farmers in western Pennsylvania threatened to secede from Pennsylvania—until icy winter winds and snows sent them all back to the shelters and warmth of their homes and hearths.

By the time Virginians elected delegates to their state ratification convention, Maryland had ratified, and with the Federalist-dominated convention in South Carolina preparing to ratify in May, only one more state—either Virginia, New Hampshire, New York, North Carolina, or Rhode Island—would have to ratify to implement the new government. Rhode Island, however, had refused even to consider the constitution. Convinced that the state's minuscule proportions would leave it impotent in the new union, its legislature refused to call a convention, and the people confirmed their legislature's decision in a popular referendum in March 1788. Although New Hampshire's legislature had called a ratification convention in February, the delegates were so divided about ratification that they adjourned without a decision and agreed to reconvene in June.

After farmers in western North Carolina seceded and formed the new state of Franklin, the eastern establishment that controlled the legislature voted to postpone the state's ratification convention until

July. Their decision left Virginia, New Hampshire, and New York as the only possible states that could become the ninth and definitive member of the new nation.

Like Patrick Henry, New York governor Clinton planned to block the call for a ratification convention as long as he could, but when that became impossible, he convinced the legislature to postpone elections for the convention until April 29, a month after the Virginia convention elections.

Patrick Henry arrived in Richmond as disconsolate as George Mason at not having the oratorically gifted Richard Henry Lee at their side. Lee nonetheless peppered both men—and other Antifederalist delegates—with suggestions.

"It becomes us to be very circumspect and careful about the conduct we pursue," Richard Henry warned George Mason as the convention began. "On the one hand, every possible exertion of wisdom and firmness should be employed to prevent danger to civil liberty. . . . On the other hand, the most watchful precaution should take place to prevent the foes of union, order and government . . . to prevent our acceptance of the good part of the [constitutional] plan proposed."[38]

Lee expressed confidence that the four overriding Antifederalist objections to the constitution would defeat its ratification. First and foremost was the lack of a bill of rights. Their second objection was the unlimited power of the new national government to tax the people without the consent of their state legislatures—one of the issues that had provoked the Revolutionary War. And their third objection was the federal government's power over the military—a power that could send a federal force into any state to enforce federal laws—again, an issue that had provoked the Revolutionary War. Their last major objection—and Mason, Henry, and Lee were adamant on this point—was the right of a bare majority of one in Congress to legislate against the interests of Virginia—or any other state, for that matter—and, indeed, the nation itself and the vast majority of the American people.

It was no surprise that Patrick Henry was first to rise after the convention had fixed the rules of order and heard the contents of the proposed constitution.[39] Henry hoped that he and the other Antifederalists could talk the convention to death. Indeed, Henry would come close to doing the job by himself, speaking on seventeen of the convention's twenty-two days, often three times a day and five times on one day. On another he was the only speaker, standing seven hours to deliver his address.

Citing Richard Henry Lee's *Letters from the Federal Farmer*, Henry accused the authors of the constitution of having usurped powers and staged a coup d'état by violating the mandate of Congress. He reminded Virginians that Congress had called a constitutional convention "for the sole and express purpose of revising the Articles of Confederation and reporting to Congress and the several legislatures such alterations and provisions therein." Instead, he charged, they effectively set out to overthrow the confederation and replace it with a national government.

"I have the greatest veneration for . . . those worthy characters who composed a part of the late federal convention," he told the Virginians, "but, sir, give me leave to demand what right they had to say, *We, the People?*

> My political curiosity . . . leads me to ask who authorized them to speak the language of *We, the People.* . . . The people gave them no power to use their name. That they exceeded their power is perfectly clear. . . . The federal convention ought to have amended the old system—for this purpose they were solely delegated. The object of their mission extended to no other consideration.[40]

Henry quoted Richard Henry Lee, who had questioned delegates' motives at the Constitutional Convention: "I would demand the cause of their conduct . . . even from that illustrious man who saved us by his valor." His unmistakable reference to Washington drew gasps of outrage from Federalists. "I would demand . . . a faithful

historical detail of the . . . reasons that actuated its members in proposing an entire alteration of government—and to demonstrate the
dangers that awaited us. . . . Disorders have arisen in other parts of
America, but here [in Virginia], Sir, no dangers, no insurrection or
tumult has happened—everything has been calm and tranquil. . . .
What are the causes of this proposal to change our government?"[41]

Without answering his own rhetorical question, he ceded the
floor to another Richard Henry Lee ally, Governor Edmund Randolph, who took the floor for what Patrick Henry and George Mason expected would be the coup de grace against ratification. Lee's
letter had, indeed, provided Randolph with all the ammunition
needed to kill the constitution as written, and Henry and Mason
gave Randolph a warm nod of approval as he stood to speak. But
the governor ignored them, fixing his eyes on the President and reminding him that, as a member of the Constitutional Convention, "I
refused to sign, and if the same were to return, again would I refuse."

"But!" He paused, then cried out,

I never will assent to any scheme that will operate a dissolution of
the Union or any measure which may lead to it. . . . The Union is the
anchor of our political salvation, and I will assent to the lopping of
this limb [he raised his right arm] before I assent to the dissolution
of the Union.[42]

George Mason's face turned red with anger at Randolph's unmistakable mockery of Mason's dramatic refusal to sign the constitution
in Philadelphia.

Randolph then looked at Patrick Henry, who blanched with anger as the governor continued, "I shall now follow the honorable
gentleman in his enquiry," he continued in tones that now mocked
Henry. "The honorable gentleman . . . inquires why we assumed the
language of 'We, the People.' I ask, 'Why not?' The government is
for the people. . . . Is it unfair? Is it unjust? I take this to be one

of the least and most trivial objections that will be made to the Constitution."[43]

As Henry's eyes bulged red with rage, Randolph shocked the convention by abruptly switching political allegiance:

> In the whole of this business, I have acted in the strictest obedience to my conscience, in discharging what I conceive to be my duty to my country. I refused my signature . . . I would still refuse; but as I think that those eight states which have adopted the constitution will not recede, I am a friend to the Union.[44]

Randolph's speech left the entire hall in stunned silence— Federalists as well as Antifederalists. It left Henry and Mason irate. When Richard Henry Lee learned of the governor's defection, he urged Patrick Henry to respond forcefully.

Henry shot to his feet to do just that, crying out that the existing Confederation of American States deserved "the highest encomium: It carried us through a long and dangerous war: It rendered us victorious in that bloody conflict with a powerful nation: It has secured us territory greater than any European monarch possesses.

"Consider what you are about to do before you part with this Government," he thundered.[45]

In arguing for perpetuation of the Confederation, Henry cited Switzerland as proof that "we might be in amicable alliance with those states without adopting this constitution. Switzerland is a confederacy . . . of dissimilar governments . . . that has stood upwards of four hundred years. . . . They have braved all the power of France and Germany. . . . In this vicinity of powerful and ambitious monarchs, they have retained their independence, republican simplicity, and valor."[46]

He went on to cite Richard Henry Lee's warning in *Letters from the Federal Farmer to the Republican* that the proposed constitution would give the American government power to send troops into any state to enforce federal laws. The same power in the hands of Parliament, he reminded the convention, had created the Intolerable Acts, with the cruel Boston Port Bill, the Quebec Act, and the Quartering Act, which together had provoked the Revolutionary War.

Henry predicted the constitution would create "a great and mighty president with . . . the powers of a king" and give Congress the power of "unlimited . . . direct taxation" and powers "to counteract and suspend" state laws. "I am not well versed in history," he argued, "but I will submit to your recollection whether liberty has been destroyed most often by the licentiousness of the people or by the tyranny of rulers? I imagine, sir, you will find the balance on the side of tyranny."

Henry repeated Richard Henry Lee's demands for a bill of rights and other amendments to the constitution prior to ratification.

By the time he closed his speech, Henry had held the floor for seven hours.

James Madison, meanwhile, had sidled between convention members, approaching the most moderate of the Antifederalists and pledging that with the help of George Washington he would win passage of Richard Henry Lee's bill of rights in the First Congress if they would now switch their votes in favor of ratification. They did, and before the convention ended, Madison succeeded in organizing an eighty-nine to seventy-nine vote in favor of ratification, allowing Virginia to become what delegates believed was the decisive ninth state to ratify the Constitution. In fact, New Hampshire had ratified the Constitution several days earlier, making Virginia the tenth state to ratify.

Although Patrick Henry made a show of publicly accepting the decision of the convention, George Mason and his "Republicans" stormed out of the hall, intent on upsetting the convention's decision by force if necessary. When Richard Henry Lee learned of the ratification vote, he expressed disbelief, predicting that the result—"a majority of ten only out of near two hundred"—had determined the fate of the nation and doomed it to failure.

"'Tis really astonishing," Richard Henry Lee sighed in disbelief, "that the same people who have just emerged from a long and cruel war in the defense of liberty should now agree to fix an elective despotism upon themselves and their posterity. . . . Nor does it augur well for the prosperity of the new government unless the wisdom and goodness of those who first act under this system shall take effective measures for introducing the requisite amendments."[47]

The Virginia convention's vote for ratification elated George Washington. "It is with great satisfaction," he told a group of supporters gathered in celebration at "a sumptuous dinner" at Wise Tavern in Alexandria, "I have it now in my power to inform you . . . that the delegates of Virginia adopted the Constitution. . . . In consequence of some conciliatory conduct and recommendatory amendments, a happy acquiescence . . . is likely to terminate the business in as favorable a manner as could possibly be expected."[48]

In Richmond, however, George Mason and his Antifederalist delegates continued shouting Patrick Henry slogans of '76— "Liberty or Death" and "We must fight!" Armed and angry, they gathered at a nearby tavern and prepared to return to the convention site and burn all records of the ratification vote.

CHAPTER 12

His Majesty the President

TWELVE YEARS HAD ELAPSED SINCE PATRICK HENRY HAD STOOD in St. John's Church in Richmond, Virginia, to cry out for liberty or death and inspire Washington, Lee, and other Founding Fathers to take up arms against Britain. In 1775 he had inspired his countrymen to go to war by crying out "We must fight!" Now he found himself in the incongruous position of trying to inspire them to accept peace.

"I will be a peaceable citizen!" he told the Antifederalists. "My head, my hand, my heart shall be at liberty to retrieve the loss of liberty and remove the defects of that system in a constitutional way. I wish not to go to violence, but will wait . . . patiently . . . in expectation of seeing this government changed so as to be compatible with the safety, liberty, and happiness of the people."[1]

Richard Henry Lee felt much the same way, but rather than stand aside as he had during the writing and ratification of the Constitution, he determined to act by capturing a seat in the new Congress and working to implement Article V:

The Congress, whenever two thirds of both houses shall deem it necessary, shall propose amendments to this Constitution, or, on the application of the legislatures of two thirds of the several states, shall call a convention for proposing amendments, which, in either case, shall be valid to all intents and purposes.[2]

Lee decided to forego a grueling campaign for popular election to the House of Representatives, where one vote among fifty-nine would count for little. Instead, he chose to ask the state legislature to appoint him to the US Senate, where his vote—and voice—would have more impact as one of twenty-six members (twenty-seven in the event of a tie).

Washington grew alarmed at Lee's appointment, fearing that he and Patrick Henry were at least discussing—if not plotting—to overthrow the new government.

"That some of the leading characters among the opponents of the proposed government have not laid aside their ideas of obtaining great and essential changes . . . may be collected from their public speeches," Washington warned James McHenry, a courageous Revolutionary War physician and a Maryland signer of the Constitution. "A considerable effort will be made to procure the election of Antifederalists in order to . . . undo all that has been done. . . . I earnestly pray that the Omnipotent Being who hath not deserted the cause of America in the hour of its extremest hazard will never yield so fair a heritage of freedom a prey to Anarchy or Despotism."[3]

Although George Washington was unquestionably a national hero and a vast majority of the people would have voted for him to be their first President, the vast majority did not get the chance. As Patrick Henry had charged, "we, the people" had not given the framers of the Constitution authorization to use their name; the framers had simply proclaimed themselves "We, the people" and repeated the charade in electing the first President. In fact, the framers had made certain that the people had as little say in the final tally for President as they had had in the writing of the Constitution.

Of 2.4 million free men and women in America, only 1.65 per-cent actually voted—43,782 white men. Indeed, only six states al-lowed any popular voting—all of it limited to property owners. Three states did not participate in the presidential election. New York's legislature had deadlocked over ratification of the Constitution and held no vote. North Carolina had not yet ratified the Constitu-tion and, therefore, held no vote. And Rhode Island had rejected the Constitution and remained an independent state. Four states—Connecticut, Georgia, New Jersey, and South Carolina—allowed no popular vote, leaving the voting for electors to state legislatures.

In the end only the propertied citizens of Delaware (685), Mary-land (7,732), Massachusetts (17,740), New Hampshire (5,909), Pennsylvania (7,383), and Virginia (4,333) voted for the President—a total of 43,782 people in a population of 3.0 million, or, stated another way, a population of 2.4 million free people and 600,000 slaves. The election results outraged Richard Henry Lee and other Virginia anti-federalists, who called in vain for another constitutional convention.

On October 20 Virginia's legislature elected Richard Henry Lee and a second Antifederalist, William Grayson, to the powerful US Senate and crushed the senatorial ambitions of Federalist James Madison.

The first Senate was divided into three groups, each with different terms of service: one-third would serve two years, a second one-third four years, and the remainder six years, thus beginning the process of staggered elections that would allow the states to elect one-third of the Senate every two years. Lee won appointment for four years and rode to New York determined to amend the Constitution with a bill of rights and to reshape the new government to ensure individual liberties and state control of internal affairs. As written, the Consti-tution gave him ample opportunity to do both.

Meanwhile James Madison, having lost his bid for a Senate seat, declared for the House of Representatives instead and won a seat by a large majority in the district including and surrounding his father's huge plantation—a pocket borough of sorts. He joined ten other

28. Virginia's James Madison stunned George Washington after yielding to antifederalist demands for a bill of rights in exchange for their agreement to ratify the Constitution.

Virginia representatives in the House, most of them Antifederalist supporters of Richard Henry Lee. A former member of the Confederation Congress and a key figure at the Constitutional Convention, the Princeton-educated Madison was a small man, five-feet-two by some estimates, and so thin and shy at times that he all but disappeared into his suit in a crowded room. It was easy to ignore him. Although Virginians constituted the largest delegation in the new House of Representatives, irate Federalists from other states shunned Madison as a turncoat for pledging to work for passage of a bill of rights. Even some moderates thought him disingenuous.

Those who knew him well, however, saw Madison's shift as a courageous political gesture aimed at reconciling legitimate differences between two groups of patriotic Americans. Although

Antifederalists led by Richard Henry Lee and Patrick Henry represented a popular majority, they had had almost no support in the overwhelmingly Federalist Confederation Congress when they called for a second constitutional convention to rewrite—or scrap—the existing document and prevent a new government from taking office.

By supporting Richard Henry Lee's most important demands for a bill of rights, however, Madison had extended a hand of compromise to Lee and other moderate Antifederalists and effectively separated them from radicals who sought to emasculate the new federal government. With Washington's reluctant approval, Madison predicted that "amendments . . . may serve the double purpose of satisfying the minds of well-meaning opponents, and of providing additional guards in favor of liberty."[4]

When Richard Henry Lee had first entered the Senate he expected to step into the same leadership role he had held in the Continental Congress—more so when he saw John Adams in the president's chair. Together they had elevated Washington to prominence as commander-in-chief of the Continental Army. Both Lee and Adams now looked forward to working together again.

In shaping a new government and giving definition to the vaguely defined executive and judiciary branches, the First Congress divided along the same fault lines as had delegates at the Constitutional Convention. Lee and the Antifederalist minority fought to preserve as much state sovereignty as possible, and Washington's Federalist majority was as intent on empowering the federal government and preventing the congressional stalemates that had almost cost them the war.

Twenty members of the First Congress—nine of fifty-nine in the House and eleven of twenty-two senators—had attended the Constitutional Convention and intended maintaining their positions in Congress. As they had at the Constitutional Convention, America's wealthiest white males made up almost the entirety of Congress, with the owners of the largest southern plantations representing the South.

Although pro-ratification Federalists had won a significant majority of seats in both houses—fifty of the fifty-nine House seats and
eighteen of the twenty-two Senate seats—they represented but a minority of the American people—namely, those who met each state's
property qualifications for voting—sometimes as much as $1 million
in today's currency. In their effort to ensure majority rule, they had
actually created rule by minority—the very oligarchy Richard Henry
Lee predicted the Constitution would produce.

Although most Americans who could not vote had opposed ratification of the Constitution because of its failure to guarantee individual rights and popular voting, Lee recognized the futility of
moving for a second constitutional convention in a Senate dominated by Federalists.

It was not until April 20—six weeks after the scheduled opening of Congress—that John Adams completed a week-long journey
from his Massachusetts home and crossed the Harlem River to the
northern end of Manhattan Island.

The next morning the Senate's president pro tempore greeted him
at the door of Federal Hall, led him up the flight of stairs, and escorted him into the Senate chamber to his chair, where he assumed
the presidency of that body without ceremony. Although the Constitution required the incoming President to take a specific oath, it
required no comparable commitment by the vice president. His election automatically installed him in office.

After calling the Senate to order, Adams, as presiding officer, immediately threw off conventional procedural restraints and pressed
the Senate to consider as one of its first orders of business what he
deemed the momentous question of how to address the President.
Infatuated by the pomp and ceremony of European courts he had
visited as an American minister during the Revolutionary War, he
suggested "Your Highness" or "Your Most Benign Highness" as appropriate titles for the President. A few senators protested Adams's
blatant violation of customary procedures by initiating and even in-
truding in a debate instead of remaining an impartial moderator. To

29. *French architect Pierre Charles l'Enfant transformed New York's City Hall into Federal Hall, the nation's most stunning public building at the time. Standing on Wall Street at the end of Broad Street, it featured a two-tiered portico that hosted the inauguration of George Washington as the nation's first President.*

restore their bond of Revolutionary War days, Richard Henry Lee immediately came to Adams's support.

Although the debate that followed seemed ridiculous to some, Lee's enemies—Robert Morris and Oliver Ellsworth—charged that Lee was flattering Adams to gain control of the Senate. Whatever his motives, Lee nonetheless agreed that throughout history "all the world, civilized and savage, called for the use of titles," while Adams argued that "the principles of government are to be seen in every scene of human life. There is no person and no society to whom forms and titles are indifferent. . . . Family titles are necessary to family government; colonial titles were indispensable to colonial government, and we shall find national titles essential to national government."[5]

In the comedy that followed, twenty-two of America's richest and most powerful statesmen responded with long, pompous arguments extoling the propriety of "His Exalted Highness," "His Elective Highness," "Most Illustrious and Excellent President," and even "His Majesty the President." When one senator proposed calling the President "George"—a wag among them responded, "Why not George IV?" Others were less oblique, stating that the President was neither a king nor an emperor and entitled to no title but plain "George." Faced with an impasse, Adams suggested naming a special committee to resolve differences. He warned that the United States would earn "the contempt, the scorn and the derision" of Europe's monarchies if Congress persisted in calling America's national leader "General" or "President."

"You may depend on another thing," Adams warned the Federalists, "the state government will always be uppermost in America in the minds of our own people till you give a superior title to your first national magistrate."[6]

After several more days of debate, one senator stunned his colleagues with a reminder that the Constitution many of them had helped write prohibited titles. The Senate had no choice but to adopt the republican simplicity of "Mr. President" as the official title with which to address George Washington and his presidential successors.

In contrast to the Swiftian proceedings in the Senate, Congressman James Madison took firm command of the House of Representatives, which was dealing with the nation's disastrous finances. Madison proposed a tariff law with duties of 7 to 8 percent on a wide range of imports. Ironically, the imports he wanted to subject to higher duties included tea and molasses—the very ones Parliament had sought to tax in 1773, provoking the Boston Tea Party.

Congressmen from New England—the biggest importer of both commodities—howled at the proposal. Madison reminded them that Americans had not objected to British *taxes* on molasses and tea but to their imposition by a legislative body in which Americans were not represented. "It was the principle upon which that tax was laid," he insisted, "that made them unpopular under the British government."[7]

As mandated by the Constitution, Madison then moved to establish executive departments—the Department of Foreign Affairs on July 27 (renamed "State" two months later), Department of War on August 7, and the Department of Treasury on August 28. The departments immediately became centers of controversy when Richard Henry Lee led the Senate in seeking control over department heads by having them serve indefinitely unless removed for cause by congressional impeachment. In effect, department heads would serve independently of the President, beholden only to Congress.

"It will nurse faction," Federalist Representative Fisher Ames of Massachusetts warned the Congress. "It is tempting the Senate with forbidden fruit. It ought not to be possible for a branch of the legislature even to hope for a share of the executive power, for they may be tempted to increase it."[8] Richard Henry Lee and other opponents of presidential power fired back, declaring, "The power of creating offices is given to the legislature," Lee insisted. "Under this general grant, the legislature have it under their supreme decision to determine the whole organization, to affix its tenure, and declare the control."[9]

Federalist Ames again leaped to the President's defense, with a barrage of references to the Constitution:

> The executive powers are delegated to the president. The only bond between him and those he employs is the confidence he has in their integrity and talents. When that confidence ceases, the principal ought to have the power to remove those whom he can no longer trust with safety.[10]

But Lee's Antifederalists refused to cede until Virginia's James Madison, Washington's principal ally in the House, lured the needed swing votes in Washington's favor. He did so with a stark warning that failure to subject department heads to presidential authority

would leave the presidency a ceremonial post and allow the secre-
taries of State, War, and Treasury—all of them appointees rather
than elected officials—to form a powerful triumvirate with all but
unchecked powers over the nation's revenues and military.

In the Senate, however, Richard Henry Lee shot to his feet to
charge that presidential power to remove executives at will all but
emasculated the Senate, leaving it with no power over executive appointments. Lee's Senate colleague from Virginia William Grayson
echoed Lee's warning, adding, "The matter predicted by Mr. [Pat-
rick] Henry is now coming to pass: consolidation of the new government. And the first attempt will be to destroy the Senate, as they are
the representatives of the state legislatures."[11]

Washington responded angrily, meeting privately with Vice
President Adams and demanding full control of every executive
department, including the right to dismiss department heads without cause. If Congress refused to relegate full control over executive
functions to the President, he hinted he might resign.

Although the House voted for the President's right to remove
department heads without Senate consent, the Senate vote resulted
in a tie. For the first time Vice President Adams now assumed a
role in shaping the new American government and cast the deciding
vote. As Lee had predicted, the vote of one man decided the fate
of 3 million people without their consent. Lee had hoped that by
allying himself with Adams on the question of titles, the two would
form the same, enduring bloc that had marked their tenure in the
Continental Congress, but he was mistaken.

Adams used his constitutional prerogative to vote in favor of the
President, breaking the Senate tie vote and ending a nearly twenty-
year-old political alliance with Richard Henry Lee—an alliance that
had, until then, knit conflicting interests of North and South. The
Adams vote so strengthened presidential powers that radical Antifederalists all but threatened James Madison with bodily harm if he
did not immediately live up to his pledge to add a bill of rights to the
Constitution. Five states threatened to secede, and powerful political

leaders such as Patrick Henry and New York governor George Clinton prepared to call for a second constitutional convention to replace the existing document if Madison did not act.

Madison responded by moving to amend the Constitution with "a declaration of the rights of the people" to ensure "the tranquility of the public mind, and the stability of the government."[12] Members then proposed almost one hundred amendments, including most of those from Lee's *Letters from the Federal Farmer*. Madison reduced them to seventeen. On September 25 Congress passed twelve, and President Washington sent them to the states for ratification. Of these, the states approved ten, which became part of the Constitution on December 15, 1791.

"The Amendments to the Constitution have at length passed the Senate with difficulty, after being much mutilated and enfeebled," Richard Henry Lee complained to his brother Francis. "It is very clear, I think, that a government very different from a free one will take place ere many years are passed."[13]

The day after writing to his brother, Richard Henry wrote to Patrick Henry, warning that the amendments "as they came from the House of Representatives were far short of the wishes of our [Virginia ratification] convention . . . they are certainly much weakened. . . . Nothing on my part was left undone to prevent this.

> We might as well have attempted to move Mount Atlas on our shoulders. . . . The great points of free election, jury trial in criminal cases, and the unlimited rights of taxation, and standing armies remain as they were. The most essential danger . . . arises . . . from its tendency to a consolidated government instead of a union of confederated states. The history of the world and reason concur in proving that so extensive a territory as the United States never was nor can be governed in freedom under the former idea.[14]

Despite his reservations, Richard Henry and William Grayson, the other Antifederalist senator from Virginia, transmitted the amendments to the Virginia state legislature for ratification, but noted, "how unfortunate we have been in this business.

> It is impossible for us not to see the necessary tendency to consolidated empire in the . . . Constitution if no further amended than now proposed. And it is equally impossible for us not to be apprehensive for civil liberty when we know no instance in . . . history that show a people ruled in freedom when subject to an undivided government and inhabiting a territory so extensive as that of the United States. The impracticability . . . of carrying representation sufficiently near to the people for procuring their confidence and consequent obedience compels resort to . . . great force and excessive power in government.[15]

Two weeks after agreeing to the amendments, Congress fulfilled the last of its inaugural constitutional obligations by passing the Federal Judiciary Act of 1789. The Act created a federal judiciary with a Supreme Court, a circuit-court system, and fifteen federal district courts—one in each state, plus one each in the districts of Maine and Kentucky, which would soon become states. Although weary of his losing confrontations with Federalists, Richard Henry Lee nonetheless objected to establishing courts that could rule without juries. He warned that the circuit court system would undermine the jurisdiction of state courts and their juries and eventually make them superfluous. As a sop to Richard Henry Lee and the Senate Antifederalists, Washington agreed to consult senators on judicial appointments and forego making nominations to which they objected. The precedent of "senatorial courtesy" that he established continues to this day.

The growing enmity between Richard Henry Lee and the President eased somewhat after the first session of Congress ended. Both men returned to their plantations on the Northern Neck—Washington to Mount Vernon and Lee to Chantilly—and reunited a few weeks later at the successive weddings of Lee's two daughters

Mary and Hannah to Washington's cousin William Augustine Washington and his nephew Corbin Washington.

Overcome by illness the following winter, however, Richard Henry Lee did not reclaim his Senate seat in New York until May. By then his fellow senator from Virginia, William Grayson, had died. It proved a lonely session for Lee for multiple reasons. An influenza epidemic swept through New York, sending him along with many Senate colleagues to the solitary confinement of their hotel bedrooms, isolating them from their friends and social life. Treasury Secretary Alexander Hamilton, however, sent them documents that kept them occupied.

Before recessing the previous autumn, Congress had charged Hamilton with determining the nation's exact debt. After digging through more than a decade of federal and state government spending records, Hamilton calculated that the newborn US government had inherited foreign debts of just over $11.7 million and domestic debts of $42.4 million. In addition to federal government debts, the states collectively owed about $25 million—$21.5 million of it from the Revolutionary War.

Arguing that the Revolution had been a national enterprise, Hamilton proposed that the national government assume all state war debts, thus putting states on a sound financial footing but tying them more tightly to federal controls. High state property taxes, Hamilton argued, lay behind Shays's rebellion and the unrest in the farmlands. By assuming state debts, the federal government would allow states to reduce property taxes—and end the political, social, and economic turmoil that had resulted from increasing those taxes.

The plan angered Richard Henry Lee and other Antifederalists, who saw no reason why states like Virginia, which had repaid all its debts, should share the burden of debts of fiscally irresponsible states. Even James Madison, the Antifederalist-turned-Federalist ally of the President, objected. Washington agreed with Hamilton: "The cause in which the expenses of the war were incurred was a common cause," the President affirmed. "The states in Congress declared it so at the beginning and pledged themselves to stand by each other. If then some states were harder pressed than others . . . it is but reasonable . . . that an allowance ought to be made them."[16]

To cover costs of assuming state debts, Hamilton proposed a new 25 percent federal tax on liquor distillers. Richard Henry Lee immediately spoke out against it, saying, it was too reminiscent of the tea tax that had provoked the revolution, and in addition, it would almost certainly provoke smuggling and associated crime. In any case, he added, it would not generate nearly enough money to reduce the huge federal government debt from the war.

Hamilton had an answer on each count, however. He said the whiskey tax would win widespread support from antiliquor churchgoers and physicians. Consumers, moreover, would hardly notice the tax, which would be hidden in the price of the finished product—much like import duties. Moreover, the tax would be but one part of Hamilton's economic program to wipe out the national debt and restore government credit. While generating an immediate flow of revenue with the whiskey tax to cover current spending, Hamilton intended to gradually redeem all outstanding government paper at *face* value with a combination of new government paper *plus* options to buy government lands in the western wilderness at substantial discounts. The new paper would carry a lower face value than the paper it replaced but would make up the difference with discounted options for "real" estate of unquestioned value.

The property component would establish faith in the government's ability to repay the new certificates because the government owned all-but-unlimited millions of acres of land, and in an agrarian nation land was far more valuable than money. Paper currency could be spent only once; its value was finite, and, once spent, it was gone. The value of land, however, seemed infinite, yielding endless wealth in crops, timber, pelts, furs, and minerals, year after year—over and above the intrinsic value of the land itself. Americans could live off the land indefinitely and trade the commodities it produced; they could do next to nothing with paper money and only guess its value each time they approached the market to buy goods.

To further public faith in the new securities and the government's financial strength, Hamilton proposed establishing a "sinking fund," or reserve account, into which he would deposit a fixed percentage of government revenues each year to ensure repayment of government debts. In addition, he suggested creating a Bank of the United States—similar to the Bank of England—as the government's own bank to buy and sell government bonds and provide ready cash to the government when spending exceeded revenues. If the economy boomed, as Hamilton hoped it would, government income would not only cover current expenses but pay interest on the national debt, retire the debt itself, put federal government finances on a sound foundation, and calm the nation's financial markets while stimulating foreign trade.

Again, Richard Henry Lee stood in opposition to what he saw as a gradual expansion of central government powers and inevitable restriction of state and individual rights. Banking, he asserted sharply, was not a government function.

"Banks are capable of great abuses," he told James Monroe, who had replaced William Grayson as Virginia's second senator, "and . . . such abuses practiced by government leave injured individuals without redress." Lee referred Monroe to Adam Smith's *The Wealth of Nations*, which had only been published in 1776 but provided "very weighty reasons . . . why government should not trade. Banking is a kind of traffic that tempts by interest to abuse. The reasons assigned by that sensible author against the government of England being so engaged must be seen by every person experienced in American affairs to apply here with very increased force."[17]

With Madison rebelling against the Washington administration, the diminutive Virginian led his home-state colleagues and other southern congressmen in rejecting Hamilton's assumption plan, thirty-one to twenty-nine, leaving Hamilton three votes short of victory.

Hamilton did not surrender, however, turning for help to his fellow cabinet member, Secretary of State Thomas Jefferson of Virginia—James Madison's mentor. Jefferson suggested a startling political trade to win the three votes needed to pass Hamilton's assumption scheme.

At the time Congress was considering sites for a permanent federal capital. No less a figure than the President himself, along with every southern congressman and senator—including Richard Henry Lee—despised the long, difficult ride north to New York to conduct the nation's business. Jefferson suggested that if Hamilton convinced enough northern delegates to support situating the new federal city midway between North and South, Madison might switch his own vote and gather the two additional southern votes needed to pass the assumption measure. Hamilton agreed, and Jefferson hosted a quiet, private dinner for the three of them—Hamilton, Madison, and Jefferson. After feasting on Jefferson's usual array of elegant food and fine French wines, Madison and Hamilton agreed to situate the new federal capital on a tract of marshland along the Potomac River, opposite Alexandria, Virginia.

Madison subsequently met with Richard Henry Lee to describe the political arrangement he had made with Hamilton. Realizing there was nothing he could now do to block assumption, Lee bowed to the inevitable and embraced the possible, shocking Antifederalists by remaining seated, immobile, and expressionless when an Antifederalist senator moved to block Hamilton's plan. Although assumption would become the law of the land, Lee reasoned, moving the federal capital southward would make it more convenient for southern congressmen to attend Congress and ensure them a greater voice in national affairs than they had had in New York.

On July 10, 1790, with Madison rallying the necessary votes, the House voted thirty-two to twenty-nine to build a new federal capital on a ten-mile-square area along the Potomac River, opposite Alexandria, Virginia, and charged President Washington with defining the exact boundaries. To further facilitate southern members, Congress named Philadelphia the temporary capital effective in December. Two weeks later it voted Hamilton's assumption plan into law. In February 1791 Congress created the Bank of the United States—a predecessor institution of today's Federal Reserve Bank—and Richard Henry Lee returned to Virginia and his home and family at Chantilly, where he remained until autumn, an unhappy victim of a political compromise that all but ended antifederalism as a national political force for the foreseeable future.

Still feeling the aftereffects of his bout with influenza, he sought nothing but rest and tranquility. Although he tried returning to Congress in the fall, his carriage overturned, tossing the fifty-eight-year-old Patriot and his traveling companions onto the road, bruising them all badly and preventing Lee's return to Congress until December 1791. He arrived in time to join the end of a heated debate on congressional representation. Using the usual voting advantages that came with their proximity to the capital, northerners moved to increase the constitutionally designated number of people represented by each member of the House from 30,000 to 33,000. Still weak from his carriage accident, Richard Henry Lee struggled to his feet to oppose the measure, charging it would "abridge the representation of the South and add to that of the North"—which, of course, was what its northern proponents had intended.[18] Although Congress passed the measure, President Washington—a good Virginian, after all—vetoed the bill, and the northerners in Congress failed to muster the two-thirds majority needed to override the veto.

Although two years younger than Richard Henry Lee, Vice President Adams was as tired—even more so than Lee—with capital life. He was bored to tears, all but sobbing, "My country has in its wisdom contrived for me the most insignificant office that ever the invention of man contrived or his imagination conceived."[19] Once one of the most active Patriots in the American Revolution, he now did nothing in the new American republic but sit in the US Senate and

listen in silence to endless debates, unable under the rules to participate and consigned to voting only in the unlikely event of a tie. His
other constitutional obligation was to wait—again in silence—for
the unlikely death of the President.

After the vote over House representation, Adams looked at the
agenda and, finding nothing of importance awaiting Senate action,
he told senators he would take a month's leave of absence. By then
Richard Henry Lee had let enough colleagues know that the current
session would be his last, and with Adams's departure, the Senate—
Federalists and Antifederalists alike—honored Lee by electing him
president pro tempore.

When he left the capital and returned to Chantilly, his four-year
term came to an end, but Virginia's legislature prepared to reelect him
to succeed himself with a six-year term. He wrote to the speakers of
both state houses, saying he had "grown gray in the service of my country" and had had enough. He expressed the "deepest sense of gratitude
and obligation for the good opinion" of the legislature, adding,

> It is not in my power to convey to you an adequate idea of the regret
> I feel at being compelled by the feeble state of my health to retire
> from the service of my country. The strong sense that I entertain of
> public duty, joined to a deep feeling of gratitude for the reiterated
> goodness of the General Assembly to me, would render the toils of
> public business a pleasure . . . were I not prevented by infirmities
> that can only be relieved by a quiet retirement.[20]

The Virginia Senate responded with a unanimous resolution recognizing that "he hath conspicuously shone forth as a statesman and
patriot" and wishing that "he may close the evening of a life in . . .
uninterrupted happiness."[21] In the US Senate Pennsylvania's William Maclay, who usually spewed nothing but vitriol at everyone in
government, including George Washington, conceded that Richard
Henry Lee was "a man of clear head . . . who gave independence to
America."[22]

Although he did his best to use his better moments productively, the "feeble state" of Richard Henry Lee's health persisted well into the new year. In December 1792 his beloved younger brother Arthur died, just shy of fifty-two. He had never married and had no children. After his return from Europe in 1781 he had won election to the Virginia Assembly and subsequently to the Continental Congress, where he grew obsessed with exposing Pennsylvania delegate Robert Morris as a wartime profiteer.

Congress had appointed Morris superintendent of Finance in February 1781, as Washington began preparing his forces for the decisive Virginia campaign. Morris had accepted commissions on transactions his firm of Morris and Willing had negotiated with European arms dealers through Silas Deane, their silent partner in Paris. Although a clear violation of the emoluments clause of the Constitution, so many members of Congress and high-level military officers other than Washington had reaped similar rewards while serving in government that Congress all but ignored Arthur Lee's charges. At $6 pay per day (less than $20 in today's dollars), few delegates to Congress could afford not to extract a percentage of the funds they disbursed to government suppliers.[*]

Arthur Lee retired from public service after ratification of the Constitution and led the life of a bachelor farmer until his death in December 1792. His and Richard Henry Lee's younger brother William would die three years later in 1795 at the age of fifty-six. William's wife had predeceased him, and, blind by then, he sent his two young daughters to live with his brother Francis Lightfoot Lee and his wife, who had no children of their own. William's son remained to care for his father and run their farm.

---

[*]Although Morris would later win election as one of Pennsylvania's first two senators under the Constitution, the panic of 1796–1797 would wipe out the value of his land speculations and send him to debtor's prison for three years—too late for Arthur Lee to savor victory. He and his brothers had all died by then.

In retirement Richard Henry Lee spent as much time as possible tutoring and mentoring his two youngest boys, thirteen-year-old Cassius and ten-year-old Francis. He kept as informed as possible about current events, but unlike many retired public officials of his day, he wrote few letters to old friends from his days in government. With one exception—President George Washington—he directed his letters only to relatives, especially nieces and nephews in need of guidance.

A continent-wide war had erupted in Europe. France had declared war on Britain, Holland, Prussia, Spain, and Sardinia and demanded that the Washington administration reciprocate for French aid during the Revolutionary War by sending American troops to support France in the European conflict. Washington responded with a Presidential Proclamation of Neutrality on April 23, 1793, stating, that "the duty and interest of the United States require that they should adopt a conduct friendly and impartial toward the [warring] powers."[23]

Washington's proclamation—the first presidential proclamation in American history—sparked political turmoil across the United States, pitting Anglophiles, whose commercial and financial interests depended on British trade, against Francophiles, who had fought alongside French soldiers in the Revolutionary War. With members of his own cabinet divided on the issue, Washington was grateful for any political support he could find.

"The success and happiness of the United States is our care," Richard Henry Lee wrote to comfort the President, "and if the nations of Europe approve war, we surely may be permitted to cultivate the arts of peace. . . . It is really a happiness to reflect that if war should befall us, our government will not promote it, but give cause to all who venerate humanity to revere the rulers here."[24]

In what may have been the last letter Richard Henry Lee ever wrote,* he turned full circle politically, acknowledging the necessity

---

*There may well have been others, but this is the last authenticated letter known to have survived his death and published with his other letters in the books listed in the Notes and Bibliography of this book.

and wisdom of unilateral action by the chief executive of the federal government, unchecked by either federal legislators or state governments. It was a remarkable political change of heart—one with political implications that continue to be felt in America to this day in the unchecked stream of executive orders effectively legislating and restricting the rights of Americans without participation by Congress or the consent of the people.

During his tenure in government Richard Henry Lee had led those Founding Fathers who fought for state sovereignty and local control in almost every political sector, leaving a slim federal government with carefully limited powers. Lee, Patrick Henry, and their Antifederalist supporters had argued passionately against ratification of the Constitution and enhancement of federal power.

The anarchy during the years of the loose-knit Confederation that preceded the Constitutional Convention, however, had changed many minds. The states—and, indeed, the American people—proved themselves incapable of governing themselves and living peacefully together, and an impotent Confederation government had been incapable of resolving interstate conflicts or mounting a successful defense against foreign enemies.

As Richard Henry Lee and Patrick Henry—and, later, Thomas Jefferson—recognized the dangers of unrestricted antifederalism to national security in a nation as large as the United States, they gradually adopted federalist positions, beginning with Lee's startling support for Washington's Neutrality Proclamation.

The struggle between the Federalist and Antifederalist successors would heat up again and again, reaching a climax of sorts with the outbreak of the Civil War and continuing in various forms long after. To a certain extent it continues to this day as those who oppose federal interference in state and local political affairs—the heirs to antifederalism—take their arguments into court or, in extreme cases, arm themselves, seize federal properties, and challenge federal law enforcement authorities at gunpoint. Today's heirs to federalism, on the other hand, argue that only federal authorities have the will, the power, and the corruption-free law-enforcement operatives to protect individual rights and combat abuses by and endemic corruption of state and local officials.

Before the Founding Fathers died, however, even the staunchest Federalists and Antifederalists acknowledged at least some defects in their own political philosophies and recognized some benefits of their opponents' philosophies. So when President Washington ignored Congress in 1793 and usurped executive powers by issuing a Presidential Proclamation of Neutrality with the force of law, Richard Henry Lee—once the ardent foe of presidential power—sent the President his support in the last political act of his life.

On April 15, 1794, Washington replied to Lee, thanking him for supporting the controversial proclamation and adding, "I learn with regret that your health has continued bad ever since I last had the pleasure of seeing you. Warm weather I hope will restore it: if my wishes could be of any avail you assuredly would have them."[25]

On June 19, 1794, sixty-two-year-old Richard Henry Lee died at Chantilly. His family buried him at the Lee family graveyard not far from Stratford Hall. On his gravestone they inscribed a message that might have come from every living American at the time, "We cannot do without you."

Afterword

No bells tolled for Richard Henry Lee when he died. No processions filled the streets of American towns and cities; no celebrants extolled his life in stentorian eulogies. In fact, there were neither celebrants nor eulogies.

Only Richard Henry Lee's wife and adolescent sons looked on as slaves carried his plain wooden casket to its grave on a barren expanse of land the Lees called Burnt House Field. It was where Richard Henry Lee's father's first plantation home had stood until it burned to the ground in 1729. Along with the ashes of their ancestral home, generations of Lees had added remains of their family members and their slaves to the earth beneath the field and gave the graveyard its name.

After Richard Henry Lee's burial, his wife, Ann, and her two young boys, Cassius and Francis, abandoned their isolated home at Chantilly in favor of a smaller place in the populated community of Alexandria, Virginia. She died two years later, in 1796.

Richard Henry Lee's two oldest sons, Thomas and Ludwell, were practicing law by then and continued doing so the rest of their lives, with Thomas, an avid farmer, practicing in rural Virginia. Ludwell,

30. Richard Henry Lee's gravestone stands in the Lee Family graveyard called Burnt House Field, where his father's first home in Virginia stood before a fire reduced it to ashes.

the more ambitious of the two, entered politics, eventually winning election as Speaker of Virginia's State Senate.

Richard Henry's younger brother Francis Lightfoot Lee died three years after Richard Henry. Their sister Alice Lee remained in Philadelphia and died there in 1817 at the age of seventy-seven, all but ending the public service and associated fame of the Lee Family—with two notable exceptions. Richard Henry's first cousin, once removed, had already gained national attention as the heroic Major General Henry "Light-Horse Harry" Lee, who commanded a daring light-cavalry unit known as "Lee's Legion" in the Revolutionary War. Lee's troops helped win critical victories that recaptured the Carolinas from the British. Elected governor of Virginia in 1791, he led the troops that President Washington sent to Pittsburgh to crush the Whiskey Rebellion, also in 1791. Eight years later Henry Lee gained lasting fame for his eloquent eulogy that called the fallen Washington "first in war, first in peace, and first in the hearts of his countrymen."[1]

In 1831 his son Robert E. Lee married Mary Anna Custis, daughter of George Washington's step-grandson, George Washington Parke Custis. Together they lived in Arlington House, the magnificent Greek-revival mansion that stands today on a hill overlooking Arlington National Cemetery.

Thirty years after his marriage Robert E. Lee assumed command of the Confederate Army in a civil war aimed at fracturing the republic his illustrious father and great cousin had fought to create. He later became president of Washington and Lee College in Lexington, Virginia. Although the Lee Family line continues today, its many members are content to serve the nation in quiet ways, without the notoriety generated by their forebears.

Ironically, when Richard Henry Lee stepped off the national stage during his last years, he all but vanished into historical obscurity. Although first of America's Founding Fathers to proclaim American independence, he remains unknown to most Americans today—for a variety of reasons.

First, he lived in a home that no longer exists and had been too isolated to become a gathering place for national and world leaders. Chantilly stood on a lonely bluff overlooking the Potomac River, far from the nearest town. In contrast, Washington's Mount Vernon lay but a dozen miles from Alexandria—less than two hours on horseback. John Adams's home was near Boston, and Jefferson's aerie at Monticello commanded a full view of Charlottesville and the towering University of Virginia dome that he had designed and directed. While surviving family, friends, and admirers preserved the homes of these and other Founding Fathers, the departure of Lee's wife and two sons left Chantilly empty, untended, and deteriorating.

Visible and deserted at the top of a cliff, Chantilly was an easy target for British warships sailing up the Potomac River to destroy Washington, DC, during the War of 1812. A derelict by then, Chantilly fell victim to the elements and rotted away, vanishing into the wind off the Potomac River without leaving a trace.

Those who maintained and continue to maintain Mount Vernon, Monticello, and the Adams house in Massachusetts have preserved not just a collection of old houses but the memories and life stories of their primary residents. In addition, hagiographic biographies have added mythological deeds—Washington and his cherry tree, for example—that reinforce the national memory of all three men as larger-then-life heroes.

John Adams grumbled that the written history of the American Revolution would evolve into myth—"one continued lie . . . the essence of which will be that Dr. Franklin's electrical rod smote the Earth and out sprung General Washington—and thence forward these two conducted all the *Policy, Negotiations, Legislatures and Wars* [Adams's italics]. These underscored lines contain the whole fable, plot and catastrophe. . . . This is the fate of all nations. . . . No nation can adore more than one man at a time."[2]

Adams may well have been thinking of his friend Richard Henry Lee, for after the Federalists had won the struggle over ratification of the Constitution, they relegated most Antifederalists to historical obscurity. Although Thomas Jefferson and James Monroe began their political careers as Antifederalists, they quickly turned Federalist when presidential powers seduced them into imposing arbitrary, unilateral—and unconstitutional—acts that bypassed the states and other branches of the federal government. Recent presidents have made a common practice of using similarly unconstitutional powers, issuing executive orders to write their own laws and bypass Congress.

Among the great Antifederalists who stood alongside Richard Henry Lee in the battle against ratification, Patrick Henry's cry for liberty or death still earns universal recognition as the clarion call for American revolution. But most Americans either don't know or ignore his historic roles as Virginia's great first governor and courageous champion of antifederalism. Lost as well is Richard Henry Lee's role as The First Founding Father and originator of the Declaration of American Independence—a declaration that Congress adopted before Thomas Jefferson had put his pen to the document we celebrate today.

Purposely or not, Jefferson helped obscure the nation's memory of Richard Henry Lee. By the time Jefferson died in 1826, both Richard Henry Lee and Patrick Henry were long dead, and no other Antifederalists—indeed, no other Founding Fathers—had survived to challenge Jefferson's claim in the inscription he wrote for his own tombstone, declaring that he had been the sole author of the Declaration of Independence.

While Lee and Patrick Henry had lived both had earned Jefferson's malevolence by demanding Jefferson be censured for his failure as governor to defend Virginia against the British invasion in 1780. Lee's grandson, Richard H. Lee II, further tarnished Jefferson's name and incurred Jefferson's enmity for the Lees by asserting that Jefferson had written only a small part of the Declaration of Independence and "stole [the rest] from *Locke's Essays.*" Nonetheless, it is Jefferson's colossal statue that stands with a copy of the Declaration of Independence in his hand in the memorial that bears his name in Washington, DC. Nowhere to be found are the name and image of Richard Henry Lee, the nation's First Founding Father.

In what may be the most ironic warp of the national memory, the Lee family member whom Americans most remember today is not Richard Henry Lee but Robert E. Lee, who fought to divide the American people and split the nation asunder. Even Stratford Hall, the beautiful ancestral Lee family home and National Historic Landmark, all but ignores its importance as birthplace of Patriot Richard Henry Lee. Sadly, most visitors come instead to see the birthplace of the secessionist Robert E. Lee, who sought to shatter the union of American states that Richard Henry Lee, our First Founding Father, helped create.

Appendix A

The Leedstown, or Westmoreland, Resolves

Richard Henry Lee prepared and proposed the following articles on February 27,
1766, in Leedstown, Virginia, to the people of Westmoreland County. Called the
Leedstown or Westmoreland Resolves and signed by six Lees and four Washing-
tons, they were Virginia's first protest against taxation without representation
and were declared treasonous by the British government.

"Roused by danger and alarmed at attempts, foreign and domestic, to
reduce the people of this country to a state of abject and detestable slavery
by destroying that free and happy condition of government under which
they have hitherto lived,

We, who subscribe this paper, have associated and do bind ourselves
to each other, to God, and to our country, by the firmest ties that religion
and virtue can frame, most sacredly and punctually to stand by and with
our lives and fortunes, to support, maintain, and defend each other in the
observance and execution of these following articles—

FIRST: We declare all due allegiance and obedience to our lawful Sovereign, George the Third, King of Great Britain. And we determine to the
utmost of our power to preserve the laws, the peace and good order of this

Colony, as far as is consistent with the preservation of our Constitutional rights and liberty.

SECONDLY: As we know it to be the Birthright privilege of every British subject (and of the people of Virginia as being such) founded on Reason, Law, and Compact; that he cannot be legally tried, but by his peers; that he cannot be taxed, but by consent of a Parliament, in which he is represented by persons chosen by the people, and who themselves pay a part of the tax they impose on others. If, therefore, any person or persons shall attempt, by any action, or proceeding, to deprive this Colony of these fundamental rights, we will immediately regard him or them, as the most dangerous enemy of the community; and we will go to any extremity, not only to prevent the success of such attempts, but to stigmatize and punish the offender.

THIRDLY: As the Stamp Act does absolutely direct the property of the people to be taken from them without their consent expressed by their representatives and as in many cases it deprives the British American Subject of his right to trial by jury; we do determine, at every hazard, and paying no regard to danger or to death, we will exert every faculty, to prevent the execution of the said Stamp Act in any instance whatsoever within this Colony. And every abandoned wretch, who shall be so lost to virtue and public good, as wickedly to contribute to the introduction or fixture of the Stamp Act in this Colony, by using stamped paper, or by any other means, we will, with the utmost expedition, convince all such profligates that immediate danger and disgrace shall attend their prostitute purposes.

FOURTHLY: That the last article may most surely and effectually be executed, we engage to each other, that whenever it shall be known to any of this association, that any person is so conducting himself as to favor the introduction of the Stamp Act, that immediate notice shall be given to as many of the association as possible; and that every individual so informed, shall, with expedition, repair to a place of meeting to be appointed as near the scene of action as may be.

FIFTHLY: Each associator shall do his true endeavor to obtain as many signers to this association, as he possibly can.

SIXTHLY: If any attempt shall be made on the liberty or property of any associator for any action or thing to be done in consequence of this agreement, we do most solemnly bind ourselves by the sacred engagements above entered into, at the risk of our lives and fortunes, to restore such associate to his liberty and to protect him in the enjoyment of his property."

In testimony of the good faith with which we resolve to execute this association we have this 27th day of February 1766 in Virginia, put our hands and seals hereto.

Richard Henry Lee * Will. Robinson * Lewis Willis * Thos. Lud. Lee * Saml. Washington * Chas. Washington * Moore Fauntleroy * Francis Lightfoot Lee * Thomas Jones * Rodham Kenner * Spencer M. Ball * Richard Mitchell * Joseph Murdock * Richd. Parker * Spence Monroe * John Watts * Robt. Lovell * John Blagge * Charles Weeks * Willm. Booth * Geo. Turbeville * Alvin Moxley * Wm. Flood * John Ballatine, Jr. * William Lee * Thos. Chilton * Richard Buckner * Jos. Pierce * Will. Chilton * John Williams * William Sydnor * John Monroe * William Cocke * Willm. Grayson * Wm. Brockenbrough * Saml. Selden * Richd. Lee * Daniel Tibbs * Francis Thorn Suggett * Henry Francks * John Bland, Jr. * Jas. Emerson * Thos. Logan * Jo. Milliken * Ebenezer Fisher * Hancock Eustace * John Richards * Thos. Jett * Thos. Douglas * Max Robinson * John Orr

Appendix B

The Signers and the Declaration

31. John Trumbull's epic 1818 painting of the Founding Fathers signing the Declaration of Independence hangs in the Capitol Rotunda. Fourteen signers are missing because Trumbull could not find likenesses to copy, and he included six who did not sign. To identify each of the signers from Trumbull's badly drawn figures, see illustration 32 on page 270.

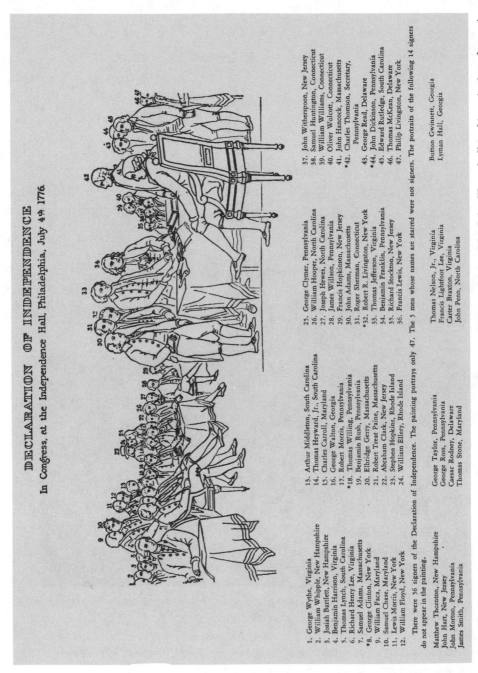

DECLARATION OF INDEPENDENCE

In Congress, at the Independence Hall, Philadelphia, July 4th, 1776.

1. George Wythe, Virginia
2. William Whipple, New Hampshire
3. Josiah Bartlett, New Hampshire
4. Benjamin Harrison, Virginia
5. Thomas Lynch, South Carolina
6. Richard Henry Lee, Virginia
7. Samuel Adams, Massachusetts
*8. George Clinton, New York
9. William Paca, Maryland
10. Samuel Chase, Maryland
11. Lewis Morris, New York
12. William Floyd, New York

There were 56 signers of the Declaration of Independence. The painting portrays only 47. The 5 men whose names are starred were not signers. The portraits of the following 14 signers do not appear in the painting.

Matthew Thornton, New Hampshire
John Hart, New Jersey
John Morton, Pennsylvania
James Smith, Pennsylvania

13. Arthur Middleton, South Carolina
14. Thomas Heyward, Jr., South Carolina
15. Charles Carroll, Maryland
16. George Walton, Georgia
17. Robert Morris, Pennsylvania
*18. Thomas Willing, Pennsylvania
19. Benjamin Rush, Pennsylvania
20. Elbridge Gerry, Massachusetts
21. Robert Treat Paine, Massachusetts
22. Abraham Clark, New Jersey
23. Stephen Hopkins, Rhode Island
24. William Ellery, Rhode Island

George Taylor, Pennsylvania
George Ross, Pennsylvania
Caesar Rodney, Delaware
Thomas Stone, Maryland

25. George Clymer, Pennsylvania
26. William Hooper, North Carolina
27. Joseph Hewes, North Carolina
28. James Willson, Pennsylvania
29. Francis Hopkinson, New Jersey
30. John Adams, Massachusetts
31. Roger Sherman, Connecticut
*32. Robert R. Livingston, New York
33. Thomas Jefferson, Virginia
34. Benjamin Franklin, Pennsylvania
35. Richard Stockton, New Jersey
36. Francis Lewis, New York

Thomas Nelson, Jr., Virginia
Francis Lightfoot Lee, Virginia
Carter Braxton, Virginia
John Penn, North Carolina

37. John Witherspoon, New Jersey
38. Samuel Huntington, Connecticut
39. William Williams, Connecticut
40. Oliver Wolcott, Connecticut
41. John Hancock, Massachusetts
*42. Charles Thomson, Secretary, Pennsylvania
43. George Read, Delaware
*44. John Dickinson, Pennsylvania
45. Edward Rutledge, South Carolina
46. Thomas McKean, Delaware
47. Philip Livingston, New York

Button Gwinnett, Georgia
Lyman Hall, Georgia

32. *A key to identify the signers of the Declaration of Independence as depicted by John Trumbull in his painting shown in illustration 31.*

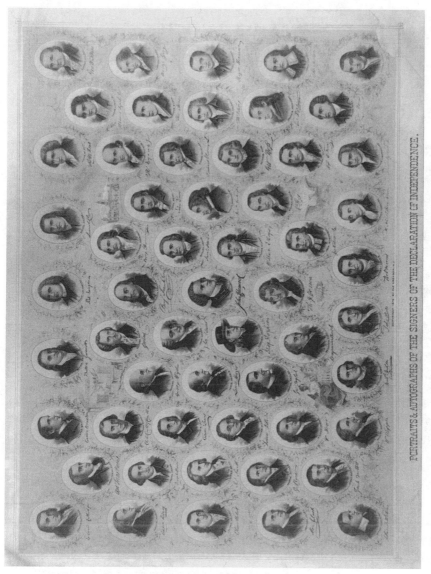

PORTRAITS & AUTOGRAPHS OF THE SIGNERS OF THE DECLARATION OF INDEPENDENCE.

33. *Portraits and signatures of the signers of the Declaration of Independence. The portraits shown are more accurate than the ones in John Trumbull's painting shown in illustration 31.*

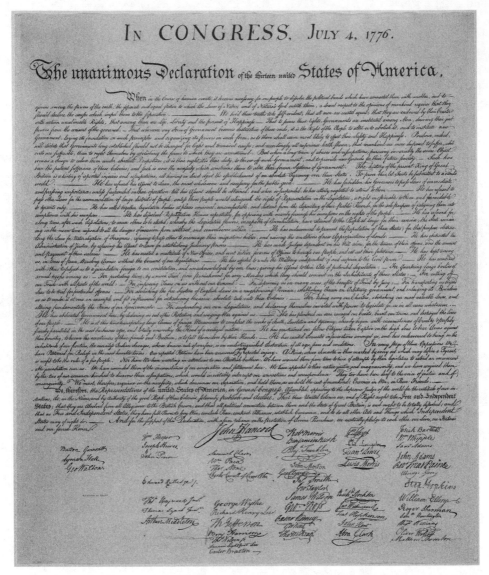

34. A copy of the Declaration of Independence with the signatures of all the signers.

Notes

Introduction

1. John Adams to Richard Bland Lee, August 10, 1819, *The Works of John Adams, Second President of the United States*, 10 vols., ed. Charles Francis Adams (Boston: Little, Brown and Company, 1856), 10:382.

CHAPTER 1   Evolution of a Dynasty

1. Joseph Randall, *An Account of the Academy at Heath, near Wakefield, Yorkshire* (London: Gough [?], 1750), 3.

2. Wilcomb E. Washburn, *The Governor and the Rebel: A History of Bacon's Rebellion in Virginia* (New York: W. W. Norton & Co., 1972), 95.

3. Ibid.

4. Michel Denis et Noël Blayau, *Le XVIIIe Siècle* (Paris: Armand Colin, 2002), 70.

5. Burton J. Hendrick, *The Lees of Virginia: Biography of a Family* (Boston: Little, Brown, and Company, 1935), 89.

6. Richard H. Lee, *Memoir of the Life of Richard Henry Lee and His Correspondence*, 2 vols. (Philadelphia: H. C. Carey and I. Lea, 1825), 1:8–9.

7. Ibid.

8. Ibid., 11.

9. Harlow Giles Unger, *The Unexpected George Washington: His Private Life* (Hoboken, NJ: John Wiley & Sons, 2008), 26–27.

10. Ibid., 27–28.

11. Philip Ludwell to George Washington (henceforth GW), August 8, 1755, *The Papers of George Washington, Colonial Series, 1748–August 1755*, 10 vols., ed. W. W. Abbott (Charlottesville: University of Virginia Press, 1983), 1:356–357. [Hereafter *PGWCol.*]

12. Richard Henry Lee to James Abercrombie, August 27, 1762, Richard Henry Lee, *The Letters of Richard Henry Lee*, 2 vols., ed. James Curtis Ballagh (New York: Macmillan Company, 1911), 1–2. [Hereafter RHL, *Letters.*]

13. RHL to Thomas Cummings, August 27, 1762, *Letters*, 1:2–4.

14. Richard R. Beeman, *Our Lives, Our Fortunes, and Our Sacred Honor: The Forging of American Independence, 1774–1776* (New York: Basic Books, 2013), 33, citing Jack P. Greene, "Foundations of Political Power in the Virginia House of Burgesses, 1720–76," *William and Mary Quarterly* 3, no. X (1959): 485–506.

CHAPTER 2   *Egyptian Bondage*

1. *Virginia Gazette*, Williamsburg, August 12, 1756.

2. Edmund Randolph, *History of Virginia* (Charlottesville: Virginia Historical Society, 1970), 167–168.

3. William Wirt Henry, *Patrick Henry: His Life, Correspondence and Speeches*, 3 vols. (New York: Charles Scribner's Sons, 1891), 1:111.

4. Lee, *Memoir*, 1:17.

5. Ibid., 18–19.

6. Ibid., 23.

7. William Wirt in S. G. Goodrich, *Biography of Eminent Men* (New York: Nafis and Cornish, 1840), 131.

8. Ibid.

9. Edmund Burke, "Speech on American Taxation," April 19, 1774, *The Works of the Right Honourable Edmund Burke*, 12 vols. (London: Holdsworth and Ball, 1834), 1:174.

10. Ibid.

11. John Locke, *The Two Treatises of Civil Government* (London: Awnsham and John Churchill, 1698), ch. 2, sect. 4.

12. William Wirt Henry, *Patrick Henry*, 1:86. Edmund Randolph recalled the speech differently, saying Henry actually retreated at the end of his attack. Here is how Randolph recalled this part of the speech: "'Caesar,' cried he, 'had his Brutus; Charles the first his Cromwell, and George the third . . .' 'Treason, sir,' exclaimed the Speaker, to which Henry instantly replied, 'and George the third, may he never have either.'" Edmund Randolph, *History of Virginia*, 169. But another burgess who heard Henry's speech rebuts Randolph: "If Henry did speak any apologetic words, they

were doubtless uttered almost tongue in cheek to give him some legal protection." Randolph, *History of Virginia*, 169n38–170n.

13. From Henry manuscript, in Moses Coit Tyler, *Patrick Henry*, 2nd ed. (Boston: Houghton, Mifflin and Company, 1898), 85.

14. RHL to Arthur Lee, July 4, 1765, *Letters*, 1:10–11.

15. RHL to the editor of the *Virginia Gazette*, July 25, 1766.

16. Ibid.

17. RHL to Arthur Lee, July 4, 1765, *Letters*, 1:10–11.

18. The American Colonies Act of 1766.

19. *Pennsylvania Gazette*, December 10, 1767.

20. RHL to John Dickinson, July 25, 1768, *Letters*, 1:29–30.

21. Soame Jenyns, MP, *The Works of Soame Jenyns*, 2 vols. (Dublin: P. Wogan et al., 1791), 1:333.

CHAPTER 3   *No Liberty, No King!*

1. RHL to Arthur Lee, May 19, 1769, *Letters*, 1:34–35.

2. RHL to William Lee, July 12, 1772, *Letters*, 1:69–74.

3. Ibid., 69–76.

4. William Lee to Court of Common Council, July 5, 1775, *Letters of William Lee, 1766–1783*, 3 vols., ed. Worthington Chauncey Ford (Brooklyn, NY: Historical Printing Club, 1891), 1:33–34.

5. Peter D. G. Thomas, *John Wilkes: A Friend to Liberty* (New York: Oxford University Press, 1996), 165.

6. Richard Henry Lee, *The Life of Arthur Lee, LLD*, 2 vols. (Boston: Wells and Lille, 1829), 1:255.

7. Junius Americanus in Richard Henry Lee, *Life of Arthur Lee*, 1:20–21.

8. RHL to Mrs. Macaulay, November 29, 1775, *Letters*, 1:160–164.

9. Committee of Secret Correspondence to Arthur Lee, December 12, 1775, Francis Wharton, *The Revolutionary Diplomatic Correspondence of the United States*, 6 vols. (Washington, DC: US Government Printing Office, 1889), 2:63–64.

10. John Adams, December 17, 1773, *Diary and Autobiography of John Adams*, 4 vols., ed. L. H. Butterfield (New York: Atheneum, 1964), 2:85–87.

11. RHL to Samuel Adams, April 14, 1774, *Letters*, 1:106–108.

12. GW to George William Fairfax, June 10[–15], 1774, *PGWCol*, 10:94–101.

13. RHL to Arthur Lee, June 26, 1774, *Letters*, 1:114–118.

14. RHL to Samuel Adams, June 23, 1774, *Letters*, 1:111–113.

15. Ibid.

16. William Lee to RHL, September 22, 1775, *Letters of William Lee, 1766–1783*, 3 vols., ed. Worthington Chauncy Ford (Brooklyn, NY: Historical Printing Club, 1891), 1:171–175.

17. RHL to William Lee, June 29, 1774, *Letters*, 1:118–122.

18. Benjamin Franklin to James Parker, March 20, 1750, *Papers of Benjamin Franklin*, 38 vols. to date [in progress], ed. Leonard W. Labaree et al. (New Haven, CT: Yale University Press, 1959–present), IV:117–121.

19. Ibid., 221.

20. John Adams, *Works of John Adams*, 9:347.

21. John Adams, *Diary and Autobiography*, 3:308.

22. Anne Hollingsworth Wharton, *Salons Colonial and Republican* (Philadelphia: J. B. Lippincott Company, 1900), 133–134.

23. John Adams, September 3, 1774, *Diary and Autobiography*, 2:120–122.

24. Joseph Galloway, as transcribed by John Adams in "Notes of Debates in the Continental Congress, September 28, 1774," *Diary and Autobiography of John Adams*, 2:141–144.

25. Ibid.

26. Richard Henry Lee's "Proposed Resolution," October 3, 1774, *Letters of Delegates to Congress, 1774–1789*, 26 vols., ed. Paul H. Smith (Washington, DC: Library of Congress, 1976), 1:140.

27. Richard Henry Lee's "Proposed Motion for Quitting the Town of Boston," October 7–8, 1774, ibid., 1:160–161.

CHAPTER 4   Poet, Playwright, Watchmaker, Spy

1. John Jay, cited in James Duane's "Notes of Debates," October 15–17, 1774, *Letters of Delegates*, 1:180.

2. RHL to William Lee, September 20, 1774, *Letters*, 1:123–124.

3. Ibid.

4. John Adams, September 17, 1774, *Diary and Autobiography*, 2:134–135.

5. RHL, "Letter of Congress to Colonial Agents," October 26, 1774, *Letters*, 1:125–126.

6. RHL to Samuel Adams, February 4, 1775, *Letters*, 1:127–130.

7. Ibid.

8. RHL to Arthur Lee, February 24, 1774, *Letters*, 1:130–131.

9. Edmund Burke, March 12, 1775, *Second Speech on Conciliation with America: The Thirteen Resolutions*, Burke, *Works of the Right Honourable Edmund Burke*, 1:177.

10. Robert Douthat Meade, *Patrick Henry, Practical Revolutionary* (Philadelphia: J. B. Lippincott Company, 1969), 3.

11. Ibid.

12. William Wirt Henry, *Patrick Henry*, 1:257–258.

13. Ibid.

14. Ibid., 267–268, citing the description of "an old Baptist clergyman who was one of the auditory."

15. Ibid., 266. No actual transcript of Henry's speech exists, and the words shown here represent a reconstruction by Henry's first biographer William Wirt, who extrapolated its contents from recollections—forty years after the event—by those present at St. John's Church, including Judge John Tyler, an intimate of Henry; Thomas Jefferson; Edmund Randolph; and Judge St. George Tucker, among others. Hardly a friend of Henry, Jefferson did not alter a word in Wirt's reconstruction of the speech and reiterated his appraisal of Henry as the greatest orator in history. In any case, word-for-word accuracy is less important here in terms of history than an accurate presentation of Henry's meaning, his passion, and his eloquence.

16. GW to John Augustine Washington, Marsh 25, 1775, *PGWCol*, 10:308–309.

17. Harlow Giles Unger, *John Hancock: Merchant King and American Patriot* (New York: John Wiley & Sons, Inc., 2000), 191.

18. RHL to Landon Carter, April 24, 1775, *Letters*, 1:132–134.

19. RHL to William Lee, May 10, 1775, *Letters*, 1:134–135.

20. RHL to Arthur Lee, February 24, 1775, *Letters*, 1:130–132.

21. *Essex Gazette*, April 25, 1775, Boston Public Library.

22. Ibid.

23. Ibid.

24. Ibid.

25. Dr. Joseph Warren to the President of Congress, June 2, 1775, *Journals of the Continental Congress*, 34 vols., ed. Worthington C. Ford (Washington, DC: Library of Congress, 1904–1937), 2:77–78.

26. Don Higginbotham, *The War of American Independence: Military Attitudes, Policies, and Practices, 1763–1789* (New York: Macmillan Company, 1971), 84–85.

27. John Ferling, *John Adams: A Life* (New York, Henry Holt and Company, 1992), 124.

28. John Adams, *Works of John Adams*, 2:416–417.

29. RHL to Francis Lightfoot Lee, May 21, 1775, *Letters*, 1:136–140.

30. RHL to GW, September 25, 1775, *PGWRS*, 2:51–53.

CHAPTER 5 **An Indispensable Necessity**

1. Louis-Léonard de Loménie, *Beaumarchais et son temps: études sur la société en France au XVIII siècle d'après des documents inédits* (Genève:

Réédition Slatkine, 1970), 226; see also Harlow G. Unger, *Improbable Patriot: The Secret History of Monsieur de Beaumarchais, the French Playwright Who Saved the American Revolution* (Hanover: University Press of New England, 2011), 84–87, 91–94.

2. Loménie, *Beaumarchais et son temps*, 266.

3. Henri Doniol, *Histoire de la Participation de la France à l'établissement des États-Unis d'Amérique*, 5 vols. (Paris: Imprimerie Nationale, 1886), 1:407.

4. The Speech of the Right Hon. John Wilkes, Esq. Lord Mayor, in Arthur H. Cash, *John Wilkes: The Scandalous Father of Civil Liberty* (New Haven, CT: Yale University Press, 2006), 319.

5. RHL, *Letter of Congress to the Lord Mayor of London*, July 8, 1875, *Letters*, 1:141–143.

6. RHL [Marine Committee] to Silas Deane, November 7, 1775, *Letters*, 1:154–155.

7. GW to RHL, July 10, 1775, *Memoir*, 1:1–3.

8. Ibid.

9. *Journals of the Continental Congress*, July 8, 1775, Library of Congress.

10. RHL to GW, August 1, 1775, *Letters*, 1:145–147.

11. GW to RHL, August 29, 1775, *Memoir*, 1:3–5.

12. RHL to GW, September 26, 1775, *Letters*, 1:149–151.

13. RHL to William Lee, September 5, 1775, *Letters*, 1:147–149.

14. RHL to GW, September 26, 1775, *Letters*, 1:149–151.

15. Ibid.

16. GW to RHL, August 29, 1775, W. W. Abbott, ed., *The Papers of George Washington, Revolutionary Series*, multivolume, in progress (Charlottesville: University of Virginia Press, 1985–present), 1:372–374. [Hereafter *PGWRS*.]

17. Ibid.

18. Richard Henry Lee, *Life of Arthur Lee*, 1:52.

19. Ibid.

20. RHL to GW, November 13, 1775, *Letters*, 1:155–157.

21. Ibid.

22. Ibid.

23. Ibid., 155–158.

24. GW to RHL, November 17, 1775, *Memoir*, 2:7–8.

25. GW to RHL, December 26, 1775, *Memoir*, 2:8–10.

26. Ibid.

27. Ibid.

28. Thomas Paine, *Common Sense, Addressed to the Inhabitants of America . . .* (Philadelphia: T. Bell, 1776).

29. RHL to GW, October 27, 1776, *PGWRS*, 7:40–41.

30. Arthur Lee [to Lieutenant Governor Cadwallader Colden], February 13, 1776, Francis Wharton, *Revolutionary Diplomatic Correspondence*, 2:71–74.

31. Ibid.

32. Ibid.

33. Doniol, *Histoire de la Participation*, 1:243–249.

34. RHL to Patrick Henry, April 20, 1776, *Letters*, 1:176–180.

35. Ibid.

36. RHL to Landon Carter, June 2, 1776, *Letters*, 1:192–200.

37. RHL to Edmund Pendleton, May 12, 1776, *Letters*, 1:190–192.

38. Doniol, *Histoire de la Participation*, 1:243–249.

39. A. Hortalez & Co. [Beaumarchais] to the Committee of Secret Correspondence, August 18, 1776, Francis Wharton, *Revolutionary Diplomatic Correspondence*, 2:129–132.

40. RHL to Landon Carter, June 2, 1776, *Letters*, 1:197–200.

41. RHL, "The Virginia Resolution for Independence, June 7, 1776," *Papers of the Continental Congress, 1774–1789* (Washington, DC: National Archives).

CHAPTER 6   *The Enemy of Everything Good*

1. Ibid.

2. John Adams, *Autobiography*, part 1, "John Adams," through 1776, sheet 38 of 53 [electronic edition], *Adams Family Papers: An Electronic Archive*, Massachusetts Historical Society, www.masshist.org/digitaladams.

3. John Adams, *Diary and Autobiography*, 3:397.

4. Thomas Jefferson, "Notes of the Proceedings in the Continental Congress, 7 June–1 August, 1776," Founders Online, National Archives, https://founders.archives.gov.

5. Beeman, *Our Lives, Our Fortunes, and Our Sacred Honor*, 356.

6. Ibid.

7. See Appendix B, Jefferson, "Notes of the Proceedings in the Continental Congress."

8. Jefferson, "Notes of Proceedings in the Continental Congress."

9. William Wirt, in Henry Howe, *Historical Collections of Virginia* (Charleston, SC: Wm. R. Babcock, 1852), 510.

10. Lee, *Memoir*, 1:172–173.

11. Ibid.

12. Jefferson, "Notes of the Proceedings in the Continental Congress."

13. RHL to Samuel Adams, June 18, 1779, *Letters*, 2:72.

14. John Locke, *Second Treatise of Government*, ed. Thomas Hollis (London: A. Millar et al., 1764), sect. 6, 7ff.

15. From the original document in the National Archives, Washington, DC.

16. Jefferson, "Notes of the Proceedings in the Continental Congress."

17. RHL, "The Virginia Resolution for Independence."

18. RHL to Landon Carter, July 21, 1776, *Letters*, 1:208–209.

19. Ibid., July 24, 1776.

20. Ibid.

21. RHL to General Charles Lee, July 6, 1776, *Letters*, 1:205–206.

22. *Connecticut Journal*, November 27, 1776.

23. John Sanderson, *Biography of the Signers to the Declaration of Independence* (Philadelphia: Thomas, Cowperthwait & Company, 1820–1827), 722.

24. Thomas Jefferson to RHL, July 8, 1776, Founders Online, National Archives.

CHAPTER 7   A Most Bloody Battle

1. Douglas Southall Freeman, *George Washington: A Biography*, 7 vols., completed by John Alexander Carroll and Mary Ashworth (New York: Charles Scribner's Sons, 1948–1957), 4:194n.

2. Joseph Reed, in ibid., 4:198.

3. RHL to Patrick Henry, September 15, 1776, *Letters*, 1:214–217.

4. RHL to Samuel Adams, July 29, 1776, *Letters*, 1:211–212.

5. James Monroe, *The Autobiography of James Monroe* (Syracuse, NY: Syracuse University Press, 1959), 24.

6. RHL to GW, October 27, 1776, *Letters*, 1:220–221.

7. RHL to Patrick Henry, December 18, 1776, *Letters*, 1:229–230.

8. GW to John Augustine Washington, November 16–19, 1776, *PGWRS*, 7:102–105.

9. RHL to Patrick Henry, December 18, 1776, *Letters*, 1:229–230.

10. Ibid., January 9, 1777, 246–249.

11. Ibid., January 17, 1777, 250–251.

12. RHL [Marine Committee to Marine Agents in Maryland], *Letters*, 1:249–250.

13. RHL to Arthur Lee, February 17, 1777, *Letters*, 1:256–258.

14. RHL to [his sons Thomas and Ludwell], May 10, 1777, *Letters*, 1:287–288.

15. RHL to Arthur Lee, June 30, 1777, *Letters*, 1:305–306.

16. GW to RHL, May 17, 1777, *PGWRS*, 9:453–454.

17. Ibid.

18. RHL to GW, May 22, 1777, *Memoir*, 2:17–18.

19. GW to RHL, June 1, 1777, *Memoir*, 2:18–19.
20. RHL to Patrick Henry, May 26, 1777, *Letters*, 1:297–302.
21. William Wirt, in Henry Howe, *Historical Collections of Virginia* (Charleston, SC: Wm. R. Babcock, 1852), 511.
22. Ibid.
23. Ibid.
24. Arthur Lee to Committee of Secret Correspondence, February 18, 1777, Francis Wharton, *Revolutionary Diplomatic Correspondence*, 2:272–273.
25. GW to RHL, April 24–26, 1777, *PGWRS*, 9:255–258.
26. Ibid.
27. RHL to Patrick Henry, April 5, 1777, *Letters*, 1:273–275.
28. GW to RHL, March 6, 1777, *Memoir*, 2:12.
29. RHL to GW, April 29, 1777, *Letters*, 1:284–285.
30. RHL to John Adams, May 13, 1778, *Letters*, 405–407.
31. RHL to John Page, August 17, 1777, *Letters*, 1:315–317.
32. RHL to Thomas Jefferson, August 25, 1777, *Letters*, 1:317–319.
33. RHL to Patrick Henry, September 13, 1777, *Letters*, 1:322–324.
34. John Adams, September 18, 1777, *Diary and Autobiography*, 2:265.
35. John Adams, *Diary and Autobiography*, 4:1.

CHAPTER 8   *To Discard General Washington*

1. RHL to Patrick Henry, October 8, 1777, *Letters*, 1:325–327.
2. GW to John Hancock, October 5, 1777, *PGWRS*, 11:393–401.
3. Ibid., October 10, 1777, *PGWRS*, 11:473–476.
4. George-Washington Lafayette [Gilbert Motier, Marquis de Lafayette], *Mémoires, Correspondence et Manuscrits du Général Lafayette, publiés par sa famille*, 2 vols. (Bruxelles: Société Belge de Librairie, Etc., Hauman, Cattoir et Compagnie, 1837), I:36–37.
5. GW to Patrick Henry, November 13, 1777, *PGWRS*,12:242–247.
6. GW to RHL, October 16, 1777, *PGWRS*, 11:529–530.
7. Ibid.
8. Ibid.
9. RHL to GW, June 1, 1777, *Memoir*, 2:15–18.
10. GW to Lund Washington, New York, July 8, 1777, Worthington Chauncey Ford, *Spurious Letters Attributed to Washington* (Brooklyn, NY: Privately Printed, 1889), 87–97, citing unsigned pamphlet entitled *Letters of George Washington to Several of His Friends in the Year 1776* (London: J. Bew, 1777).
11. GW to RHL, February 15, 1778, *PGWRS*, 13:549–550.

12. GW to Martha Washington, June 24, 1776, Ford, *Spurious Letters*, 69–79.

13. GW to RHL, May 25, 1778, *PGWRS*, 15:216–218.

14. GW to Horatio Gates, January 4, 1778, *PGWRS*, 13:138–140.

15. Unknown to Patrick Henry, January 12, 1778, *PGWRS*, 13: 610n-611n.

16. Ibid.

17. Patrick Henry to RHL, April 4, 1778, Moses Coit Tyler, *Patrick Henry* (Boston: Houghton, Mifflin Co., 1887), 253.

18. GW to Patrick Henry, March 27, 1778, *PGWRS*, 14:328–329.

19. GW to Patrick Henry, March 28, 1778, *PGWRS*, 14:335–337.

20. GW to RHL, February 15, 1778, *Memoir*, 2:20.

21. RHL to GW, January 2, 1778, *PGWRS*, 13:120–121.

22. Patrick Henry to GW, March 29, 1777, *PGWRS*, 9:12–13.

23. Arthur Lee to the Committee of Foreign Affairs, January 15, 1778, Francis Wharton, *Revolutionary Diplomatic Correspondence*, 2:470–471.

24. Patrick Henry to RHL, April 7, 1778, William Wirt Henry, *Patrick Henry*, 2:559–560.

25. GW to RHL, November 18, 1777, *PGWRS*, 12:307–309.

26. RHL to GW, November 20–22, 1777, *PGWRS*, 330–333.

27. Ibid.

28. Franklin and Deane to the President of Congress, February 8, 1778, Francis Wharton, *Revolutionary Diplomatic Correspondence*, 2:490–491.

29. General Orders, May 7, 1778, *PGWRS*, 15:68–70.

30. Jared Sparks, *The Life of Washington* (Boston: Tappan and Denner, 1843), 267–268.

31. Ibid.

32. RHL to GW, February 15, 1778, *Memoir*, 2:21.

33. GW to RHL, May 25, 1778, *PGWRS*, 15:216–218.

34. GW to John Augustine Washington, July 4, 1778, *PGWRS*, 16:25–26.

35. GW to RHL, August 10, 1778, *Memoir*, 2:22–23.

36. Arthur Lee to the Committee of Foreign Affairs, June 9, 1778, Francis Wharton, *Revolutionary Diplomatic Correspondence*, 2:608–609.

37. RHL to *Virginia Gazette*, January 1, 1779.

38. RHL to Silas Deane, January 22, 1779, *Letters*, 2:614.

CHAPTER 9   *President Richard Henry Lee*

1. RHL to GW, April 28, 1779, *PGWRS*, 20:252–253.

2. GW to RHL, April 30, 1779, *PGWRS*, 20:271–272.

3. Ibid., May 25, 1779, *PGWRS*, 20:629–631.

4. Francis Lightfoot Lee to RHL, June 30, 1776, Lee Family Digital Archive, Stratford Hall.

5. RHL to Samuel Adams, April 1, 1781, *Letters*, 2:218–219.

6. RHL to Arthur Lee, June 4, 1781, *Letters*, 2:230.

7. RHL to William Lee, July 15, 1781, *Letters*, 2:242.

8. RHL to James Lovell, June 12, 1781, *Letters*, 2:237.

9. RHL to GW, June 12, 1781, *Letters*, 2:238.

10. GW to RHL, August 10, 1778, *Memoir*, 2:22–23.

11. Julian P. Boyd, ed., *The Papers of Thomas Jefferson*, multivolume, in progress (Princeton, NJ: Princeton University Press, 1943–present), 6:204–205; Robert Douthat Meade, *Patrick Henry: Practical Revolutionary* (Philadelphia: J. B. Lippincott Company, 1969), 250.

12. Randolph, *History of Virginia*, 295–296.

13. William Wirt Henry, *Patrick Henry*, 2:151.

14. GW Address to Congress on Resigning His Commission, December 23, 1783, *The Writings of George Washington, from the Original Manuscript Sources, 1745–1799*, 39 volumes, ed. John C. Fitzpatrick (Washington, DC: US Government Printing Office, 1931–1944), 27:284–285. [Hereafter *GW Writings*.]

15. Paul C. Nagel, *The Lees of Virginia: Seven Generations of an American Family* (New York: Oxford University Press, 1990), 131–132.

16. The President of Congress [RHL] to General George Washington, September 14, 1785, *Letters*, 2:329–330.

17. RHL to Patrick Henry, February 14, 1785, *Letters*, 2:332–333.

18. Ibid.

19. Ibid.

20. Ibid.

21. RHL to GW, April 18, 1785, *Letters*, 2:349.

CHAPTER 10   Riots and Mobbish Proceedings

1. John Steele Gordon, *An Empire of Wealth: The Epic History of American Economic Power* (New York: Harper Collins, 2004), 61–63.

2. GW to Jacob Read, November 3, 1784, *GW Writings*, 27:489.

3. GW to James Madison, November 30, 1785, *The Papers of George Washington, Confederation Series, January 1784–September 1788*, 6 vols. (Charlottesville: University of Virginia Press, 1992–1997), 3:419–421. [Hereafter *PGWCon.*]

4. RHL to Theodoric Lee, January 27, 1786, *Letters*, 410–411.

5. RHL to Col. Martin Picket, March 5, 1786, *Letters*, 2:411–412.

6. Ibid.

7. Gordon, *Empire of Wealth*, 61–63.

8. Henry Lee Jr. to GW, February 16, 1786, *PGWCon*, 3:562.

9. George Washington Circular to the States, *GW Writings*, 26:483–496.

10. GW to John Jay, May 18, 1786, *PGWCon*, 4:55–56.

11. James Madison, *Notes of Debates in the Federal Convention of 1787 Reported by James Madison* (New York: W. W. Norton, 1987), 7. [Hereafter, *Notes.*]

12. Ibid.

13. RHL to Edmund Randolph, March 26, 1787, *Letters*, 2:415.

14. William Short [citing Henry] to Thomas Jefferson, May 15, 1784, in Meade, *Patrick Henry, Practical Revolutionary*, 273.

15. Henry Knox to GW, January 31, 1785, *PGWCon*, 2:301–306.

16. GW to Benjamin Harrison, October 10, 1784, *PGWCon*, 2:86–99.

17. GW to Jonathan Trumbull Jr., January 5, 1784, *GW Writings*, 27:293–295.

18. RHL to George Mason, May 15, 1787, *Letters*, 2:419–422.

19. Ibid.

20. Ibid.

21. US Constitution, Article IV, Section III.

22. Lee, *Memoir*, 1:17.

23. RHL to GW, July 15, 1787, *PGWCon*, 5:258–260.

24. GW to the Marquis de Lafayette, August 17, 1787, Freeman, *George Washington*, 6:105; GW to George Augustine Washington, May 27, 1787, *PGWCon*, 196–199.

25. Madison, *Notes*, 98.

26. Ibid., 68.

27. Ibid., 652.

28. Ibid., 566.

29. Ibid., 651.

30. GW to Patrick Henry, Benjamin Harrison, and Thomas Nelson, September 24, 1787, *PGWCon*, 5:339–340.

31. Madison, *Notes*, 653.

32. Ibid., 652–654.

33. RHL to George Mason, October 1, 1787, *The Documentary History of the Ratification of the Constitution*, multivolume, in progress, ed. Merrill Jensen et al. (Madison: State Historical Society of Wisconsin, volumes beginning 1976), 1:345–346. [Hereafter *DHRC*.]

34. Richard Henry Lee's Proposed Amendments, September 27, 1787, *DHRC*, 1:337–339.

35. Ibid.

36. *Journals of Congress*, September 28, 1787, *DHRC*, 1:340.

CHAPTER 11   The Farmer and the Federalist

1. RHL to Elbridge Gerry, September 29, 1787, *DHRC*, 1:347.
2. RHL to Edmund Randolph, October 16, 1787, *Letters*, 2:450.
3. Ibid.
4. Ibid.
5. *New York Journal*, September 27, 1787, *DHRC*, 19:9–10.
6. Patrick Henry to GW, October 19, 1787, *PGWCon*, 5:384.
7. GW to David Humphreys, GW's secretary, and forwarded to Lee, October 19, 1787, *PGWCon*, 5:365–366.
8. Max Farrand, ed., *The Records of the Federal Constitution of 1787*, 4 vols. (New Haven, CT: Yale University Press, 1911), 3:88.
9. Ibid., 303–304.
10. Ron Chernow, *Alexander Hamilton* (New York: Penguin, 2004), 248.
11. Richard Henry Lee, *Observations Leading to a Fair Examination of the System of Government Proposed by the Late Convention and to Several Essential and Necessary Alterations in It*, in *Letters from the Federal Farmer to the Republican*, ed. William Hartwell Bennett (New York: Thomas Greenleaf, 1787; reprint: Tuscaloosa: University of Alabama Press, 1777), Introduction, 3–4.
12. Ibid., 19.
13. Ibid., 27.
14. Ibid., 65.
15. Ibid.
16. Ibid., 94, 96.
17. Ibid., 58.
18. Ibid., 95.
19. Ibid., 14–15.
20. Ibid., 51.
21. Ibid., 16.
22. Ibid., 58.
23. Ibid., 67.
24. Ibid., 7.
25. RHL, *Letters from the Federal Farmer*, XVI: Arguments for a Bill of Rights, 105–112; II: Essentials of a Free Government, 10–13.
26. Ibid., 15.
27. Alexander Hamilton, James Madison, and John Jay, *The Federalist Papers* (New York: New American Library, 1961), 1: Hamilton, 33–37.
28. Ibid., 68: Hamilton, 414.
29. RHL, *Letters from the Federal Farmer*, I: Introduction, 3.
30. David Stuart to GW, December 4, 1787, *PGWCon*, 5:480.

31. Ibid.

32. GW to Benjamin Lincoln, April 2, 1788, *PGWCon*, 6:187–188.

33. *American Mercury*, December 24, 1787; *Connecticut Gazette*, January 4, 1788, *DHRC*, 3:506.

34. *Pennsylvania Gazette*, January 2, 1788, *DHRC*, 8:284.

35. Arthur Lee to RHL, February 19, 1788, *DHRC*, 9:619–620.

36. *Massachusetts Centinel*, November 17, 1787, *DHRC*, 4:259–262.

37. Philadelphia *Freeman's Journal*, September 26, 1787, *DHRC*, 13:243–245.

38. RHL to George Mason, May 7, 1788, *Letters*, 2:466–469.

39. The most complete text of Henry's speeches to the Virginia Ratification Convention can be found in two sources. William Wirt Henry (Patrick Henry's grandson), *Patrick Henry, Life Correspondence and Speeches*, 3 vols. (New York: Charles Scribner's Sons, 1891, reprinted by Sprinkle Publications, Harrisonburg, Virginia, 1993), 3:431–600, contains his speeches with brief summaries of other delegates' responses. There is also the complete proceedings of the Virginia Ratification Convention, including Henry's speeches, which can be found in volumes 8–11 of *DHRC*.

40. Patrick Henry, to the Virginia Convention, June 21, 1788, *DHRC*, 9:929–931.

41. Ibid.

42. Ibid., 931–936.

43. Ibid.

44. Ibid.

45. Ibid.

46. Ibid.

47. RHL to General John Lamb, June 27, 1788, *Letters*, 2:474–476.

48. GW to Charles Cotesworth Pinckney, June 28, 1788, *PGWCon*, 6:360–362.

CHAPTER 12   *His Majesty the President*

1. Patrick Henry, to the Virginia Convention, June 25, 1778, *DHRC*, 10:1537.

2. The Constitution of the United States, National Archives.

3. GW to James McHenry, July 31, 1788, *PGWCon*, 6:409–410.

4. Richard Labunski, *James Madison and the Struggle for the Bill of Rights* (New York: Oxford University Press, 2006), 64.

5. RHL in Charlene Bangs Bickford et al., eds., *The Documentary History of the First Federal Congress*, 17 vols. (Baltimore, MD: Johns Hopkins University Press, 1972–1998), 9:27; John Adams to Benjamin Rush, MD,

July 5, 1789, *Old Family Letters* (Philadelphia: J. B. Lippincott Company, 1892), 41–43.

6. John Adams to Benjamin Rush, July 24, 1789, Charlene Bangs Bickford and Kenneth R. Bowling, *Birth of the Nation: The First Federal Congress, 1789–1791* (Lanham, MD: Madison House Publishers, 1989), 28.

7. Ibid., citing Thomas Lloyd, *The Congressional Register*, 4 vols. (New York: 1789–1790), 1:299.

8. Ibid., 557.

9. Ibid., 531.

10. Ibid.

11. Bickford et al., *Documentary History*, 9:5.

12. Robert R. Rutland, ed., *The Papers of James Madison*, 16 vols. (Charlottesville: University Press of Virginia, 1989), 12:203.

13. RHL to Francis Lightfoot Lee, September 13, 1789, *Letters*, 2:300–301.

14. RHL to Patrick Henry, September 14, 1789, *Letters*, 2:501–504.

15. RHL and Wm. Grayson to Speaker of the House of Representatives of Virginia, September 28, 1789, *Letters*, 2:507–508.

16. GW to David Stuart, June 15, 1790, *The Papers of George Washington Presidential Series, September 1788–May 1793*, multivolume, in progress (Charlottesville: University of Virginia Press, 1987), 5:523–528. [Hereafter *PGWP*.]

17. RHL to James Monroe, January 15, 1791, *Letters*, 2:541–542.

18. RHL to Virginia governor Henry Lee, January 21, 1792, *Letters*, 2:545.

19. John Adams to Abigail Adams, December 19, 1793, Massachusetts Historical Society, *The Adams Papers: Adams Family Correspondence*, multivolume, in progress (Cambridge, MA: Belknap Press of Harvard University Press, 2009), 9:476–477.

20. RHL to the Speaker of the House of Delegates, October 8, 1792, *Letters*, 2:550–551; RHL to the Speaker of the [Virginia] Senate, November 5, 1792, *Letters*, 2:552–553.

21. Speaker of the [Virginia] Senate, November 5, 1792, *Letters*, 2:552n1.

22. Bickford et al., *Documentary History*, 9:290.

23. *A Compilation of the Messages and Papers of the Presidents, 1789–1897*, 10 vols. (Washington, DC: US Government Printing Office, 1897), 1:148.

24. RHL to the President of the United States, March 8, 1794, *Letters*, 2:580–583.

25. GW to RHL, April 15, 1794, *PGWP*, 15:601–602.

Afterword

1. Major-General Henry Lee, *Funeral Oration on the Death of General Washington* (Boston: Joseph Nancrede and Manning & Loring, 1800).

2. John Adams to Benjamin Rush, April 1790, Founders Online.

Bibliography

Abbott, W. W., ed. *The Papers of George Washington, Colonial Series, 1748–August 1755*. 10 vols. Charlottesville: University of Virginia Press, 1983.

———, ed. *The Papers of George Washington, Confederation Series, January 1784–September 1788*. 6 vols. Charlottesville: University of Virginia Press, 1992–1997.

Abbott, W. W., Dorothy Twohig, Philander D. Chase, and Theodore J. Crackel, eds. *The Papers of George Washington, Presidential Series, September 1788–May 1793*. Multivolume [in progress]. Charlottesville: University of Virginia Press, 1987.

———, eds. *The Papers of George Washington, Revolutionary War Series, June 1775–April 1778*. Multivolume [in progress]. Charlottesville: University of Virginia Press, 1984.

Adams, Charles Francis, ed. *Letters of John Adams Addressed to His Wife*. 2 vols. Boston: 1841.

———, ed. *The Works of John Adams*. 10 vols. Boston: Little, Brown and Company, 1850–1856.

Adams, John. *Diary and Autobiography of John Adams*. 4 vols. Edited by L. H. Butterfield. New York: Atheneum, 1964.

[Adams, John]. *The Adams Papers: Adams Family Correspondence*. Multivolume [in progress]. Cambridge, MA: The Belknap Press of Harvard University Press, 2009.

———. *Old Family Letters*. Philadelphia: J. B. Lippincott Company, 1892.

Alden, John R. *A History of the American Revolution*. New York: Alfred A. Knopf, 1969.

Annals of Congress. See [Congress], *Debates and Proceedings in the Congress of the United States.*

Beeman, Richard R. *Our Lives, Our Fortunes, and Our Sacred Honor: The Forging of American Independence, 1774–1776.* New York: Basic Books, 2013.

Bickford, Charlene Bangs, and Kenneth R. Bowling. *Birth of the Nation: The First Federal Congress, 1789–1791.* Lanham, MD: Madison House Publishers, 1989.

Burke, Edmund. *Thoughts on the Cause of the Present Discontents.* Dublin: M. H. Gill & Son, 1882.

———. *The Works of the Right Honourable Edmund Burke.* 12 vols. London: Holdsworth and Ball, 1834.

Cash, Arthur H. *Arthur Wilkes, The Scandalous Father of Civil Liberty.* New Haven, CT: Yale University Press, 2006.

Chernow, Ron. *Alexander Hamilton.* New York: Penguin, 2004.

[Congress]. *The Congress of the United States, Its Origins and Early Development, 1789–1989.* Edited by Joel Silbey. Brooklyn, NY: Carlson Publishing, 1991.

———. *The Debates and Proceedings in the Congress of the United States.* Washington, DC: Library of Congress, 1834–1856.

———. *The Documentary History of the First Federal Congress.* 14 vols. Baltimore, MD: Johns Hopkins University Press, 1972–1996.

———. *Journals of the Continental Congress.* Washington, DC: Library of Congress, 1904–1937.

———. *Letters of Delegates to Congress, 1774–1789.* 26 vols. Edited by Paul H. Smith. Washington, DC: Library of Congress, 1976.

[Constitution]. *The Documentary History of the Ratification of the Constitution.* Multivolume [in progress]. Edited by Merrill Jensen, et al. Madison: State Historical Society of Wisconsin, 1976–present.

Doniol, Henri. *Histoire de la participation de la France à l'établissement des États Unis.* 5 vols., quarto. Paris: Imprimerie Nationale, 1886.

Durand, John. *New Materials for the History of the American Revolution* New York: Henry Holt and Company, 1889.

Farrand, Max. *The Fathers of the Constitution: A Chronicle of the Establishment of the Union.* New Haven, CT: Yale University Press, 1921.

———, ed. *The Records of the Federal Convention of 1787.* 4 vols. New Haven: Yale University Press, 1911.

Ferling, John. *John Adams: A Life.* New York, Henry Holt and Company, 1992.

Fitzpatrick, John C., ed. *The Writings of George Washington, from the Original Manuscript Sources, 1745–1799.* 39 vols. Washington, DC: US Government Printing Office, 1931–1944.

Flassan, Gaëtan de Raxi de. *Histoire générale et raisonnée de la diplomatie française depuis la foundation de la monarchie jusqu'à la fin du règne de Louis XVI.* 17 vols. Paris: Laboulaye et Da-Resie, 1811.

Ford, Paul Leicester, ed. *The Writings of Thomas Jefferson.* 10 vols. New York: G. P. Putnam's Sons, 1892–1899.

Ford, Worthington Chauncey. *Spurious Letters Attributed to Washington.* Brooklyn, NY: Privately Printed, 1889.

Franklin, Benjamin. *Papers of Benjamin Franklin.* 38 vols. to date [in progress]. Edited by Leonard W. Labaree et al. New Haven: Yale University Press, 1959–present.

Freeman, Douglas Southall. *George Washington.* 7 vols. Completed by John Alexander Carroll and Mary Wells Ashworth. New York: Charles Scribner's Sons, 1957.

Goodrich, S. G. *Biography of Eminent Men.* New York: Nafis and Cornish, 1840.

Goutel, Hennet de. *Vergennes et l'indépendance américaine.* Paris: Éditions de la Nouvelle revue nationale, 1918.

[Hamilton, Alexander, James Madison, and John Jay]. *The Federalist Papers.* New York: New American Library, 1961.

Hendrick, Burton J. *The Lees of Virginia: Biography of a Family.* Boston: Little, Brown, and Company, 1935.

Henry, William Wirt. *Patrick Henry: Life, Correspondence, and Speeches.* 3 vols. New York: Charles Scribner's Sons, 1891.

Higginbotham, Don. *The War of American Independence: Military Attitudes, Policies, and Practice, 1763–1789.* New York: The Macmillan Company, 1971.

Howe, Henry. *Historical Collections of Virginia.* Charleston, S.C.: Wm. R. Babcock, 1852.

Jefferson, Thomas. "Notes of the Proceedings in the Continental Congress." Founders Online. National Archives.

[Jefferson, Thomas]. Julian P. Boyd, ed., *The Papers of Thomas Jefferson.* Multivolume [in progress]. Princeton, NJ: Princeton University Press, 1943–present.

Jensen, Kaminski, Gaspare Saladino, Richard Leffler, and Charles H. Schoenleber, eds. *The Documentary History of the Ratification of the Constitution.* Multivolume [in progress]. Madison: State Historical Society of Wisconsin, 1976–present.

Jensen, Merrill. *The New Nation: A History of the United States During the Confederation, 1781–1789.* New York: Alfred A. Knopf, 1950.

Jenyns, Soame, MP. *The Works of Soame Jenyns.* 2 vols. Dublin: P. Wogan et al., 1791.

Journals of the Continental Congress, 1774–1783. 34 vols. Edited by Worthington C. Ford et al. Washington, DC: US Government Printing Office, 1904–1937.

Kaminski, John P., ed. *The Founders on the Founders: Word Portraits from the American Revolutionary Era*. Charlottesville: University of Virginia Press, 2008.

Knollenberg, Bernhard. *Growth of the American Revolution, 1766–1775*. New York: Free Press, 1975.

Labunski, Richard. *James Madison and the Struggle for the Bill of Rights*. New York: Oxford University Press, 2006.

Lafayette, George-Washington [Gilbert Motier, Marquis de Lafayette]. *Mémoires, Correspondence et Manuscrits du Général Lafayette, publiés par sa famille*. 2 vols. Bruxelles: Société Belge de Librairie, Etc., Hauman, Cattoir et Compagnie, 1837.

[Lee, Richard Henry]. *Letters from the Federal Farmer to the Republican* [Full title: *Observations Leading to a Fair Examination of the System of Government Proposed by the Late Convention and to Several Essential and Necessary Alterations in It, in a number of Letters from the Federal Farmer to the Republican*]. Edited by William Hartwell Bennett. New York: T. Greenleaf, 1787, 1788; reprint: Tuscaloosa: University of Alabama Press, 1777.

Lee, Richard Henry. *The Letters of Richard Henry Lee*. 2 vols. Edited by James Curtis Ballagh. New York: Macmillan Company, 1911.

———. *The Life of Arthur Lee, LLD*. 2 vols. Boston: Wells and Lille, 1829.

———. *Memoir of the Life of Richard Henry Lee and His Correspondence with the Most Distinguished Men in America and Europe*. 2 vols. Philadelphia: H. C. Carey and I. Lee, 1825.

Lee, William. *Letters of William Lee*. 3 vols. Edited by Worthington Chauncey Ford. Brooklyn, NY: Historical Printing Club, 1891.

———. *A Yankee Jeffersonian: Selections from the Diary and Letters of William Lee of Massachusetts, Written from 1796–1840*. Cambridge, MA: Harvard University Press, 1958.

Letters of Members of the Continental Congress. 8 vols. Edited by Edmund C. Burnett. Washington, DC: Carnegie Institution, 1924–1936.

Locke, John. *The Two Treatises of Civil Government*. London: Awnsham and John Churchill, 1698.

Loménie, Louis de. *Beaumarchais et son temps: Études sur la société en France au XVIIIe siècle*. 2 vols. Paris: Michel Lévy frères, 1856.

Macaulay, Catherine. *History of England from the Accession of James I to the Revolution*. 8 vols. London: Edward and Charles Dilly in the Poultry, 1769.

Madison, James. *Notes of Debates in the Federal Convention of 1787 Reported by James Madison*. New York: W. W. Norton & Co., 1987.

Maier, Pauline. *American Scripture: Making the Declaration of Independence*. New York: Alfred A. Knopf, 1997.

———. *The Old Revolutionaries: Political Lives in the Age of Samuel Adams*. New York: Alfred A. Knopf, 1980.

Matthews, John Carter. *Richard Henry Lee*. Williamsburg: Virginia Independence Bicentennial Commission, 1978.

McGaughy, J. Kent. *Richard Henry Lee of Virginia*. Lanham, MD: Rowman & Littlefield Publishers, 2004.

Meade, Robert Douthat. *Patrick Henry, Practical Revolutionary*. Philadelphia: J. B. Lippincott Company, 1969.

Monroe, James. *The Autobiography of James Monroe*. Syracuse, NY: Syracuse University Press, 1959.

Nagle, Paul C. *The Lees of Virginia: Seven Generations of an American Family*. New York: Oxford University Press, 1990.

Paine, Thomas. *Common Sense, Addressed to the Inhabitants of America . . . .* Philadelphia: T. Bell, 1776.

Potts, Louis W. *Arthur Lee: A Virtuous Revolutionary*. Baton Rouge, LA: Louisiana State Press, 1981.

[Presidents of the United States]. *A Compilation of the Messages and Papers of the Presidents*. Washington, DC: Library of Congress, 1902.

Randolph, Edmund. *History of Virginia*. Charlottesville: Virginia Historical Society, 1970.

Rutland, Robert R., ed. *The Papers of James Madison*. 16 vols. Charlottesville: University of Virginia Press, 1984–1989.

Sanderson, John. *Biography of the Signers to the Declaration of Independence*. Philadelphia: Thomas Cowperthwait & Company, 1820–1827.

Soulavie, Jean-Louis. *Mémoires historiques et politiques du regne de Louis XVI, depuis son marriage jusqu'à sa mort*. Paris: Treuttel et Würtz, 1801.

Sparks, Jared. *The Life of Washington*. Boston: Tappan and Denner, 1843.

Thomas, Peter D. G. *John Wilkes: A Friend to Liberty*. New York: Oxford University Press, 1996.

Tyler, Moses Coit. *Patrick Henry*. 2nd ed. Boston: Houghton, Mifflin and Company, 1898.

Unger, Harlow Giles. *John Hancock: Merchant King and American Patriot*. New York: John Wiley & Sons, 2000.

———. *The Unexpected George Washington: His Private Life*. Hoboken, NJ: John Wiley & Sons, 2008.

Van Doren, Carl. *The Great Rehearsal*. New York: The Viking Press, 1948.

Washburn, Wilcomb E. *The Governor and the Rebel: A History of Bacon's Rebellion in Virginia*. New York: W. W. Norton & Co., 1972.

Wharton, Anne Hollingsworth. *Salons Colonial and Republican*. Philadelphia: J. B. Lippincott Company, 1900.

Wharton, Francis. *The Revolutionary Diplomatic Correspondence of the United States*. 6 vols. Edited under Direction of Congress. Published in conformity with Act of Congress of August 13, 1888. Washington, DC: US Government Printing Office, 1889.

Periodicals

American Mercury
Connecticut Gazette
Essex Gazette
Freeman's Journal
Massachusetts Centinel
New York Journal
Pennsylvania Gazette
(Philadelphia) *Independent Gazetteer*
Virginia Gazette

Archives

Archives de l'Ancien Régime, Département de la Maison du roi, Ministère des Affaires Étrangères, Quai d'Orsay, Paris, France.
Archives des Affaires Étrangères et Papiers Diplomatiques, Ministère des Affaires Étrangères, Quai d'Orsay, Paris, France.
Centre Historique des Archives Nationales, Paris, France.
National Historical Publications and Records Commission of the National Archives, Washington, DC. Founders Online. https://founders.archives.gov.
Massachusetts Historical Society, Boston, MA.

Index